Creating an Effective Couples Therapy Practice

Most clinicians seek guidelines and indicators as to the effectiveness of their interventions with clients. Some may even be implementing evidence-based interventions and seek an in-depth understanding of their results. This book helps clinicians who provide couple or marriage therapy and counseling go from the ambiguous realm of "thinking" or "knowing" their effectiveness to being able to demonstrate it. It identifies effective strategies for common treatment concerns that connect to the successful outcomes of therapy. Here, the process starts even before the couple enters therapy and goes beyond the final session. Dr. Losey discusses specific outcome measures and how they can be used in session so that the couple can assess their relationship and develop specific goals and interventions for treatment. The author also examines session notes, pretreatment change, and quality post-treatment goals in his discussion of clinical effectiveness.

Butch Losey, EdD, PCC-S, is an assistant professor for Xavier University's Department of Counseling in Cincinnati, Ohio. He has over thirty years' experience in the mental health field and is a licensed professional clinical counselor with supervisor endorsement. Dr. Losey is an assistant professor in the Counseling Department of Xavier University, the CEO of Waybridge Counseling Services, and a couples therapist helping couples recover from infidelity, high conflict, and problems with intimacy. He is also an international speaker on a variety of mental health topics.

Creating an Effective Couples Therapy Practice

Butch Losey

Routledge
Taylor & Francis Group
NEW YORK AND LONDON

First published 2018
by Routledge
4 Park Square, Milton Park, Abingdon, Oxon, OX14 4RN

and by Routledge
605 Third Avenue, New York, NY 10017

Routledge is an imprint of the Taylor & Francis Group, an informa business

British Library Cataloguing-in-Publication Data
A catalogue record for this book is available from the British Library

Library of Congress Cataloging-in-Publication Data
Names: Losey, Butch, author.
Title: Creating an effective couples therapy practice / Butch Losey.
Description: Milton Park, Abingdon, Oxon ; New York, NY : Routledge, 2018.
Identifiers: LCCN 2017028744 | ISBN 9781138780309 (hbk : alk. paper) | ISBN 9781138780347 (pbk : alk. paper) | ISBN 9781315770826 (ebk)
Subjects: LCSH: Couples therapy. | Marital psychotherapy.
Classification: LCC RC488.5 .L675 2018 | DDC 616.89/1562—dc23
LC record available at https://lccn.loc.gov/2017028744

ISBN: 978-1-138-78030-9 (hbk)
ISBN: 978-1-138-78034-7 (pbk)
ISBN: 978-1-315-77082-6 (ebk)

Typeset in Goudy
by Apex CoVantage, LLC

Contents

Foreword

Mary and John described their marriage as a cake, or, in their case, more a lack of cake. The couple was married over twenty years and avoided conflict so consistently that their "marriage cake" became depleted to a point where they no longer saw any salvageability for their relationship. John remarked that "over the years, we just kept taking pieces from the cake until one day there was nothing left." The couple sought couple counseling before coming to the conclusion of divorce. My personal reaction at the time was "what a waste", and to this day, I believe Mary and John had strengths and complementary characteristics to be successful in therapy. I wonder about their experience with the counselor. John later told me that after the first session, the counselor was weighing divorce as an option for the couple. They left the first session feeling hopeless for their relationship, affirming their decision to end their marriage.

John could be described as conflict avoidant, as he often stayed at work or out of the home to reduce opportunity for conflict. He also had the propensity to refuse confronting Mary regarding his core values and needs. John felt that he was frequently exploited due to his inability to challenge Mary to advocate for his needs, which explains why he envisioned their cake slowly disappearing and Mary the main culprit for taking the pieces.

Mary felt deep hurt because of John's long absences and avoidance of the relationship. Though her tendency was to be intimacy-avoidant, she expressed resentment that John did not attempt to intimately connect with her. John failed to take the emotional risk and be vulnerable to Mary, fearing a negative emotional response. Mary also failed to be vulnerable and emotionally transparent in order to encourage John to approach her.

On the surface, these relational dynamics seem dangerous or doomful for a relationship. For the clinician, however, it is their role in interrupting the ineffective patterns that plague the couple's day-to-day interactions that will aid the couple in creating change. For Mary and John, their relationship depends on the expertise of the clinician for breaking John's pattern of physically distancing himself from Mary during stints of tension or conflict or for thwarting Mary's withholding emotional intimacy by stonewalling.

Many clinicians will look at the story of Mary and John as a familiar one: a couple who came to therapy experiencing some form of relational crisis. This is a very delicate place for the relationship, and the couple is most vulnerable to the influence of the clinician. Couples are looking to us for guidance until they can achieve stability again. Our success in this critical role is dependent on our effectiveness in what we do.

Creating an Effective Couples Therapy Practice by Butch Losey examines issues, such as John and Mary's, that are common in clinical practice. He challenges us to consider the clinical interventions that we are using and discusses the efficacy research that supports them and how we might evaluate ours and our client's success.

Caitlin Yilmazer, M.A., LPCC
Licensed Professional Clinical Counselor
Chief Operating Officer, Waybridge Counseling Services

Introduction

There are a number of benefits of private practice. For the clinician, the pace is relaxed, the demands are within the clinician's control, there is autonomy in decision-making, freedom to work from a preferred theoretical orientation, opportunity to create one's own schedule, and the pride that comes with ownership. For the client, the setting is serene and private practice offers the option of selecting a clinician from a variety of specialties. This helps couples find a clinician that is a best fit for their particular circumstance.

There are many different types of private practices and practitioners. There are solo practitioners and others that are in large group private practices. Some practitioners may have a part-time private practice while working a full-time position elsewhere, which offers security of income and insurance benefits. Some will be affiliated with physician offices or faith-based organizations. How do we go about knowing the quality and effectiveness of private practice services? With so many different models of private practice, can we be assured that there are business and clinical practices that are standard among the different practices? This I see as a challenge for us private practitioners.

It is important to take a moment to recognize that community mental health is different than private practice in a very important way: community mental health is different in how it approaches the delivery of services and monitoring of outcomes of programs and therapy. Most community mental health agencies have numerous entities that demand oversight of service delivery and outcomes.

Mental health agencies tend to have a number of funding lines. For example, Child Focus, Inc., located in Cincinnati, Ohio, has thirty-two funding lines (Carter, 2017). Most funding lines, such as local, state, or federal grants or mental health board initiatives, have specific outcomes that require programs to collect and report data back to the funder.

Mental health agencies seek certification or are required to have certification by governmental agencies or funding sources, which have expectations for the agency, and its programs, to conform to specific standards. One accrediting organization, the Commission for Accreditation of Rehabilitation Facilities (CARF), states that conformance to quality standards is a way to identify areas for improvement and growth and help the service provider focus on improved service outcomes, satisfaction of the persons served, and quality service delivery. Each standard sets a guideline for the subject addressed (CARF, 2017). CARF-certified agencies regularly report their adherence to these standards.

Corporate governance also offers a layer of accountability. Community mental health programs tend to have directors and middle managers who manage the delivery of services and report performance towards outcomes. Middle managers also serve as both administrative and clinical supervisors.

Mental health agencies also have review boards. If the agency is a non-profit agency, they will have a board of directors that will have specific directives for outcomes of programs. Most agencies also have quality assurance committees who regularly review charts to assure adherence to clinical standards.

The private-practice world is starkly different. There are typically no accrediting bodies, no grants that require outcome data, limited (if any) governance other than that of the owner of the practice, and most likely no quality assurance committee. Clinical supervision is the most common method of monitoring services. In a solo practice, oversight is left to the clinician. Larger group practices who operate within managed care may have more oversight related to insurance billing and chart reviews.

Specific to couples therapy, clinicians in private practice also vary in skill and in their ability to serve couples. Couples seeking therapy are unaware that many clinicians in private practice have limited formal training in couples therapy, nor have they had supervised experience working with couples. For example, clinical mental health counselors have little classwork on couples therapy in their graduate program, and it is possible that they have had only one class session (not class, but class session) on couples therapy in a broader course on family therapy.

This leads me to the reason that I chose to write this book. My focus is to consider some of the critical issues that couple therapists in private practice are likely to face and consider the therapeutic efficacy and effectiveness of treatment with these issues. I hope to discuss the research relevant to the issue, what is considered efficacious and effective, what is considered best practice, and how outcomes might be measured with each issue.

The scope of this book is not to support one particular theoretical lens. I have intentionally avoided advocating for a particular theory. I am more interested in considering an integrative approach, meaning couples therapy that takes a combined approach and brings together different elements of specific therapies. In practice, even when clinicians ascribe to a particular theory, most still practice an integrative approach that tailors different strategies from different theories to match the individual needs of the couple. As a systemic counselor, I am very willing to use cognitive approaches to help someone managing intrusive thinking as they recover from infidelity.

I hope that what I have written here will give you an opportunity to think critically about how you are intervening with couples and why you choose the interventions that you use. The book has led my thinking in this direction.

Butch Losey

References

CARF. (2017). *Quality standards*. Retrieved April 4, 2017 from www.carf.org/Accreditation/QualityStandards/

Carter, J. (2017, April 4). Funding lines for Child Focus, Inc. Personal Communication.

1 Effective Couples Therapy

Couples therapy is difficult work. Couples come to therapy with a high level of stress and emotional volatility, leaving the clinician to feel like they have little control at times in the session. Couples are at different places in their motivation for change and may have differing timelines for their recovery. Each partner may view the relationship in a very different way, resulting in very different goals for the relationship. With all the challenges, how is it possible for clinicians to be successful in their work and for couples to create significant changes in their relationships?

The Gap Between Efficacy and Effectiveness

There is a distinction to be made between the terms *research efficacy* and *clinical effectiveness*. *Efficacy* refers to treatment effects observed in a randomized control trial, whereas *effectiveness* refers to treatment effects in routine practice. In routine practice, couples are self referred and have multi-problem focus, and clinicians use a wide range of techniques without relying on treatment manuals (Klann et al., 2011). As you can imagine, there is a preference in the research literature for randomized trials because researchers like to control as many confounding variables as possible. For this reason, we have a great and more confident understanding of research efficacy than we do clinical effectiveness.

To answer the question of whether couples therapy is effective, it is important to know that when most clinicians are talking about the effectiveness of a particular model or technique, they are likely referring to their understanding of the research and implying that the outcomes from the research studies translate to their practice setting. Effectiveness actually only speaks to the outcomes of treatment in a clinical setting, whereas efficacy is specific to the outcomes in a highly controlled research study. Efficacy may not translate to a clinical setting because the same controls are not in place in a private practice or community mental health agency. Clinicians would be more correct to say that a particular model has research efficacy and then discuss effectiveness of their practice by identifying the outcomes they have measured post-treatment with their clients. Therefore, there is a blending of the words *efficacy* and *effectiveness* because this is our common language. It should be mentioned that through the course of this book, the same blending of terms will occur.

Efficacy of couples therapy is quite good. A review of eight meta-analyses, mostly research on behavior couples therapy or emotion-focused couples therapy, shows strong outcomes as compared to control groups (Baucom, Hahlweg, & Kuschel, 2003).

Couple counseling shows a high level of efficacy yet much lower levels of effectiveness. In clinical effectiveness studies, couple recovery rates are less than half that reported in research efficacy trials. In addition, about 60% of couples studied showed no reliable benefit from couples therapy in effectiveness studies, compared to 35% in efficacy studies (Halford, Pepping, & Petch, 2015). From the perspective of a practitioner in private practice, one has to wonder if there is a disparity between the number of clinicians providing couples therapy and the number of clinicians that are actually trained in couples therapy. Research indicates that about 70%–80% of clinicians do couples therapy, yet most never took a course in couples therapy and never did their internships under supervision from someone who mastered the art (Doherty, 2017; Orlinsky & Ronnestad, 2005). This may be a strong reason for less-positive outcomes in practice than in research.

From observation, it is evident that inexperienced and untrained couple therapists do not manage sessions well. They struggle with the techniques of couples therapy, and clients often sense that these clinicians are not skillful. Inexperienced clinicians tend to lack structure in their sessions, they do not recommend changes for the couple, and they give up on the relationship because they feel overwhelmed by the couple's problems (Doherty, 2017).

Researchers point to other variables that are within the design of research that may not be translated into the clinical setting, providing four potential explanations for the difference between research efficacy and clinical effectiveness (Halford, Pepping, & Petch, 2015). First, it could be the type of therapy provided in research studies. Most research studies focus on behavioral- or emotion-focused therapy and show efficacy; most practicing clinicians do not espouse allegiance to either of those models. Keep in mind, though, that there is no clear evidence that either model is better than the other.

The characteristic of the couple is a second explanation. In research, couples are held to stringent inclusion/exclusion criteria. There are likely more couples in the clinical setting that are ambivalent about staying in the relationship. Clinical effectiveness, then, would logically be lower.

Efficacy studies use comprehensive assessments and typically more than one. They are used pretreatment, throughout treatment and post-treatment. In contrast, practicing couple therapists are likely not to use assessments at all and prefer to use unstructured conjoined couple interviews.

The fourth explanation is quality control. Research studies are highly controlled with strong support by the researchers. In addition, the clinicians are highly trained in the treatments being evaluated, and they maintain strict adherence to the model.

Research informs practice. Understanding this divide between efficacy and effectiveness should be taken note of by clinicians. It is possible that some of these explanations described here might be keys to creating more positive outcomes of treatment.

Ingredients of Effective Couples Therapy

It may be beneficial to look beyond the evidence that supports a particular model. A primary reason for this is that in practice, clinicians who provide evidence-based treatment actually do not stick to one particular theoretical orientation. Instead, they adapt their approach to ensure that they are following a best practice model that takes into consideration both evidenced-based research and practice-based evidence. Following is a review of some of the general principles of effective couples therapy.

Consider for a moment the general framework of the total clinical experience for the couple. Even before therapy starts, pretreatment role expectations are a factor that has been shown to predict strong treatment alliance. The client's expectation that they will have a personal commitment to therapy plays a strong role in the development of the treatment alliance early on in the treatment process. Couples expecting to take responsibility for the work of therapy create a stronger collaborative bond with the therapist and create a more productive relationship, and this can happen within the first three sessions of treatment (Patterson, Uhlin, & Anderson, 2008).

These early successes in treatment are critical to overall treatment outcomes. Lewis et al. (2012) led a study at the University of Indiana of 173 individuals ranging in age from eighteen to sixty-four. These individuals came in for treatment of depression and anxiety. Lewis found that decreases in depressive symptoms in the first five sessions of treatment directly predicted overall outcome in the participants. Interestingly, those in the study who continued to have symptom declines during the first five sessions had the most benefit from therapy.

Bradley Erford (Shallcross, 2012) offers a good summation of five clinical considerations that will increase the effectiveness of couples therapy. Effective treatment will start with the establishment of a strong *therapeutic alliance*. Without early development of the therapeutic alliance, a couple seeking treatment in a private practice setting will tend to move on to another clinician. Effective treatment will also require a focus on the needs of the couple and will be *centered on achieving objectives*. Without setting treatment goals the couple will lose confidence in the clinician, and gains of treatment will be stalled at best or not achieved. The clinician will need to stay aware of current *evidenced-based practice* standards and implement the necessary interventions based on the presentation of the couple's concerns. The clinician will *facilitate treatment adherence* and challenge the couple to stay focused on the goals they set out to accomplish. Lastly, the clinician will identify and *follow up on treatment gains*. This will include the necessity of implementing outcome measure through the course of treatment and monitoring gains post-treatment.

Benson et al. (2012) identify five basic behaviors of the clinician for effective couples therapy. These are influential strategies of the clinician that will affect changes in the relationship and changes in the perception of the partner and the relationship.

The Clinician Helps Alter the View of the Relationship

Throughout the therapeutic process, the therapist attempts to help both partners see the relationship in a more objective manner rather than one sided and blaming. Most couples do not fully recognize that their own behaviors contribute to the relationship problems. From their perspective, the clinician can help this by creating a strong working alliance and sharing a casual analysis of the central relationship issue. The clinician can share their hypothesis of how the analysis may affect the dynamic of the relationship. Different therapists will use different strategies, but as long as they focus on altering the way the relationship is understood, the couple can start to see each other, and their interactions, in more adaptive ways.

The Clinician Modifies Dysfunctional Behavior

Effective clinicians attempt to change the way that the partners behave with one another. This means that in addition to helping them improve their interactions, therapists also need to ensure that their clients are not engaging in actions that can cause physical or psychological harm. In order to do this, therapists must conduct a careful assessment to determine whether their clients are, in fact, at risk. If there is risk, they need to intervene and may need to refer one partner to individual counseling and not continue with couple counseling, for example in cases of domestic violence.

The Clinician Challenges and Reduces Emotional Avoidance

Distressed couples tend to avoid expressing their private feelings, and this put them at greater risk of becoming emotionally distant and growing apart. Emotional avoidance perpetuates dysfunctional communication patterns such as the demand-withdraw pattern, in which one partner demands or requests change and the other withdraws by being defensive or avoidant. Effective clinicians will disrupt these patterns and elicit emotions and thoughts from each partner in hopes of opening up the perspectives of each partner.

The Clinician Takes the Necessary Steps to Improve Communication

Healthy communication requires more than just stopping abusive ways of talking. It may require the clinician to take a coaching approach to help the couple successfully navigate difficult conversations. Couples will need to be encouraged to create vulnerability in disclosure and may need help in responding to disclosures in appropriate ways. These can be guided, in-session experiences called enactments. The clinician may also provide the couple with didactic instruction early on in treatment to give the couple the basis for knowing what types of communication are effective and what types will only cause more conflict.

The Clinician Promotes Strengths

Couples therapy often focuses on difficulties in the relationship, but successful couples therapy does not end with removal of the identified problems. Effective couples therapy results in a more deeply satisfying relationship sustainable from the perspective of both partners. Helping a couple focus on the strengths and the good aspects of their relationship will increase the likelihood that they will enjoy the relationship. It is important that the clinician keep in mind the client's perspective because if the clinician offers false praise or claims success that truly is not there, the couple will fail at implementing this principle.

Behaviors of the Clinician That Increase Positive Outcomes

Not all clinicians are created equal. There is great variance in clinicians, and even though they may be equally trained in technique they may not help clients achieve the same level of positive outcomes. There is convincing evidence that differences among therapists contribute more to the success of clients than the treatments they practice (Wampold, 2001).

Estrada and Holmes (1999) interviewed fifteen couples and asked them about helpful and hindering aspects of their couples therapy. The couples were interviewed after receiving eight sessions of couples therapy, and their responses were sorted into twelve effective behaviors of the clinician and five ineffective behaviors. The results of their study indicate that couples expect clinicians to be active, directive, and focused while providing a safe and empathic therapeutic environment. The clinician behaviors are identified in Table 1.1 and are listed in descending order of frequency identified by the couple.

There is consistent evidence in the research that clinicians need to adapt to client preferences, expectations, and characteristics (Sprenkle, Davies, &

Table 1.1 Effective and Ineffective Behaviors of the Clinician

Effective Behaviors	*Ineffective Behaviors*
Clinician moderates and controls discussion	Clinician wastes time in therapy
Clinician facilitates communication	Clinician techniques are unclear
Clinician increases awareness of patterns	Clinician does not help in resolving issues
Clinician reflects and provides feedback	Clinician is not acting empathically
Clinician provides safe environment	Clinician is unfocused in therapy
Clinician provides structured therapy	
Clinician is an objective third party	
Clinician encourages participation	
Clinician is empathic	
Clinician helps in resolving problems	
Clinician challenges couple	
Clinician asks questions	

Lebow, 2009, p. 52). For example, when resistance is high, the clinician should decrease directedness. When the couple becomes highly emotional, the clinician will need to adjust their technique. Yet, even though expert clinicians vary their approach based on the client context, expert clinicians consistently help couples achieve positive outcomes. It makes sense, then, to look at what these expert clinicians have and do in common.

According to Meichenbaum (2008), expert clinicians begin by developing a collaborative therapeutic relationship with the couple and help each individual "tell" his or her story. They work on an ongoing basis to educate the couple about their problem and possible solutions. At times this requires the clinician to re-conceptualize the client problem in a more hopeful and solvable way. Expert clinicians are also well aware that the couple is the primary agent of their own change and work to ensure that the couple takes credit for the changes they make in the relationship.

Characteristics of the Couple That Increase Positive Outcomes

Client motivation has to be a primary factor in the success of couple counseling. Clinicians can do a great deal to influence this motivation positively or negatively. Simply maintaining a positive hopeful presence can give the encouragement a couple needs when they have lost all hope. Sometimes, we as clinicians put too much responsibility on our role in the therapeutic process or the outcomes of therapy. Just as there are helpful characteristics of clinicians, there are also characteristics of the couple that contribute to success or hinder the outcomes.

Sells and Yarhouse (2011) identify five characteristics of couples, listed in Table 1.2, that are predictors of positive outcomes.

Age is a potentiating characteristic because younger couples tend to do better at changing their relationships. One assumption for this is that they are catching their problems earlier in the relationship. By some estimates, couples wait seven years too long to get into therapy.

Most couples come to therapy with different levels of motivation for change and *commitment* to the relationship. Some couples will say that they are committed to staying in the marriage "for better or worse" and will do whatever it takes to save the marriage. These couples certainly have a strong commitment to the relationship, but they also tend to have a strong commitment to the counseling process.

Table 1.2 Five Characteristics of Couples Related to Positive Outcomes

Age
Commitment
Emotional connection
Mutual partnership
Shared beliefs and goals

Couples that are *emotionally connected*, in other words, are able to be vulnerable to share thoughts and feelings, are better able to nurture each other when times are difficult. They are also able to share positive experiences through shared interest and activities.

Couples that have a *mutual partnership* with equality in decision-making, have flexibility in roles, and have a shared vision of the relationship that includes *shared beliefs and goals* tend to have higher levels of positive therapeutic outcomes.

The Influence of Common Factors

When clinicians and researchers talk of common factors, they are considering the notion that different treatment methods in counseling share common factors that account for much of the effectiveness of treatment. In other words, the common factor opinion is that elements common to all methods have more of an effect in the treatment outcome than the method itself. Of particular interest to researchers and clinicians alike is to understand the strength of the effect of the clinician in regards to the outcomes of treatment. Common factors include the therapeutic relationship, strength of the alliance between client and clinician, client factors, hope, and expectancy.

The connection between common factors and client outcomes is consistently shown in the research. According to the most recent review of the clinician-effects literature, approximately 5% of outcome variance is attributable to clinician. Treatment method accounts for only 1% of total outcome variance. Strong evidence suggest that the clinician has a stronger effect than the treatment method (Laska, Gurman, & Wampold, 2014).

Common Factors Unique to Couples

There are specific common factors for couple counseling. Effective couple therapists consistently conceptualize the couple's problems in relational terms. They are more apt to look for circular patterns than linear causes. There is an intentional focus on the interactional cycles, and when dysfunctional relational patterns do emerge, they work to disrupt them. Couple therapists will expand the direct treatment system. This is relative to couples because there is a preference to keep the couple together even when one may be struggling with an issue, such as depression, more than the other. Lastly, they expand the therapeutic alliance. The clinician makes special effort to create a strong bond with both partners (Sprenkle, Davis, & Lebow, 2009).

The Act of Measuring Outcomes Increases Positive Outcomes

Private practitioners are busy people, and the truth of the matter is that if measuring outcomes is not required, it will likely not occur. There are a number of reasons that clinicians choose not to routinely collect data on client outcome measures. Some reasons include that the clinician does not believe there is enough time to do so, the client does not like completing the evaluation, the clinician is concerned that the outcomes will not truly reflect how much the client has been helped, the clinician does not believe that the measures are therapeutic, or, worse, may hinder the therapeutic alliance, and finally the clinician worries that the outcomes might be misused by their supervisor (Streatfield, 2012).

Data about the couple's well-being and the problems that brought them to treatment should be collected at the beginning of the treatment process and measured at regular intervals throughout and at the end of treatment. Data can also be collected post-treatment through surveys or in-person reports.

Measuring progress, effectiveness, or outcomes, and using the information to help guide or adjust treatment, has been shown to significantly improve therapy outcomes. Measurement of progress toward treatment goals, effectiveness of a specific intervention, level of client symptomology, and even heart rate during session conflict creates an opportunity for the couple and the clinician to discuss what appears to be working, what does not seem to be working, and any need for adjustments to the treatment approach or interventions. Measuring progress, effectiveness, and outcomes also helps determine when therapy is complete (Brown, Dreis, & Nace, 1999; Duncan & Miller, 2000).

Effective Clinicians Use Client Feedback

Clinicians will readily admit that they use client feedback in every session by virtue of the nature of their interactions with the client. Many relational clinicians are less likely to use informal or formal measures in session because they have concerns about the time it will take to implement the outcome measure or the time it will take to interpret the scores, and by some estimates, the majority of clinicians would not tolerate a five-minute, session-by-session measurement (Tarescavage & Ben-Porath, 2014; Miller et al., 2003).

There are a number of benefits, though, for using ongoing formal or semi-formal couple feedback measures in session. When used regularly, client feedback leads to fewer premature terminations, improved outcomes for clients at the time of termination (Brown & Jones, 2005; Whipple et al., 2003), increased opportunities to repair alliance ruptures, and improvements in the therapeutic relationship (Ackerman et al., 2001). Couples using feedback with their clinician demonstrate significantly greater treatment gains than those not receiving feedback (Anker, Duncan, & Sparks, 2009; Miller et al., 2006).

One example is the Norway Couple Study (Sparks, 2015). The study included 205 Euro-Scandinavian, heterosexual couples, ranging in age from twenty to seventy-one, receiving treatment from one of ten clinicians in an outpatient setting. In the study, the clinicians could choose the clinical approach that they thought would be most appropriate for the couple they were treating. The only difference between the control and experimental

Table 1.3 Evaluation Methods

Client satisfaction survey	To evaluate the degree that the client feels that the services have been helpful
Goal attainment scaling	To help determine if goals were attained based on predetermined criteria
Assessment of client functioning	To determine functional status on general or specific criteria
Assessment of client symptomology	To determine rate or frequency of presenting issues

group was the routine use of a simple feedback approach in session. The results were pretty amazing. The couples that received feedback had nearly four times the rate of clinically significant change than the couples not receiving feedback, and six months after they completed treatment, those receiving feedback were still doing significantly better (two times better) than those not receiving the feedback. Overall, the couples receiving feedback were 46% less likely to be separated or divorced at six months post-treatment than couples not receiving feedback.

It does not take a complicated outcome measure or assessment process to increase the possibility of positive outcomes for the couple. For example, Miller and Duncan (2004) developed two simple surveys that are brief and are meant to track client outcomes and the clinician-client relationship in every session. Both are used together at the end of the session and just take a few minutes to complete. Each survey has four items, and the couple simply marks their impression of each item on a continuum. The two measures and the discussion between couple and clinician takes less than five minutes to complete.

Possible Outcome Measures for Couples

There are a variety of evaluation methods when considering client outcomes. With so many outcome measures too numerous to identify, it might be easier to identify the different methods used and what they measure. In Table 1.3, several common outcome measures are identified (Newsome & Gladding, 2013; Loesch, 2001; Steenbarger & Smith, 1996):

Generally Accepted Guidelines for Working With Couples

There are a number of guidelines that are accepted by a majority of clinicians. For the most part, clinicians of differing clinical orientations will still see the value in many of the following guidelines.

The Relationship Is the Client

Recently, Janis Abrahms-Spring stated in a workshop (Abrahms-Spring, 2012) that she keeps, and even encourages, the secrets that couples tell her.

There was an audible groan from the 500 or more attendees in the audience, clearly indicating the concern of most clinicians about keeping secrets. Her argument for keeping secrets was that this will allow her to know "what she is working with." Ethically, she is correct in her statement as long as she does not reveal information from the individual session to the couple session without proper authorization. The American Association for Marriage and Family Therapy (Standard 2.2; p. 4) states directly that "In the context of couple, family or group treatment, the therapist may not reveal any individual's confidences to others in the client unit without the prior written permission of that individual." Clinically, the negative clinician response at the workshop was more likely related to the concern most clinicians have that they will be placed in a conflict of interest in keeping a secret that might be harmful to the couple's relationship. These clinicians likely have policies and processes up front that directly state how the clinician will manage secrets. Most likely they opt to inform the couple of their policy not to keep secrets and seek authorization for disclosure. The topic of secrets will be discussed in greater detail in Chapter 3, when I discuss ethical practice.

Keeping secrets also has the potential to create anger towards the clinician, particularly if the secret is held by the clinician and then discovered later in the treatment process. Secrets can also result in a board licensing complaint or even legal action by the couple.

Define Goals Early and Monitor Progress

Without goals, there is no direction and no need for monitoring progress. Progress towards what? Clinicians that help couples develop a well-defined problem statement and goals to address the identified problem will have a better understanding of the interventions to employ, when course corrections need to be made and when treatment is completed. According to Clifton Mitchell (2007), failure to mutually develop goals with the client will increase the likelihood that the client will be resistant to treatment.

Infidelity Has a Specific Protocol

Intervention for couples recovering from infidelity has a specific protocol. Failing to have a strong understanding of the complex issue of infidelity and the treatment protocol can lead to further damage to the couple's relationship. Seek training and practice under supervision before taking on couples recovering from infidelity.

Teaching Communication Is a Limited Intervention

Many couples enter therapy stating that they have trouble communicating. Though this can be true, also true is that most of these couples have deeper underlying issues. Teaching communication skills may have short-term benefits early in treatment process to create structure in the session, but clinicians need to address the underlying problem to make any significant change for the couple that will last post-treatment.

Not Neutral but Multi-Perspective

Though clinicians want to believe they are neutral, they are not. Clinicians have specific values about healthy relationships and the process of change, they have process goals that may challenge the couple's way of interacting, they value specific expectations for outcomes over others, and they have beliefs about love, intimacy and sexuality, and what constitutes appropriate communication patterns. Neutrality may not be appropriate if one partner's behavior is hurting the relationship or the other partner. Though the clinician is not neutral, they can work to be multi-perspective. A multi-perspective clinician will consider the perspective of both partners and their own perspective in hopes of creating alternative ways to address the relationship problems.

Identify Relational Issues in Circular Terms

Couples have a tendency to put less emphasis on how their own behaviors contribute to the problem. It can be a logical step for one partner to believe that a problematic interaction has a start point and an end point, with one partner causing the problem for the other. Most relationship clinicians will, however, challenge this linear perspective and define the issue in circular terms, helping the couple understand how both partners influence and perpetuate that particular problem. In most cases, the clinician will challenge the linear assumption that one partner is the problem and define the problem relationally. This is usually done in the first session.

Have a Clinical Reason to See Partners Individually

Relational therapists prefer to see the couple together because they recognize the power of influencing the system when both partners are present. Some clinicians will see the partners individually as part of their assessment, though this comes with the risk of supporting linear attribution, in other words, supporting one partner's view that the other partner is the problem. The risk is also greater that the clinician will be put in a position to keep a secret. Another reason for an individual session is for assessment of the individual psychopathology of one partner. Since most relational therapist prefer not to pathologize individuals, individual sessions can help the clinician make an assessment without supporting the notion that one partner is "sick" and one partner is "well". Careful consideration should be made when deciding to see the partners separately.

Maintain Structure in Session

The inexperienced clinician will allow the couple to argue in session, which can quickly escalate out of control. Structure begins by explicitly telling couples the expectations for how they will interact in session. Volatility and defensiveness can be monitored and modified. Raised voices, name-calling, and threatening are out-of-bounds behavior in session and will be interrupted, and alternative interactions will be suggested by the clinician.

Have the Courage to Tell the Couple What They Are Doing Wrong

Couples have consistently reported that they would prefer to work with a clinician that is familiar with their problem, who has a method for treating it, and who has had success with treating it. They prefer the clinician who will interrupt what they are doing wrong and offer them corrective ideas so that they can be better as a couple.

Implement Out-of-Session Procedures

Clinicians typically see their clients just one hour a week. That means that there are 167 hours each week for the couple to integrate the work they do in therapy to their daily lives. This highlights the limited power of the weekly session. Since generalizing the learning in therapy to the couple's real-world relationship is important, most clinicians assign, or co-create with the couple, out-of-session procedures. These can be in the form of between-session tasks that encourage the couple to interact in different ways or experiments that create awareness for the couple. Obviously, the between-session tasks should be relevant to the treatment goals, an extension of the clinician's theoretical orientation, and meaningful to the couple.

Assessment

Most clinicians assess aspects of the couple relationship and relationship history. Assessment is usually quick. The key is to continue to assess and use client feedback from start to finish to create better possibility for success in achieving positive outcomes.

Assume a "Not Knowing" Approach

Assuming a one-up hierarchal relationship with the couple, in which the clinician is the expert, can lead to opportunities for resistance to the clinician's efforts to influence the couple relationship. It is best to take a collaborative approach with the couple where there is a negotiation of goals and interventions.

Potential Problematic Use of Individual Sessions

The involvement of both partners is strongly preferable in treating couple distress. There are two common diversions from treating the couple together: 1) individual counseling when one partner is not involved in treatment and 2) the clinician's referral of one or both partners to individual counseling while continuing treatment with the couple.

One person attending individual therapy for a relationship problem can be very risky for the relationship and may increase the odds that the relationship will end. The clinician will need to be careful to resist the temptation to validate how bad the other partner seems, which may inadvertently encourage the client to leave the relationship. Treatment can focus on creating insight around what the in-session partner is doing to contribute to the problems in the relationship, developing and implementing systemic change processes by the in-session partner, and monitoring for effectiveness of the change strategies.

In my practice, there have been occasions that I have referred one partner to another clinician for individual counseling as I continued my work with the couple. I have made the referral when it seemed that one partner needed to do individual work around an issue. One example of this would be when one partner was struggling with rumination or obsessive and/or intrusive thinking. My hope was that cognitive therapy would speed the process of symptom reduction. In a majority of the cases, I found that it was not as productive as I had hoped, and I discontinued the practice of referring individuals to individual counseling in these situations.

There have long been indications, both in research and in clinical experience, that individual therapies are highly risky ways to try to resolve couple distress, often promoting relationship breakup (Gurman & Kniskern, 1978; Gurman, 2008, p. 504). Even riskier would be three clinicians (one for the couple treatment and one for each partner to work with individually).

Another argument against couples' participating concurrently in individual therapy is the growing body of research that indicates that the couple treatment context has distinct advantages for helping with a range of other problems, including those that are typically thought of as residing within individuals (Lebow, 2013). For these reasons, I am more likely to suggest that couples stop their involvement in individual counseling when starting couples therapy and less likely to refer out for individual therapy once they have started.

An Interview With Jon and Steph

Putting sex to the side and getting us focused on the relationship;
This helped show us that lack of sex was a symptom, not a problem.

Jon, former client

The following conversation was an interview conducted with Steph and Jon at the conclusion of their couples therapy (Steph and Jon, Personal Communication,

February 9, 2013). Their presenting issue is undisclosed intentionally, along with other aspects of their relationship, to respect the privacy of the couple. However, they did give permission for the publication of this interview.

The focus of this interview was to ask the couple about specific components of treatment and how helpful they were to the couple. As with most counseling experiences, there were certainly less helpful moments of therapy, but the interview was solely focused on what was effective. For that reason, the discussion did not identify negative or less helpful experiences.

Dr. Losey: During the very first session, I helped you assess your relationship based on satisfaction and intimacy, among other things. What was it like to assess your relationship the way we did it?

Jon: It was actually scary. We didn't know if we would like what we would find. It was certainly eye-opening. We never had broken down the relationship before in terms of friendship, communications, or the like. I always thought of "the marriage" and not its parts. It really showed the position of the relationship.

Steph: It also gave me confidence in some areas. I was able to see specific areas that needed improvement and where things were acceptable to good. It also showed the relationship disconnects. Once we completed the assessment, we saw where the issue was, and not where it wasn't.

Dr. Losey: We have worked for some time together. What comments can you make about the client-counselor relationship? What would be your description?

Steph: It was supportive. We both felt very comfortable and safe to disclose our issues. You were non-judgmental, but not automatically neutral. You valued our opinions and we valued yours.

Dr. Losey: Any thoughts about what effects the relative strength of the relationship had on completion of treatment?

Jon: The safe environment allowed honesty, and this sped treatment. The probing questions really required critical thought about the relationship from me that I had never had before. I also thought the ability to veer off the initial treatment path to handle crises as they arose helped show the importance of treatment.

Dr. Losey: How did this relationship affect other parts of the treatment experience?

Steph: By having a constant example of what kind of support we both needed from the counselor, we were better able to learn what support to look for in not only ourselves but in our network of friends and family.

Jon: We looked at not only the mental but potential physical causes of our emotions such as Stephanie's use of vitamins, her hormones and IUD situation.

Dr. Losey: Okay, switching gears for a minute, overall, what do you think was most helpful in counseling?

Jon: Putting sex to the side and getting us focused on the relationship. This helped show us that lack of sex was a symptom, not a problem.

Steph: You gave us constant positive reinforcements. For example, saying we were a great couple, and I was not being crazy or Jonathan had some valid points.

Dr. Losey: Did you notice any specific techniques? Can you speak to that?

Jon: You challenged us on discounting by breaking down our everyday conversations and discussing what we were each actually wanting and needing.

Steph: Forcing a conversation every night the first week.

Dr. Losey: Yes, I strongly suggested that you bare your soul to Jonathan every evening to the point of crying if possible. After the first week of doing it, I actually asked you to do it for another week.

Steph: Yes, that's right. It broke down a lot of barriers and made sure nothing remained hidden. Sometimes it highlighted where we both really agreed and definitely broke a lot of assumptions for Jonathan. Most of all it taught us to have hard conversations.

Dr. Losey: The point of that activity from my perspective was to reduce your emotional intensity by getting you what I thought you needed most, which was a caring ear. It was difficult for you to stop crying during session, and within a few weeks you seemed so much more emotionally stable. It was certainly not something you would teach in grad school, but it seemed so effective. So, speaking of between-session tasks, were they useful?

Steph: They really helped bring the lessons from counseling into our daily lives. The initial homework we both were asked to do without the other knowing really helped break the ice.

Dr. Losey: Oh yes, I asked both of you to create some small change in what you were doing, as I remember, and then see if you could figure out what the other was doing.

Steph: The later tasks I don't really remember.

Dr. Losey: My guess is there were fewer tasks as we continued our work. So, every session I started with a reflection statement to offer my perspective; what did you think of that?

Jon: It did help to focus on the session. I think it helped to lend perspective that we were moving down a path, and not just rehashing something again and again.

Steph: It also kept outside issues like our jobs, kids, and family out until it was time to discuss them.

Dr. Losey: Okay, let's move to how treatment was concluded. What was the final session like for you?

Jon: It was awkward for me. I had already talked about this to Stephanie, so I thought, "Why do we need to discuss it again with the counselor?" However, after the session ended we were proud and relieved.

Dr. Losey: What do you think of the report you received at the end of treatment, the one I sent by email?

Steph: The report was helpful in showing where the issues were in the relationship and how much improvement was made. The goals at the end are nice to have in writing so we know what to continue working on.

Dr. Losey: You mean the post-treatment goals?

Steph: Yes.

Dr. Losey: What do you think of having post-treatment consultation?

Steph: I recommend it just to see if goals listed in the final report are being focused on and also to see if there are other adjustments to make.

Following the interview, Steph and Jon met for one three-month post-treatment consultation. At the three-month consultation they disclosed that following treatment, the couple created a wellness plan together and each had lost a considerable amount of weight. They had two post-treatment goals, one to do a symbolic activity to recognize the success of treatment and the second to utilize foreplay to increase sexuality. For their first goal, they did several small symbolic activities and then booked a trip to South Africa. They confided that they did not work on the second goal regarding sexuality because they both believed that they were more satisfied than ever with their sexuality, making the second goal unnecessary.

Lessons From Steph and Jon: Effective Components From Clinical Practice

Assessment

- Assessment of specific aspects of the relationship showed the condition of the relationship
- Assessment created confidence because it highlighted the strengths, not just weaknesses
- Assessment considered physical as well as mental health causes
- Assessment considered the underlying condition, not the symptom

Therapeutic Relationship

- The clinician was supportive, non-judgmental but not neutral
- The clinician modeled support, which helped the couple learn how to support each other and understand the support they needed from friends and family
- The clinician valued each partner's opinion, which led to respect for the counselor

- The safe environment allowed honesty, and this sped treatment
- The clinician noticed strengths

Interventions

- Flexibility in the initial treatment path to manage crisis showed the importance of treatment
- The clinician used probing questions, requiring critical thought and resulting in new perspectives for the couple
- The clinician intervened and directed conversation between the couple
- Between-session task of daily conversations within the first week of therapy broke down barriers for the couple
- Skills learned in session were transferred to the daily lives of the couple

Termination

- Receiving post-treatment goals and plan helped keep couple focused post-treatment

A Final Thought: Prevention Before Intervention

There are an increasing number of marriage and relationship education programs available to couples as an alternative to therapy. The question is when, and if, they are effective. Most marriage and relationship education programs have two core components: the primary focus is on developing better communication and problem-solving skills, and the other component offers didactic presentations on relationship quality. For most programs, the emphasis is on communication skills training (Hawkins et al., 2008).

The intent of most programs is to intervene with couples before the problems become too serious. A number of studies over the last twenty-five years have shown that marriage and education programs are effective in enhancing both relationship quality and communication skills, with programs showing a stronger success with communication skill development. Though follow-up outcome studies are limited, most studies show maintained improvement three to six months after attendance to the program, with a couple of studies showing benefits twelve months or longer (Hawkins et al., 2008). The key is to remember that these programs are preventative in nature and not designed for couples in severe distress or in crisis.

References

AAMFT. (2017). *Code of ethics*. Retrieved March 12, 2017 from http://aamft.org/iMIS15/AAMFT/Content/Legal_Ethics/Code_of_Ethics.aspx.

Abrahms-Spring, J. (2012). *Don't ask me to forgive you: A radical approach to healing from interpersonal wounds*. Clinical Workshop, Cincinnati, Ohio, April 11, 2013.

Ackerman, S. J., Benjamin, L. S., Beutler, L. E., Gelso, C. J., Goldfried, M. R., Hill, C., & Rainer, J. (2001). Empirically supported therapy relationships: Conclusions and recommendations of the division 29 task force. *Psychotherapy: Theory, Research, Practice, Training*, *38*, 495–497.

Anker, M. G., Duncan, B. L., & Sparks, J. A. (2009). Using client feedback to improve couple therapy outcomes: A randomized clinical trial in a naturalistic setting. *Journal of Consulting and Clinical Psychology*, *77*(4), 693–704.

Baucom, D. H., Hahlweg, K., & Kuschel, A. (2003). Are waiting-list control groups needed in future marital therapy outcome research? *Behavior Therapy*, *34*, 179–188.

Benson, L. A., McGinn, M. M., & Christensen, A. (2012). Common principles of couple therapy. *Behavior Therapy*, *43*(1), 25–35.

Bernard, J. M., & Goodyear, R. (2013). *Fundamentals of clinical supervision* (5th ed.). Boston, MA: Merril.

Brown, G. S., & Jones, D. R. (2005). Implementation of a feedback system in a managed care environment: What are patients teaching us? *Journal of Clinical Psychology*, *61*, 187–198.

Brown, J., Dreis, S., & Nace, D. K. (1999). What really makes a difference in psychotherapy outcome? Why does managed care want to know? In M. A. Hubble, B. L. Duncan, & S. D. Miller (Eds.), *The heart and soul of change: What works in therapy* (pp. 389–406). Washington, DC: APA Press.

Carroll, K. P. (2011). *The use of outcome measures by licensed marriage and family therapists in Iowa*. A dissertation presented to the school of education Drake University.

Doherty, W. (2017). Bad couple's therapy. *Psychotherapy Networker*. Retrieved January 8, 2017 from www.psychotherapynetworker.org/blog/details/369/bad-couples-therapy.

Duncan, M., & Miller, S. (2000). *The heroic client: Principles of client-directed, outcome-informed therapy*. San Francisco, CA: Jossey-Bass.

Estrada, A. U., & Holmes, J. M. (1999). Couples' perceptions of effective and ineffective ingredients of marital therapy. *Journal of Sex & Marital Therapy*, *25*(2), 151–162.

Gurman, A. S., & Kniskern, D. P. (1978). Research on marital and family therapy: Progress, perspective, and prospect. In S. L. Garfield & A. E. Bergin (Eds.), *Handbook of psychotherapy and behavior change* (pp. 817-902). New York: Wiley.

Gurman, A.S. (2008). Clinical handbook of couple therapy. 4th Edition. *Guilford Publications*, Inc. New Yok, NY.

Halford, W. K., Pepping, C. A., & Petch, J. (2015). The gap between couple therapy research efficacy and practice effectiveness. *Journal of Marriage and Family Therapy*, *42*(1), 32–44.

Hawkins, A. J., Blanchard, V. L., Baldwin, S. A., & Fawcett, E. B. (2008). Does marriage and relationship education work? A meta-analytic study. *Journal of Consulting and Clinical Psychology*, *76*(5), 723–734.

Jon and Steph. (2013, February 9). Personal Communication.

Klann, N., Hahlweg, K., Baucom, D. H., & Kroeger, C. (2011). The effectiveness of couple therapy in Germany: A replication study. *Journal and Marital Therapy*, *37*(2), 200–208.

Laska, K. M., Gurman, A. S., & Wampold, B. E. (2014). Expanding the lens of evidence-based practice in psychotherapy: A common factors perspective. *Psychotherapy*, *51*(4), 467–481. doi:10.1037/a0034332.

Lebow, J. (2013). Editorial: Couple therapy and family therapy. *Family Process*, *52*(1), 1–4. doi:10.1111/famp.12027.

Lewis, C., Simons, A., & Kim, H. (2012). The Role of Early Symptom Trajectories and Pretreatment Variables in Predicting Treatment Response to Cognitive Behavioral Therapy. *Journal of consulting and clinical psychology*, 80, 525–534. 10.1037/a0029131.

Loesch, L. C. (2001). Counseling program evaluation: Inside and outside the box. In D. C. Locke, J. E. Myers, & E. L. Herr (Eds.), *The handbook of counseling* (pp. 513–525). Thousand Oaks, CA: Sage.

Meichenbaum, D. (2008). *Core task of psychotherapy/counseling: What "expert" therapists do.* Presentation at the 12th Annual Melissa Institute Conference May, 2008. Reducing Violence by Nurturing Emotional and Behavioral Well-being: Application to Schools, Communities and Social Agencies. Miami Florida.

Miller, S.D., & Duncan, B.L. (2004). The Outcome and Session Rating Scales: Administration and scoring manual. Chicago: Institute for the Study of Therapeutic Change.

Miller, S. D., Duncan, B. L., Brown, J., Sparks, J. A., & Claud, D. A. (2003). The outcome rating scale: A preliminary study of the reliability, validity, and feasibility of a brief visual analog measure. *Journal of Brief Therapy*, *2*, 91–100.

Miller, S. D., Duncan, L. L., Brown, J., Sorrell, R., & Chalk, M. (2006). Using formal client feedback to improve outcome and retention: Making ongoing, real-time assessment feasible. *Journal of Brief Therapy*, 5, 5–22.

Mitchell, C. (2007). *Effective techniques for dealing with highly resistant clients* (2nd ed.). Clifton W. Mitchell Publishing. Jackson City, TN.

Newsome, D. W. & Gladding, S. T. (2013). *Clinical mental health counseling in community and agency settings* (4th Edition). Upper Saddle River, NJ: Pearson Education.

Orlinsky, D. E. & Ronnestad, M. H. (2005). *How psychotherapists develop: A study of therapeutic work and professional growth.* American Psychological Association.

Patterson, C. L., Uhlin, B., & Anderson, T. (2008). Clients' pretreatment counseling expectations as predictors of the working alliance. *Journal of Counseling Psychology*, *V4*, 528–534.

Prepare/Enrich. (2014). *Why should you assess your relationship with the #1 relationship assessment tool?* Retrieved December 12, 2014 from www.prepare-enrich.com/webapp/pe/couples/template/DisplaySecureContent.vm?id=pe*couples*for_couples.html.

Sells, J. N., & Yarhouse, M. A. (2011). *Counseling couples in conflict: A relational restoration model.* Downers Grove, IL: InterVarsity Press.

Shallcross, L. (2012). The recipe of truly great counseling. *Counseling Today.* Retrieved December 21, 2014 from http://ct.counseling.org/2012/12/the-recipe-for-truly-great-counseling/

Sparks, J. A. (2015). The Norway couple project: Lessons learned. *Journal of Marital and Family Therapy*, *41*(4), 481–494. doi:10.1111/jmft.12099.

Sprenkle, D. H., Davis, S. D., & Lebow, J. L. (2009). *Common factors in couple and family therapy.* New York: The Gilford Press.

Steenbarger, B. N., & Smith, H. B. (1996). Assessing the quality of counseling services: Developing accountable helping systems. *Journal of Counseling and Development*, *75*, 145–150.

Streatfield, N. (2012). Measuring outcomes. *Therapy Today*, *24*(2), 28–31. Retrieved February 22, 2016 from www.therapytoday.net/article/show/2899/measuring-outcomes/

Tarescavage, A. M., & Ben-Porath, Y. S. (2014). Psychotherapeutic outcomes measures: A critical review for practitioners. *Journal of Clinical Psychology*, *70*, 808–830. doi:http://dx.doi.org/10.1002/jclp.22080

Wampold, B. E. (2001). *The great psychotherapy debate: Models, methods and findings.* New York: Routledge.

Whipple, J. L., Lambert, M. J., Vermeerch, D. A., Smart, D. W., Nielsen, S. L., & Hawkins, E. J. (2003). Improving the effects of psychotherapy: The use of early identification of treatment failure and problem-solving strategies in routine practice. *Journal of Counseling Psychology*, 50, 59–68.

2 The Hidden Beginning of Treatment

Distal colors move in and out on the summer grass
Quietly she sits and sees the wave and plume
Yet perceives no feature of the day
Further approach shows symmetry and form
A children's game much like a dance
Running, laughing, almost choreographed
Enjoyment discovered
By the discerning glance

—Butch Losey

Josh and Emily began quarreling as usual one Thursday evening. The argument escalated with Emily's complaints of Josh's lack of concern for the deepening desperation of their relationship. From a heated moment of frustration, Emily threatened divorce. This was the one threat the couple had not voiced, and yet both had probably thought about in the past. Josh was shocked and fearful and no longer clung to his refusal to go to counseling. He went to his computer and began exploring clinicians online.

He discovered that there were many private practitioners listed on many different websites. He found one that seemed like a good fit and asked his wife of five years to join him for the call. Josh called the clinician, and Emily quietly listened in. Soon both were talking with the clinician, who listened as they explained their problem. The twenty-minute call left the couple calm, reassured, and scheduled for an appointment for the following Monday.

The skilled clinician took the short time needed to facilitate the client's goals for the call. She joined in a way that gave hope to the couple. She also recognized that this call was the primary first therapeutic exchange and was deliberately purposeful in her approach. She has set the stage for positive outcomes in treatment

Pretreatment change is happening here. Truly, it may have actually begun weeks or months prior to this conversation. This phone call is a crucial first step that is linked to positive outcomes of treatment. If the clinician manages this well, there is a possibility that the treatment process will include higher show rates and less drop-out rates, greater satisfaction for the treatment process and satisfaction with the clinician, more sessions overall devoted to treatment and higher rates of treatment completion.

Evidence for Pretreatment Change

The research literature supports that pretreatment change does occur. Weiner-Davis, de Shazer, and Gingerich (1987) conducted an informal survey of thirty families and showed that 67% or approximately two-thirds of the families reported having observed pretreatment changes. The researchers also noted that although the remaining ten clients initially reported observing no differences, it was quite common for them to recall pretreatment changes later in the session.

Larger studies also confirm the presence of pretreatment change. Allgood et al. (1995) found that 30% of 200 clients reported pretreatment improvement in the situation that led them to seek therapy. Another study reviewing data from 2,400 clients found that 15% made significant improvement before attending their first session (Howard et al., 1986).

In practice, I have found that the majority of couples can identify some small change that has occurred prior to the first session. Some of course do not. Some may even say that no change has occurred, but then go on to say that they felt relief once making the appointment. My guess is that as clinicians maintain a perspective of curiosity and question the pretreatment experience, subsequent sessions may uncover previously unidentified pretreatment change. The discovery could lead to new solutions and potential goals for treatment: an important endeavor indeed.

Defining Pretreatment Change

For the purpose of this book, I am defining pretreatment change in a very specific way. The reason I need a definition is because I am interested in targeting all components of the definition in my treatment process. In this case, the definition informs my treatment. Pretreatment change from my perspective is defined as follows:

> *Change "without treatment" that occurs by the client to solve the current problem prior to entering treatment (this could include making an appointment).*
>
> *Subtle changes in the couple relationship as the result of conversations facilitated by the clinician, focused on expectations for change prior to their first session.*
>
> *Changes that occur in the couple relationship that occur because of interventions prescribed by the clinician and implemented by the couple prior to the first session.*
>
> *Any or a combination of all three.*

Pretreatment change questioning is rooted in solution-focused therapy. The process is quite useful (and hope-focused) for clinicians practicing with couples from a variety of different theoretical orientations. You do not need to be a solution-focused clinician. As a systemic counselor, I believe discussing pretreatment changes is a good discussion starter for the first session. Pretreatment change processes for treatment in my practice will include conversations during the intake phone call that presumes change has already occurred, assigning tasks to the couple at intake to target the clients' identification of pretreatment change prior to the first session, pretreatment change talk in the first and subsequent sessions, and goal setting based on identified changes.

Pretreatment Change and Outcomes for Therapy

The factors that contribute to positive outcomes in therapy have long been studied, including in-session factors such as the clinician's characteristics, the therapeutic relationship, therapeutic conditions, and specific therapeutic techniques. Between-session variables have also been considered, and it has been estimated that things that clients do outside the session could account for as much as 40% of the variance in change that occurs (Lambert, 1986). Research supports that there is an association between the client's identification of pretreatment change and positive outcomes for treatment. Identification of pretreatment change by the client and the clinician accomplishes four specific outcomes.

Shifts Focus to Solutions

Solution-focused clinicians are aware that asking about pretreatment change by the clinician is applying a solution-focused process of shifting clients' focus on the problem to the solutions. This change talk also holds clues to the clients' goals. It is possible that moving clients in the first session towards solution-oriented thinking could quickly get the clients some symptom relief and increase possible positive outcomes for treatment.

Increases Likelihood for Completion of Treatment

A strong indication of the importance of pretreatment change comes from Beyebach (2014). The researchers found that clients reporting pretreatment changes were four times more likely to successfully complete treatment than were clients who did not experience pretreatment change. Early identification of changes could lead to multiple components of treatment, including early goal setting and symptom relief translating to the staying power of the clinical experience.

Increases the Number of Sessions Involved in Treatment

Terminations in one university counseling clinic could be predicted with 76% accuracy based on the identification of pretreatment change. There was a correlation between the number of sessions and a lack of pretreatment change. Reviewing session-by-session dropout rates, it was found that clients without pretreatment change had significantly fewer sessions (Allgood et al., 2007).

Reduces Dropout Rates

Johnson, Nelson, and Allgood (1998) investigated the prevalence and duration of pretreatment change, as well as the impact of clinicians' noticing and inquiring about pretreatment change. Their results showed that clients who reported pretreatment changes also noticed by counselors had a lower unplanned termination rate than did those who did not report pretreatment changes.

So asking pretreatment change questions is an important treatment concern, and yet, interestingly, asking about pretreatment changes is apparently not an easy endeavor. Of the four primary solution-based brief therapy questions (miracle, scaling, exception, and pretreatment change), therapists rate the miracle question as the most therapeutic. Scaling questions were the most frequently used by clinicians, and clinicians rate these questions as the best way to evaluate a client's progress. Clinicians described exception questions as typically leading the client to report exceptions and improvements in his or her problems and to describe what he or she did to achieve the change. Clinicians, however, find questions about pretreatment change to be the most difficult to use effectively and therefore are less commonly used (Skidmore, 1993). The contradiction is apparent, then: pretreatment changes are more likely to emerge in therapy if targeted by the therapist in the first session, but therapists have to feel capable and willing to ask the questions.

Stages of Change

Prochaska and DiClemente (1983) developed a change model characterized by a series of stages of change to describe a person's motivational readiness and progress towards changing a particular problem behavior. The model recognizes that people in different stages of change need different types of interventions to help them progress. The stages include Pre-contemplation, Contemplation, Preparation, Action, and Maintenance. I see pretreatment change processes as falling in Prochaska's Preparation stage. I specifically see pretreatment change in the Preparation stage as "transitioning action." The clinician can play a key role in the client's transition from Preparation to Action, and this process can start just prior to the first session. In Table 2.1, I compare the change model to treatment processes highlighting the "transitioning action" of the Preparation stage.

Table 2.1 Comparison of Stages to Change and Stages of Treatment

Stage of Change	*Stage of Treatment*	*Client Process/Interventions*
Pre-Contemplation	Pretreatment	Couple does not acknowledge or recognize relationship problems.
Contemplation	Pretreatment	Couple begins considering there may be a problem.

(*Continued*)

Table 2.1 Continued

Stage of Change	*Stage of Treatment*	*Client Process/Interventions*
Preparation	Pretreatment (transitioning action)	The couple considers possible ways to address relationship problems. Has initial contact with a professional, makes appointment and the individual may notice change, make change, or feel relief. Clinician creates dialogue and task related to pretreatment change.
Action	Treatment	The couple attends first session. Discusses pretreatment change that has occurred. Assesses relationship and sets goals. Completes treatment.
Maintenance	Post-treatment	Implements post-treatment goals. Participates in post-treatment consultation. Maintains therapeutic gains.

The Intake Phone Call

The intake phone call is the primary first therapeutic encounter with the client. It should not be dismissed as just a means to set an appointment. There are multiple goals of the intake phone contact. Goals need to be seen from both the client perspective and the clinician perspective. The nice thing is that the clinician and client goals are similar and overlap. The clinician should take the lead to facilitate a purposeful, directed conversation that matches the goals of both parties. Too many times I hear clinicians do little in facilitating this discussion. They basically collect some data, and then they may or may not set an appointment. They do this without any consideration that the phone call is a critical clinical intervention. In Table 2.2 I have outlined the shared goals of the intake phone call.

The client's goals are primarily to describe the presenting problem to the clinician and to have their views understood and validated. They also want to hear that the clinician is capable of managing their problem, and a small number of couples will want to know the education and theoretical background of the clinician.

The clinician should support these goals and give time for the client to express their understanding of the problem. I generally allow the intake call to last fifteen to twenty minutes. As they talk I paraphrase and validate. Once the client completes their description of the problem, I move to my goals.

The first task, and a very important one, is to tell them how I can help them. This generally includes a *global* outlay of treatment over time and the specific interventions that might be helpful. I then solicit from them questions about my clinical process or my background and answer these questions as needed. We then negotiate a time for the appointment, and I clearly state that by virtue of

Table 2.2 Client and Clinician Goals of Intake Phone Call

Client Goal	*Clinician Action*	*Clinician Goal*
Describe presenting problem	Paraphrase and validate	Therapeutic responsiveness and develop therapeutic bond
Be understood and validated	Paraphrase and validate	Therapeutic responsiveness and develop therapeutic bond
Confirm clinician competence	Propose course of treatment and specific interventions Solicit questions about process, clinician background, or theoretical orientation	Conceptualize treatment course and indicated interventions
Obtain appointment	Confirm length of time of appointment and negotiate time Confirm "client" status	Obtain appointment and define client-clinician relationship
	Prescribe pretreatment change task	Move client from problem focus to solution focus and heighten pretreatment change opportunities and focus

making the appointment they are now my client. I say that since they are my client, the counseling process starts at this phone call, and I have a therapeutic task that I would like the couple to do prior to their scheduled appointment.

Here is where I introduce the pretreatment change task (if the phone call is only with one of the partners, I direct them to share this task with their partner). To set up the task I will say to the client, "Nothing is constant, and though it is difficult for you right now there will be times when things will be a little easier." I then prescribe this task for them to complete before their first session:

> Between now and the time of our first meeting, I want you to be an observer of your relationship. I want you to notice those things in the relationship that are just a little bit better. What small changes do you notice as you go through each day? You may want to write this down so that we can talk about them when we meet.

Ethical Considerations

The Initiation of the Counseling Relationship

The challenge with this process for the intake phone call is determining when you, the clinician, initiate the counseling relationship and the clinician has established the professional relationship. I suggest that the clinician refrain from giving advice or making recommendations. These indicate the beginning of the counseling relationship and may add liability for the clinician. Definitely do not offer diagnostic impressions because this could be both unethical and illegal.

First Contact by Email

First contact by email is best handled differently. Too much can be assumed or inferred. When an email comes in to me from prospective clients accessing websites such as Psychology Today or Good Therapy, I will only answer basic information. I then request that they set up a phone appointment with me. A good professional policy is to only use email for non-urgent and non-confidential information. It would be wise to respond to the email with a brief comment and request a phone call.

Pretreatment Change

"Nothing personal, but I've been dreading this phone call for the last month!" the woman explained in an exasperated voice. "Often making that call can be the beginning of the relief you've been looking for," I responded encouragingly. When Andrea arrived at her appointment later in the week, she appeared cautious but happy and ready to explain her reasons for being in therapy. "What has improved since you made that phone call?" I asked. Andrea launched into how she felt so much better just reaching out to a therapist.

Since the call, Andrea began writing a list of behaviors she wanted to change. I asked how making this list improved her life situation. She exclaimed that by making this list, she had already noticed positive changes! As we explored the list, I inquired as to how she saw improvement in each behavior. My pretreatment question inquiring about what improved since Andrea made the phone call encouraged

Andrea to find hope. She began constructing solutions rather than just noticing the negatives of her situation. Andrea was obviously eager and willing to embrace change.

An important consideration in using pretreatment questions successfully is the recognition of how motivated the client is to change. Often an unconscious or conscious reason (secondary gain) exists that creates an obstruction against change. If I asked what improved since the phone call was made and Andrea responded, "Absolutely nothing!" another scenario would be cast. Andrea may be in great pain with very little hope for positive change. Helping her to find any positive possibilities, without invalidating her present experience, can be challenging.

In both cases, having a list of pretreatment questions may be useful to help the client experience hope and begin construction of solutions. When a client responds favorably to a pretreatment question, asking her more specific questions to continue the process of finding solutions can be easy. When the response is negative, as it so often can be, having questions available to help the client kick-start change is important. The following questions can be used to help facilitate solution construction:

"It took courage to make the call for help. What have you noticed in the past when you were this determined to make change happen?"

"What would you like to happen instead (Walter & Peller, 1992, p. 228)?"

"What would you like to continue to happen (de Shazer & Molnar, 1984, p. 298)?"

"What were the 'exceptions' to the problem (Weiner-Davis, de Shazer, & Gingerich, 1987, p. 360)?"

Linda Mika has worked in the mental health field since 1985. She received her M.S. in Family Studies and Child Development from Purdue University, where she was awarded the Graduate Research Award for her work with abusing families, which was later published. She attended the University of Cincinnati for further study in sexual disorders, dysfunctions, and issues. She became certified in Eye Movement Desensitization and Reprocessing (EMDR) to assist clients in overcoming trauma and abuse. She has presented seminars on trauma and sexual abuse, EMDR using puppets, sexual addiction, and attachment issues in adults and children. She has been in private practice since 1993 and currently practices in Fort Thomas, Kentucky, where she uses Brief Solution-Focused Therapy as one of her treatment modalities.

Linda can be reached at
(859) 441–3020
L.Mikalmft@zoomtown.com
lindamika.com

Pretreatment Change Questioning During the First Session

In my practice the first session is considered a double session. There is just so much to complete that a fifty-five-minute session will not be enough time. I set the first appointment at one and a half hours, and this is a long enough period of time to complete my intake process. I do know of a few private practice clinicians who will schedule the first session for three hours. Obviously, it would be difficult to accomplish this time frame in an agency setting that takes insurance reimbursement.

Since I consider myself a systemic therapist and not a solution-focused therapist, I will not dedicate the entire session to pretreatment change questioning. This is, however, the first conversation that I start with, following the joining and consent process. I find it useful to have a three-step procedure to guide me through this questioning.

1. *Consideration*

The first step is to remind the client of the pretreatment change task and confirm that the other partner was given the directive. The discussion is then directed to an exploration of any changes that have occurred between the time the client made the appointment and this first session. This conversation is useful for a number of reasons:

- It creates a framework of fluidity emphasizing that nothing is static
- It helps the client and therapist recognize any skills or resources that may have been utilized recently
- It helps clients identify steps to take to continue helping their situation
- It can highlight exceptions to the problem
- It helps clients feel encouraged because they realize their situation can improve

Rarely will the client report pretreatment change spontaneously. It will require the clinician to solicit this information in the first and even subsequent sessions. When potential changes and solutions are not identified or are ignored by the clinician and client, they quietly disappear and sadly go unused.

Here are a few possible pretreatment prompting questions:

What things are just a little bit better (this is the pretreatment task you assigned on the first phone call)?
What things have you done that worked well between the moment you called and now?
Which steps forward have you taken since the moment you called me?

When the answer indicates change, it is important to track the context of their answer: the who, what, where, when, and how of the pretreatment change and how it was useful. If the couple does not indicate change, I continue to explore and broaden the exploration to include positive, negative, and neutral changes.

2. *Utilization*

Once changes are identified, the clinician can assist the client in making meaning for the changes that they are noticing. The clinician can ask a variety of questions for exploration:

How are these changes different than before?
Do these changes relate to the reason you have come to counseling?
How helpful has the change been to the current problem?
What has this change most helped in your relationship?
Are these changes that you would like to see happen more frequently in your life?
What did you do to help bring about these changes?

3. *Amplification*

Now that the clinician knows the positive pretreatment changes and the context, it is important to amplify the changes. Presuppositional questions are a good way to amplify pretreatment changes and also the exceptions to the problem. These questions are used by solution-focused therapists to introduce possibilities or discover exceptions, improvements, or steps toward solutions. They are leading questions which assume and communicate a positive expectation about the client, their situation, or their ability to accomplish their goals (McKeel, 2011). The following are a few presupposition questions (Clarke & Dembkowski, 2006):

How did you do that?	*Presupposes that the client had influence on the outcome*
How did you know to do that?	*Presupposes the client has knowledge*
What else?	*Presupposes that the client could say more*
What might you do differently next time?	*Presupposes choice*
What helped?	*Presupposes that something was helpful*
What did you learn from that?	*Presupposes reflection*

Pretreatment change occurs and beckons to be noticed. If the discerning clinician can help the client recognize, understand, and apply these changes to the process of therapy, they can affect positive change. Clients will be more engaged in treatment, they will see symptom reduction earlier, and they will be more likely to complete therapy. The clinician needs to take an active part in the discovery of pretreatment change, and this happens at the entryway into therapy: the first phone call.

References

Allgood, S. M., Parham, K. B., Salts, C. J., & Smith, T. A. (1995). The association between pretreatment change and unplanned termination in family therapy. *American Journal of Family Therapy*, *23*(3), 195–202.

Allgood, S. M., Parham, K. B., Salts, C. J., & Smith, T. A. (2007). The association between pretreatment change and unplanned termination in family therapy. *The American Journal of Family Therapy*, 195–202.

Beyebach, M. (2014). Change factors in solution-focused breif therapy: A review of the Salamanca studies. *Journal of Systemic Therapies*, Vol. 33, N1, 62–77.

Clarke, C., & Dembkowski, S. (2006). The art of asking great questions. *International Journal of Mentoring & Coaching*, *IV*(2).

de Shazer, S., & Molnar, A. (1984). Four useful interventions in brief family therapy. *Journal of Marital and Family Therapy*, *10*(3), 297–304.

Howard, K. I., Lopta, S. M., Krause, M. S., & Orlinsky, D. E. (1986). The dose-effect relationship in psychotherapy. *American Psychologist*, *41*, 159–164.

Johnson, L. N., Nelson, T. S., & Allgood, S. M. (1998). Noticing pretreatment change and therapeutic outcome: An initial study. *American Journal of Family Therapy*, *26*, 159–168.

Lambert, M. J. (1986). Implications of psychotherapy outcome research for eclectic psychocounseling. In J. C. Norcross (Ed.), *Handbook of eclectic psychotherapy* (pp. 436–462). New York: Brunner/Mazel.

McKeel, J. (2011). *Solution-focused therapy research: A common factors perspective.* Workshop at the SFBTA Annual Conference November 11.

Prochaska, J., & DiClemente, C. (1983). Stages and processes of self-change of smoking: Toward an integrative model of change. *Journal of Consulting and Clinical Psychology*, *51*(3), 390–395.

Walter, J., & Peller, J. (1992). *Becoming solution-focused in brief therapy*. New York: Brunner/Mazel.

Weiner-Davis, M., de Shazer, S., & Gingerich, W. (1987). Building on pretreatment change to construct the therapeutic solution: An exploratory study. *Journal of Marital and Family Therapy*, *13*(4), 359–363.

3 Ethical Practice

Adherence to professional ethics and common professional values will create the foundation for the clinician to provide effective treatment. This chapter is not meant to offer an exhaustive review of ethics related to couples therapy but moreso a review of common issues that a couple therapist might encounter in their therapy practice.

Common Ethical Considerations for Couples Therapy

Competency to Practice

Core ethical responsibilities include beneficence, which is the clinician's efforts to do good on the clients' behalf and non-malfeasance, which is the clinician's obligation to interact with the client without doing harm. As I have mentioned earlier, couples therapy is quite commonly practiced by clinicians with little or no specific training. It is highly important that clinicians get additional training and supervision if they are interested in working with couples. Additional training should include developing skills to work with severe attachment disruptions, violence and abuse, sexual concerns, infidelity and other betrayals, high conflict, disruption in trust, relational boundaries, and therapeutic boundaries and assessment, just to name a few. These issues make couple counseling highly complex and specialized. Without this training, there is great risk of not offering the best service to the client (beneficence) and worse, causing harm to the couple (malfeasance).

Individual Sessions

Clinicians may occasionally arrange to see one or both partners individually. If clinicians choose to do so, there must be a clear and strong clinical rationale. There are three clinical reasons that clinicians may consider individual sessions in the context of couples therapy (Weeks, Odell, & Methven, 2005). First, it may be that one partner needs to share information that might be hurtful to the other partner. In this case, having an individual session to plan for the disclosure in an upcoming session can be helpful in considering the best way to share the information. Second, the clinician may believe that one partner may need to bond more with the clinician. This could occur when one partner has high levels of defensiveness with the clinician, possibly because of not trusting or "believing in" therapy. A third reason would be when the clinician suspects that a secret is being hidden, in which the secret is inhibiting progress. In these cases, the clinician may work to uncover the secret and help the partner facilitate disclosure of the secret, if discovered. Sometimes, the partner may state that there is a secret and ask for help to disclose it.

It is important that the clinician consider the consequences of the decision to see the couple individually, even before discussing the possibility with the couple. Usually, to avoid a conflict of interest, these sessions are conducted under the rule that there will be no secrets and anything spoken in the individual sessions can be brought back to the couple session. Secondly, once confidentiality and parameters of the individual sessions are discussed, it is important to have both partners in agreement before proceeding.

Confidentiality and Informed Consent

Confidentiality is the foundation of effective therapy and is one of the most important aspects of informed consent. In couples counseling, the clinician is required to clearly define who is considered "the client" and to discuss expectations and limitations of confidentiality. I clearly explain to the couple that "the relationship" is my client and, therefore, I am guided by what is best for my client: the relationship.

This is true for confidentiality as well. We are expected to document in writing the agreement among all involved parties regarding the confidentiality of information. Confidentiality is covered in my standard informed-consent paperwork but I also have an additional process of detailing my policy on how I will manage secrets: in other words, how I will deal with one partner privately sharing information to me and requesting that I not share it with the other partner. My particular take on this issue is that I prefer not to keep secrets and try to not put myself in the situation of needing to do so. For that reason, I have a no-secrets policy. You will need to decide how you will deal with secrets.

Many clinicians now have a no-secrets policy. A no-secrets policy is sufficient in offering informed consent but not sufficient for disclosing a secret of one partner, shared in confidence to the clinician, to the other partner. The American Association of Marriage and Family Therapy directly states this in their code of ethics section 2.2: "In the context of couple, family or group treatment, the therapist may not reveal any individual's confidences to others in the client unit without the prior written permission of that individual" (AAMFT, 2017).

For this reason, I recommend a policy statement in the no-secrets policy on informed consent, and within that policy statement, the clinician should include an authorization for release of information. This release should cover disclosure to each partner of all communication that is considered part of the couple treatment, including couples therapy sessions, individual sessions that are considered part of the couple treatment, phone calls, emails, and texts.

This chapter's next section contains an outline of statements in my no-secrets policy that I believe are important for informed consent and authorization for release. Certainly, vet this with your own attorney to consider applicable laws in your professional discipline and state of practice. Please note that a sample no-secrets policy is included in Appendix 3.1.

Neutrality

Clinicians want to believe they are neutral, but in truth, they are not. Clinicians may have strong beliefs about healthy relationships, the process of change, beliefs about love, intimacy and sexuality, and what constitutes appropriate communication patterns. These beliefs will guide their work with couples. There are also times when neutrality may not be appropriate: for example, in situations in which one partner's behavior is hurting the relationship or hurting the other partner.

Though the clinician is not neutral, they can work to be multi-perspective. A multi-perspective clinician will consider the perspectives of both partners and their own perspective. In doing so, they may help create new awareness for the couple, generate perspective-taking between the partners, and offer new possibilities for solutions that may not have been considered by the couple.

Role Changes

Any time there is a clinical role change during treatment, there is added risk for the clinician and the client. Though there is not an outright ban on changing roles, many professions do, however, have a statement about role changes in their code of ethics. Consider for a moment the American Counseling Association's (2014, Standard A.6.d.) statement on role changes:

> When counselors change a role from the original or most recent contracted relationship, they obtain informed consent from the client and explain the client's right to refuse services related to the change. . . . Clients must be fully informed of any anticipated consequences (e.g., financial, legal, personal, therapeutic) of counselor role changes.

A primary challenge of changing roles is the treatment alliance. A client can create a strong bond with the clinician in individual counseling, which would make it next to impossible for the clinician to be impartial if a partner is brought into the treatment session. Likewise, changing from couple therapist to individual therapist would make it difficult to return back to couples therapy and be impartial.

All role changes need to be clearly documented in the client record. The clinician should document reasons considered, arguments for and against the

Table 3.1 Role Changes in Couples Therapy

From couple to individual due to separation or divorce
From couple to individual due to one partner's dropping out of treatment
From individual to couple due to changing treatment focus
Guest invitations

decision to change the role, results of consultation with other clinicians, and the informed-consent process of the clinician.

There are several situations in which clinicians will consider changing their role. Table 3.1 identifies the most common role changes.

From Couple to Individual: Due to Separation or Divorce

One conclusion of couples therapy is the decision to separate or divorce. On many occasions, one partner will request to continue with the clinician in individual counseling. What would you do? Would it make a difference if the couple were separating versus divorcing? Is there reason to notify the exiting partner that the other partner is continuing without them, in the case of divorce?

I believe I would be more comfortable changing the role to individual counseling in a situation of divorce. The person continuing with individual counseling would be informed that by choosing individual counseling, I would not see the two of them as a couple again. Strange as it might sound, some couples decide to stay together after a decision to divorce, and others decide to re-marry each other after they have divorced. If I am authorized to release information, I would also inform the other partner that I was continuing with their partner in individual counseling and the consequences of that decision.

If one partner wants to continue with individual counseling after the couple's decision to separate, I will encourage each to seek an individual therapist. I am more open to seeing the partner individually in these cases; however, I find it best if I can serve in just one role. There is always a possibility the couple will reunite. In many cases, the client will make the argument that he or she would prefer not to "start over" with another clinician. I definitely understand that, when the treatment alliance is set, it is easier to stay with the clinician than tell the backstory all over again to another clinician. This is the primary reason that I consider the role change. If there is a strong treatment alliance, I will consider moving to individual counseling.

From Couple to Individual: Due to One Partner Dropping Out of Treatment

Couples join treatment with different commitments to the relationship and different commitments to therapy. In this situation, the couple attended therapy for a period of time, and when one partner lost interest in therapy, he dropped out of treatment yet still stayed in the relationship with his partner.

I agreed to continue with individual counseling with the remaining partner because the couple was adamant about not returning to couples therapy. I stated that my expectation would be that I would not see them as a couple in the future, if they were so inclined, but that I would be willing to refer them to a couples therapist.

From Individual to Couple: Due to Changing Treatment Focus

This is one of the most difficult role changes and one that is pretty clear. There are very few reasons for changing from individual to couples therapy. The primary problem with this role change is the therapeutic alliance that is established in individual therapy. It is difficult to be impartial in couples therapy following any period of time with someone in individual counseling. The only exception that I consider is when I have met with an individual for one session and it is determined that couples therapy would be a better option.

I have had quite a number of couples share with me that their past couples therapy began with one partner in individual counseling for a number of sessions and then transitioned to couples therapy. I have yet to meet one couple that had positive things to say about the experience. I typically hear statements such as "the therapist did not seem to know what they were doing" or "the therapist was on his/her side." Some couples will ask if the role change is considered inappropriate, without elaborating further. Others will state that they reported the clinician to the board or that they had considered reporting the clinician to the board. My guess is that in these cases there was difficulty trusting the clinician. So, my recommendation to you here is to be cautious when considering this role change.

Guest Invitations

I believe guest invitations are a blending of roles that can take on some of the feeling and dynamics of couples therapy. Guest invitations typically occur in individual counseling in which the clinician or client suggests having the client's partner attend treatment for a session or a number of sessions to support the person's individual treatment. Trouble arises when the clinician is unprepared for the couple dynamic that occurs in session, the clinician lets the session linger without any predetermined agenda, the clinician inappropriately discloses information to the guest partner, or the clinician changes the roles of individual counseling to couple counseling (this usually happens without appropriate, informed consent).

Guest attendance in individual counseling is more appropriate when it is brief. There are a number of guidelines that I would suggest for clinicians considering inviting a spouse/partner to attend individual counseling.

Inviting a guest to individual counseling should not be happenstance. Without goals in mind, the clinician can do more harm than good. Without clear rules, the clinician can inadvertently breach confidentiality. The guest session should be highly structured to meet a specific goal in mind.

Table 3.2 Guidelines for Guest Attendance

Schedule a planning session prior to guest attendance.
Clarify goal of guest session prior to guest attendance.
Clarify rules for interaction with guest.
Obtain informed consent from guest at first session.
Obtain authorization for release of information to speak to guest.
Do not change role from individual therapist to couple therapist.

A planning session is important to have prior to bringing a guest into session. In the planning session, I help the client identify one or two primary goals of the guest session. I am structured to the point of identifying what will occur in each fifteen-minute increment. I have the client identify specific topics to discuss with the guest. The plan includes what might be facilitated in session or requested of the guest.

I also want to make it very clear what the individual client is authorizing me to say and what topics are off limits. Accidental disclosers are a substantial risk with inviting a guest, particularly when inviting the spouse or partner. In this discussion, I have the client complete an authorization for release of information to talk to the guest, and I will specifically list the topic areas that are planned for discussion. I also clarify the differences between a "client" and a "guest," particularly regarding rights and privacy.

There are a number of informed-consent requirements for guests (see Appendix 3.2, Guest Agreement). For example, who are guests? A guest is usually a spouse, family member, or friend who participates in therapy to assist the client. The guest is not considered to be a client, nor are they considered to be receiving treatment. Due to this, they do not have the same rights as clients.

Clients do have a right to be treated in a way that is consistent with state and federal law and have access to my privacy and client-rights policies, which I provide to guests. However, many of the privacy-policy rights apply only to clients and not to someone who joins in a counseling session as a guest.

Being a guest affects how records are managed. Since guests are not receiving treatment, they will have no file, they will not have a treatment plan, and records will not be released to them. Any records that are created during the visit as a guest will be part of the file of the client. The client is able to access or release these records as needed, including any references to the attendance as a guest that are included in the file. The guest, however, does not have access to these records unless the client signs a waiver to release them to the guest.

If the guest, client, or clinician believes that the guest's relationship with the client should be the main focus of treatment, then couple counseling would be suggested and a referral made to a couples therapist. The clinician could continue with individual counseling if that meets the client's needs and is within their financial ability. I would caution the clinician to resist making guest invitations permanent.

Ethical Business Practice

We usually associate ethics with the clinical aspect of our work. There are also a number of ethical considerations for managing private practice. If clinicians are not careful, they may unknowingly participate in unethical business practices.

1. *Self-Referrals*

Many clinicians in a clinical or school setting also manage their own private practice. It may make sense that some clients in one setting might benefit from the services in the clinician's private practice, and consequently clinicians may refer to themselves. Clinicians need to be careful in approaching self-referrals. Ethical codes suggest that clinicians should not self-refer to their private practice unless the policies of a particular organization make explicit provisions for self-referrals (ACA Standard A.10.a). In such instances, the clients must be informed of other options open to them should they seek private counseling services.

2. *Payments, Incentives, and Discounts for Referrals*

Clinicians should not participate in fee splitting with other clinicians or agencies, nor should they give or receive commissions, rebates, or any other form of remuneration when referring clients for professional services (ACA Standard A.10.b; NASW Standard 2.06c).

3. *Use of Collection Agencies*

If clinicians plan to use collection agencies, it is important that this policy is identified during the informed consent process (ACA Standard A.10.d.). Also, be aware that using collection agencies also increases the risk of board complaints.

4. *Advertising and Soliciting Clients*

It is important that clinicians advertise their practice and credentials truthfully and not in a misleading or deceptive manner (ACA Standard C.3.a.). If clinicians choose to use testimonials, they do not solicit them from current clients, former clients, or any other persons who may be vulnerable to undue influence. They should also discuss with their clients the implications of and obtain permission for the use of any testimonial (ACA Standard C.3.b.; NASW Standard 4.07b).

5. *Representations of Credentials*

Clinicians claim only the professional qualifications actually completed and correct any known misrepresentations of their qualifications by others (ACA

Standard C.4.a.; NASW Standard 4.06c). Counselors do not imply doctoral-level competence when possessing a master's degree in counseling or a related field by referring to themselves as "Dr." in a counseling context when their doctorate is not in counseling or a related field. Counselors do not use "ABD" (all but dissertation) or other such terms to imply competency (ACA Standard C.4.d.).

6. *Accepting Gifts*

Clinicians understand the challenges of accepting gifts from clients and recognize that in some cultures, small gifts are a token of respect and gratitude. When determining whether to accept a gift from clients, clinicians take into account the therapeutic relationship, the monetary value of the gift, the client's motivation for giving the gift, and the clinician's motivation for wanting to accept or decline the gift (ACA Standard A.10.f.).

7. *Domestic Violence/Partner Abuse*

Approximately 10% of men and women will experience physical aggression from their partners in the context of an argument. Most, if not all, will be preceded by psychological aggression (O'Leary & Woodin, 2009). Couples therapists understand that they will at times need to work with couples in which aggression is present. Domestic violence, however, which includes force, intimidation, or manipulation, is considered different by many clinicians because it hinders the effectiveness of treatment. It is our ethical and professional obligation to carefully assess factors that may undermine treatment, and when partner abuse is assessed and determined, most clinicians believe that it is an exclusionary criterion for couples therapy and will prefer to refer the partners to individual counseling.

Clinicians struggle with knowing when to continue to treat the couple or when it is appropriate to refuse to provide couples therapy and refer one or both partners to individual therapy. According to Albert Dytch (2017), before he will treat an abusive couple together, the individuals would have to meet several conditions as outlined in Table 3.3. He emphasizes that couples therapy is appropriate when the dynamics of the relationship, not the abuse, is the focus of treatment (Dytch, 2017).

Table 3.3 Parameters for Treating Abusive Couples Together

Past abuse was moderate to mild; currently, abuse is extremely mild or entirely absent.
The couple can adhere to a contract of no further abuse.
The abused partner is safe, unafraid, and able to mobilize resources if needed.
Both partners are motivated for treatment out of a sincere desire to grow and change.
Both partners are willing to be accountable for their behavior, without blaming the other.
The couple can use basic communication skills in a non-manipulative manner.

States also differ on how they require reporting of suspected domestic violence. For example, here in Cincinnati where I live, Ohio clinicians are not required to report domestic violence. Across the river in Kentucky, clinicians are required to report. Make sure to understand your state's reporting law because it could likely create an added layer of legal, ethical, and professional considerations.

References

AAMFT. (2017). *Code of ethics*. Retrieved March 12, 2017 from http://aamft.org/iMIS15/AAMFT/Content/Legal_Ethics/Code_of_Ethics.aspx

American Counseling Association. (2014). *Code of ethics: As approved by the governing counsel.*

Dytch, A. (2017). *Assessing partner abuse in couples therapy*. Retrieved March 23, 2017 from www.psychotherapy.net/article/couples-abuse-assessment#section-obligation-to-assess.

O'Leary, D. K., & Woodin, E. M. (2009). *Psychological and physical aggression in couples: Causes and interventions*. American Psychological Association. Washington, D.C.

Weeks, G. R., Odell, M., & Methven, S. (2005). *If only I had known: Avoiding common mistakes in couples therapy*. New York: W.W. Norton & Company.

Appendix 3.1

"No Secrets" Policy

Confidentiality

This written policy is intended to inform you, the participants in therapy, that when I agree to treat a couple, I consider the couple to be my client (the treatment unit). For this reason, my responsibility for confidentiality is to the couple, not just the individual.

These sessions are confidential and I will not release any confidential information to a third party unless I am required by law to do so or unless I have written authorization from all members of the treatment unit.

For instance, if there is a request for the treatment records of the couple, I will seek the authorization of all members of the treatment unit before I release confidential information to third parties. If any member of the treatment unit refuses authorization to release information, I will decline to do so. Also, if my records are subpoenaed, I will assert the counselor-client privilege on behalf of the client, which is the treatment unit.

Management of Communication

During the course of my work with a couple, I may see one of you individually for one or more sessions. Though individual sessions are rare in my practice, these sessions should be seen by you as a part of the work that I am doing with you as a couple. In addition, any communication with me outside of the couple session should be considered part of the couple treatment.

Management of Secrets

At some point, I may need to share information learned from you or your partner in an individual session (or other communication outside the couple session) with the entire treatment unit (the couple) if I am to effectively serve the unit being treated. I will use my best judgment as to whether, when, and to what extent I will make disclosures to the treatment unit. I will also, if appropriate, first give the individual or the smaller part of the treatment unit being seen the opportunity to make the disclosure.

Thus, if you feel it necessary to talk about matters that you absolutely want to be shared with no one, you might want to consult with an individual therapist who can treat you individually.

This "no-secrets" policy is intended to allow me to continue to treat the couple by preventing, to the extent possible, a conflict of interest to arise in which an individual's interests may not be consistent with the interests of the unit being treated.

For instance, information learned in the course of an individual session may be relevant or even essential to the proper treatment of the couple. If I am not free to exercise my clinical judgment regarding the need to bring this information to the couple during their therapy, I might be placed in a situation where I will have to terminate treatment of the couple. This policy is intended to prevent the need for such a termination.

I, ______________________________ (Client Name), acknowledge by my signature below that I have read this policy, that I understand it, that I have had an opportunity to discuss its contents with Dr. Butch Losey, Ed.D., LPCC-S, and that I enter couples therapy in agreement with this policy.

Signature___________________ Date___________________________

I, _________________________ (Client Name), hereby authorize Dr. Butch Losey, Ed.D., LPCC-S to release and disclose to _________________________ (Partner/Spouse) all information shared, during the course of treatment, that is considered part of the couple treatment, including couples therapy sessions, individual sessions that are considered part of the couple treatment, and phone calls, emails, and text messages during the authorized period identified below. The purpose of this ongoing disclosure is to provide competent treatment that allows Dr. Butch Losey, Ed.D., LPCC-S to treat the couple by preventing, to the extent possible, a conflict of interest to arise in which an individual's interests may not be consistent with the interests of the unit being treated.

[ ] This authorization expires six months from today on ____________ (Date).
[ ] This authorization expires less than six months from today on______ (Date).

Signature___________________ Date___________________________

Appendix 3.2

Guest Agreement

Waybridge Counseling

Counseling Guest Agreement Form

Thank you for accepting the invitation to join ______________________ (our client) as a guest in a counseling session. This document is to inform you about the risks, rights, and responsibilities of your participation as a guest.

WHO IS A GUEST?

A guest is usually a spouse, family member, or friend, who participates in therapy to assist our client. As a guest you are not considered to be the client and are not receiving treatment. Generally a guest comes to therapy sessions only one or two times. If you (the guest), our client, or a counselor believe that your relationship with our client should be the main focus of the counseling, then being a guest to the therapy session may not be appropriate. If this happens we may either 1) suggest counseling in which both you and our client are considered clients of the counselor and we would create a file that represents both of you equally or 2) refer the two of you to another clinician.

YOUR RIGHTS AS A GUEST

Being a guest affects how records are held and what services you receive. Since you are a guest and are not receiving treatment, counselors at Waybridge Counseling will not create a file for you, develop a treatment plan for you, or release any records created to you. Any records that are created during your visit as a guest will be part of the file of our client. Our client is able to access or release these records as needed, including any references in the file to your attendance as a guest. You do not have access to these records unless our client signs a waiver to release them to you. Please let the counselor at Waybridge know if you have concerns about certain information and prefer not to discuss certain things. You do have a right to be treated in a way that is consistent with state and federal law and have access to our privacy and client rights policies, which we can provide to you. However many of the privacy policy rights apply only to clients of Waybridge Counseling and not to someone who joins in a counseling session as a guest.

BENEFITS AND RISKS

Counseling can be an intense emotional experience, and your participation as a guest may be stressful or create anxiety. While your participation may result in better understanding of our client or an improved relationship, or may even help in your own growth and development, there is no guarantee that this will be the case. Joining in a counseling session as a guest is a positive experience for many, but it is not helpful to all people.

GOALS FOR THIS SESSION

The session you are attending has been carefully planned prior to your attendance. The following goals or content areas have been identified as a focus for this session:

1) ____
2) ____
3) ____
4) ____

FEES

As a guest you are not responsible for paying for professional services unless you are financially responsible for our client (for instance if you are a parent of a minor child who is doing individual counseling).

CONFIDENTIALITY

Both federal and state law protect the confidentiality of information in our client's chart, including the information that you provide during any session you attend as a guest at Waybridge Counseling that may become part of our client's file. Client information can only be released if our client specifically authorizes Waybridge Counseling to do so.

There are some exceptions to this general rule:

1) If a counselor suspects a child or vulnerable adult is being abused or neglected (or has been abused or neglected), that counselor is required to file a report with the appropriate agency.
2) If a counselor believes that a guest or a client is suicidal, the counselor will take actions to protect the guest's or the client's life even if he or she must reveal client information or information about the guest to do so.

3) If the guest or a client threatens serious bodily harm to another, the counselor will take necessary actions to protect that person, even if he or she must reveal client information or guest information to do so.
4) If a guest or a client is involved in a lawsuit, and a court requires that a counselor submit information or testify, the counselor must comply.
5) Waybridge Counseling may use or disclose client health information for treatment purposes including presentation of a client's case in consultation with other professionals or consultants who are bound by the legal framework of privacy and confidentiality for professional development and guidance purposes.
6) With your signature below you agree that you will maintain our client's identity and any information provided/gained in session as confidential.

DO GUESTS EVER BECOME CLIENTS?

Guests may discuss their own problems in a counseling session, especially problems that interact with issues of our client. The therapist may recommend independent counseling for a guest. Most often, but not always, a Waybridge Counseling counselor will refer you to another clinician for treatment.

RELEASE OF INFORMATION

The presence of the guest with the consent of our client is adequate; however, it is Waybridge Counseling practice to require such a release. This provides some assurance that full consent has been given to the therapist for our client's confidential information to be discussed with the guest in therapy. The release is also helpful to the counselor on those occasions when receiving a telephone call from a guest or when the counselor calls a guest for one reason or another. In most instances the counselor cannot take a call from a guest without having a signed release.

SUMMARY

If you have questions about being a guest in a counseling session, Waybridge Counseling procedures, or your role in this process, please discuss them with the counselor. Remember that the best way to assure quality and ethical treatment is to keep communication open.

By signing below you indicate that you have read and understood this document.

Signature of Guest ______________________________ Date __________
Name of Guest ____
Signature of Clinician ____________________________ Date __________
Signature of Client ______________________________ Date __________

[ ] Release from our Client completed.

4 Principles of Assessment

A variety of specific assessment is covered throughout this book. There are truly too many assessments available to describe them all. With that said, to increase effectiveness in assessing couple relationships, it will require the clinician to move beyond a formulaic approach of asking questions and seeking responses. Lee Williams et al. (2011) discuss that effective assessment follows certain principles. They believe that using the seven guiding principles in Table 4.1 will increase the clinician's assessment skills.

The therapeutic alliance is critical to the outcomes of therapy, and the alliance begins when the clinician joins with the couple at the first session. Joining is a means to establish trust between the couple and clinician. Couples need to feel that they are not being judged and that the clinician is listening deeply and coming from an unbiased position. In the first session, they are assessing best fit with the clinician and hope to see that the clinician has seen their problem before, knows what to do about it, and has had success with it.

In a later chapter, I will discuss the importance of curiosity to creating intimacy in relationships. The same is true in the therapeutic relationship. The curious clinician who approaches the couple without defensiveness will be in a better position to develop a strong therapeutic alliance. This curiosity leads to more disclosure by the couple, which helps the clinician obtain a complete understanding of the current problems and couple functioning.

Assessment is not a point-in-time intervention. Beginning clinicians will view assessment as what therapists do in the first session or two. Assessment, along with ongoing evaluation and feedback about the progress of treatment and the outcomes of interventions, is critical to long-term change for the couple.

Assessment is considered an intervention because the act of questioning can open up new understanding for the couple around perpetuating factors that maintain the current problem or offer insight for future solutions. From a basic view of assessment, most of the clinician's questions seemingly are designed to help them formulate an assessment. The questions themselves are not usually regarded as interventions to help the couple. Yet, many questions do have therapeutic effects on the partners, either directly through the implications of

Table 4.1 Seven Guiding Principles of Assessment

Joining is critical to assessment.
Be curious.
Think assessment all the time.
Assessment is intervention, and intervention is assessment.
Assess for strengths.
Assessment includes the clinician.
Assess using multiple perspectives.

the questions and/or indirectly through the verbal and nonverbal responses of the couple to the questions (Tomm, 1987).

Interventions are also assessment. How couples respond to the clinician's interventions can also offer insight for the clinician that can be incorporated into his or her understanding of the couple. The couple's response can also indicate what is working and what is not working, guiding the clinician's future interventions with the couple.

Assessing strengths can easily be overlooked by clinicians as they work to determine the primary problem from the couple's and clinician's perspectives and the factors that perpetuate them. Strengths though can be called upon to address issues from the personal and unique skill set of the couple.

Assessment includes the clinician because from the moment we joined with the couple, we joined their system. Therefore, we are impacted by the interactions that we have with them. Careful awareness of this impact may give us clues to what is occurring with the couple and how they relate to each other. It may also call to us to pay close attention to the countertransference that may lie just below our awareness.

There are many advantages to multi-perspectives. Assessing using multiple perspectives would include information from both partners and use a variety of assessment methods. For example, depression could be understood from each partner's perspective and several assessment instruments.

Methods of Assessment

Clinical Interview

The clinical interview is one of the primary ways in which most clinicians address assessment in couples therapy. Although defined differently by different authors, John and Rita Sommers Flanagan (2014) define the clinical interview to be inclusive of an informed-consent process and has as its primary goals 1) initiation of a therapeutic alliance, 2) assessment or diagnostic data collection, 3) case formulation, and/or 4) implementation of a psychological intervention. In the clinical interview, questions are focused on understanding thought, feelings and behaviors, and how each partner observes and understands the other. The usefulness of the clinical interview requires that the couple is cooperative, insightful, and honest, which is not always the case.

Assessment Instruments

Embedded in the clinical interview is the use of assessment measures. There are some distinct advantages to using assessment along with clinical interviewing. First, it is a quick way of gathering information. Second, it offers quantitative data for clinical decision-making. For example, two people reporting depression will experience depression differently. Using an assessment measure will allow the clinician the opportunity to quantitatively assess the depression. Third, since assessment is consistent in the questions, we are able to assess at different points in time and make observations about improvement occurring during the course of treatment (Williams et al., 2011).

Clinical Observation

Considerable information can be obtained by simply observing the couple. Observations can occur spontaneously in session (or during transition before and after session). The clinician can structure observation of the couple as happens when the clinician structures an enactment.

Assessment Focus in the Clinical Interview

Clinicians will vary in their focus during the initial clinical interview based on their theoretical orientation since most clinicians, even those who profess allegiance to a specific theoretical lens, are integrative. Table 4.2 lists some common focus areas in the clinical interview.

Presenting Problem and Attempted Solutions

Couples may fail to bring up problem areas in their relationship or may minimize the importance of the problems. There are a number of reasons for this, including fear of how the other partner will respond to the disclosure,

Table 4.2 Common Assessment Focus

Presenting problem and attempted solutions
Safety
Strengths
The couple's goals
Relationship history
External relationships
Addictions
Potential past or current partner abuse
Severe psychopathology
Communication/Conflict resolution
Core vision, shared values, and beliefs about the relationship
Satisfaction
Intimacy and closeness
Commitment and motivation
Forgiveness

embarrassment of the situation or issue, or the couple's collusion in some way to hide the problem. One couple that I worked with was participating in swinging events and colluded to keep this hidden from me, in spite of intimacy and trust issues that were directly linked to the relationships they were experiencing at the swingers' club. Two good principles to keep in mind while assessing couple problems are 1) the clinician should assume that the couple will reveal what seems important to them when it feels safe for them to bring it up, and 2) the clinician needs to ask about major areas of couple functioning, regardless of whether or not the couple brings it up (Weeks, Odell, & Methven, 2005). Alternately, once problems have been identified, the clinician can ask the couple how they went about trying to solve the problem and what were the most- and the least-successful solutions.

Safety

The clinician should have a third ear open for potential safety issues and have the courage to explore any issue of concern in terms of emotional and physical safety. Clinicians should be prepared to assess for suicidal thought and intent and aggression and threats of violence.

Strengths

Counseling can be a problem-focused endeavor, at least early on in the process. As mentioned a little earlier, calling upon strengths of the couple can lead to new relationship dynamics and improved functioning.

The Couple's Goals

One way to create resistance in treatment and stall progress is to not have clear, collaborative goals with the couple. It is helpful to hear each partner's goals for the relationship independently. This will give the clinician an understanding of whether the couple sees their future relationship in similar ways. The clinician can use these goals as a foundation to help the couple develop goals for the relationship that are change directed, specific, and measurable.

Relationship History

The genogram is a wonderful assessment process in itself. It is quick and offers multiple layers of information. Structurally, it helps the clinician understand who are the important players in the family and the relationship characteristics between family members. Other topics that can be discussed include the career of each partner, spiritual and cultural influences, and generational transmission of physical and mental health issues.

Taking a timeline of the relationship is a simple, quick assessment process that results in considerable historical information about the relationship. The couple is asked to create a timeline of the relationship that includes the significant changes or events in the relationship that are either positive or negative. The couple starts by describing how their relationship formed and what they found appealing in the other partner. Couples can be asked how these perceptions changed over time. From there, they share significant events and changes over the course of the relationship. The completed timeline helps the clinician assess individual struggles of each partner, relationship issues through time, external stressors that have applied pressure to the relationship, and adaptive and maladaptive responses to the stressors.

External Relationships

External relationships include those that are problematic as well as those that are supportive to the couple relationship. Parents and in-laws can exert considerable positive or negative influence with the couple. Infidelity, swinging and inappropriately close relationships could be hidden and not immediately disclosed to the clinician. The clinician should ask directly about past and current infidelity. Lastly, people who are supportive to the couple relationship and its preservation should be identified.

Addictions

One in ten people who come to therapy are addicted (Gottman Institute, 2017). Clinicians should be prepared to look for indications of problematic substance use and addiction. Clinicians should also look for process addictions such as porn and sex addiction. If addiction is an issue, a thorough understanding is needed of the relationship between the addicted and non-addicted partner.

Potential Past or Current Partner Abuse

Clinicians have an ethical and professional obligation to carefully assess factors that may undermine treatment. Clinicians should carefully look for possible use of force, intimidation, or manipulation (or the threat to use any of those methods) to control, hurt, or frighten the partner (Dytch, 2017). If partner abuse is suspected, the Abusive Behavior Inventory, developed by Albert Dytch (2017), or the Self-Assessment: Abusive Behavior Inventory, developed by Melanie Shepard and James Campbell (1992), could be good options to uncover behaviors that indicate partner abuse.

Severe Psychopathology

Partners suffering from severe psychopathology are characterized by chronic, complex problems that often result in a relatively large degree of functional impairment. Most clinicians view severe psychopathology as an exclusionary criterion for couples therapy. The chances of the couple making therapeutic progress as a couple are highly unlikely when there is severe psychopathology in one partner (Weeks, Odell, & Methven, 2005).

Communication/Conflict Resolution

Communication patterns can be assessed through observation in the clinical interview or through structured enactments. An important element in assessment is the extent and nature of disagreements and how they interact in the context of stress and differing opinions. Understanding how couples begin engagement in conflict and process for resolution will be useful. Problematic patterns around communication will need to be interrupted and modified by the clinician.

Core Vision, Shared Values, and Beliefs About the Relationship

A couple that has a shared vision will flourish. The vision in relationship begins with a combination of what was observed in the family of origin, what is integrated through culture, and what is learned through past romantic relationships. These experiences, combined with aspiration and direction toward a future time in the relationship, create a vision of the relationship. Many couples entering counseling are lacking a shared vision for the future.

Values are principles that govern our actions and give meaning to our life. Couples can definitely have different interests and still have healthy relationships. Couples of different religions, or non-religion, and couples differing in cultural backgrounds can have healthy relationships as well; what distinguishes healthy and troubled relationships is sharing of core values.

Beliefs about the relationship that are negative can have a corrosive effect on its health and vitality. It is important to understand the type and extent of negative beliefs. These beliefs can take on a life of their own when partners hold to the beliefs even when change may be attempted or occurring. Examples of negative beliefs include pigeonholing one partner (she is passive-aggressive), fortune-telling a partner's actions or thoughts (he will never change), and mind-reading (I don't need to ask you, I know what you are thinking).

Satisfaction

Perceived satisfaction can be assessed concerning a variety of aspects within the relationship. I tend to assess satisfaction about closeness, expression of feelings, positivity in the relationship, sexuality and sensuality, financial decision-making, positivity in the relationship, and the quantity and quality of the time spent together as a couple. Later in this chapter, I will discuss the Global Assessment of Relationship Dimensions, which is a useful assessment to identify satisfaction and confidence about a variety of relationship dimensions.

Intimacy and Closeness

Intimacy requires a great deal of trust, vulnerability, and mutual disclosure. Many people struggle with intimacy, and fear of intimacy is a common concern in therapy. While intimacy for many people is associated with romantic relationships, a variety of close relationships can have intimacy. Intimacy will need to be assessed by considering the multiple dimensions of intimacy, including trust, vulnerability, disclosure, sexuality and sensuality, shared meaning and goals, interest, social interest, recreation, and spirituality.

Commitment and Motivation

People may be committed to a relationship for very different reasons. Each person has a different combination of reasons for commitment, or lack of commitment, to a relationship. According to Adams and Jones (1999), there are three dimensions of commitment in relationships. First is the commitment as an attraction. Some people are committed to a relationship because of the rewards and satisfactions of the relationship. Such people may not only experience satisfaction in their relationship but also be held to the relationship by love and closeness. Second is commitment as a moral obligation. Some people stay in a relationship even when it is unhappy because they see it as a vow, an obligation, or a duty. For many people, commitment to the relationship is a part of their religious or family values. Third is commitment as a constraint. Some people stay in a relationship because of the children, because of social consequences of divorce, or because of financial limitations. Some stay in a relationship simply because getting out seems too risky. Since commitment has multiple dimensions, it functions differently in different relationships.

Forgiveness

Forgiveness is transformative. It is the displacement of negative attitudes, such as anger, resentment, and punishment towards damaging situations or people, with positive attitudes such as compassion and tolerance. It is important to understand to what extent the couple is open to forgiving each other for the transgressions in the relationship.

Assessing Issues of Safety

There can be an assumption that most couples enter therapy in crisis. Associated with high stress in couples is the potential for suicidal ideation and intent, as well as potential threats of harm towards others. Effective assessment of suicide ideation and potential threats to others includes assessing the extent of thoughts, feelings, and behaviors and intervening based on level of risk.

Suicide

Clinicians can ensure an individual's safety through their interviewing process. In doing so, the clinician's primary task is to uncover the extent of the person's planning, past attempts, and current behavior and respond accordingly. Shawn Shea (2011) developed the CASE Approach, which is a flexible, practical, and easily learned interview strategy for eliciting suicidal ideation, planning, and intent. It is designed to increase validity, decrease errors of omission, and increase the person's sense of safety with the interviewer. One assumption is that the person will increasingly disclose their intent as they become comfortable with the clinician.

The CASE approach gives the clinician a specific sequence or structure for asking questions about suicide with the data-gathering process, segmented in the following four time frames:

1) Presenting ideation and suicidal behavior in the past forty-eight hours

   The person is asked to help the clinician create a "verbal videotape" of the attempt or experiences that have occurred in the past forty-eight hours. The person is asked to sequence, step by step, what occurred during this time frame.

2) Recent ideation and behaviors during the preceding two months

   The person is asked about other ways in which the person considered killing themselves. It is important to ask for specifics and the amount of time that they spent thinking about killing themselves. The more the person is engaged in thinking about suicide, the more likely they are in behaving in self-destructive ways.

3) Past suicidal ideation and behaviors

   This time frame is focused on uncovering the person's perspective of the most serious past attempt. Considerations include the approximate number of past attempts and which one was the most serious. It is important to obtain specific information about the serious attempt. It is important to also know the reasons for the serious attempt and whether the reason is similar to the current crisis.

4) Immediate suicidal ideation that occurs during the interview itself

   Once trust has been maximized, it is an opportune time to explore immediate suicidal plans and intentions, a critically important area of suicide assessment. Asking for information such as 1) thoughts the person is having about suicide, 2) what actions they have taken towards ending their life, 3) by what method and means they plan to employ to end their life and if it is available to them, and 4) what level of emotional distress they are experiencing.

Mobility

The clinician's response can be considered a pairing of action and mobility. Action refers to the extent the clinician takes control of the developing crisis with a person. Mobility refers to the person's ability to change and cope in response to differing moods, feelings, emotions, needs, and conditions. Immobility indicates the person is not immediately capable of this (James & Gilliland, 2017).

The counselor moves on a continuum of nondirective to collaborative, and then to more directive approaches based on the mobility presented by the person. The person who is fully mobile is relatively autonomous to address situations in their life, and for the most part the clinician can take a nondirective approach. For people who are partially mobile, the clinician can collaborate with the person, their partner, and their family to create safety strategies and other interventions to mediate the issues at hand. When the person is immobile, the clinician will need to put strategies in place to ensure the safety of the person, which could include hospitalization.

Threats of Harm to Others

In my book *Bullying, Suicide, and Homicide* (Losey, 2011), I talk about the "triple P" strategy for assessing threat. The "triple P" of persistence, plausibility, and preparation is a good way to determine the risk of a potential threat. Persistence considers whether the threat lasts longer than the immediate situation. Someone who is harboring highly elevated anger and hostility a day after a situation would be considered having increased risk. Plausibility considers the credibility of the threat. For example, does the threat have details, is there a method, is the method available, and is it logical? Is it implied or direct? Preparation speaks to both the developmental nature of a threat, such as leakage (the intentional or unintentional conveyance of the threatener's intent, such as drawings, poems, and comments to others), and the planning that may have taken place (practiced with a weapon, stalked the victim). In considering preparation, the clinician should assess the person's resistance with attempts by the clinician to help the person identify alternatives to harming others.

A high-risk situation is one in which the person's threat lasts beyond the immediate situation; has a detailed, logical plan that has strong potential for follow-through; and has planning behind the threat. The person has leaked comments or violent writings or has concerned others by their behavior and may be resistant to alternatives to the threat.

Other factors to consider include the person's history of violence towards others and their mental-health history. The nature and seriousness of the threat will indicate the level of involvement of the clinician. Clinicians should consider their state laws regarding duty to warn. For example, Ohio law requires that if a clinician believes that if a client has the intent and ability to carry out an explicit threat of inflicting imminent and serious physical harm to a clearly identifiable potential victim(s), the clinician will initiate the duty to protect process. This includes the clinician's informing the potential victim and the appropriate law enforcement agency.

Partner Abuse

Partner abuse can be physical violence, sexual violence, stalking, coercion, and psychological aggression. Characteristics of partner abuse include force, intimidation, or manipulation and is considered by clinicians to hinder the effectiveness of treatment. Another primary concern is that therapy requires open and honest discussion, but in the case of partner abuse, this type of communication may be dangerous for the victim. It is our ethical and professional obligation to carefully assess factors that may undermine treatment, and when partner abuse is assessed and determined, most clinicians believe that it is an exclusionary criterion for couples therapy and will prefer to refer the partners to individual counseling.

As there are complications associated with treating couples experiencing partner abuse, there is also a danger in treating couples and not knowing that partner abuse is occurring. Since clinicians are careful to make sure that partner abuse is not occurring in the couples they treat, how do they go about screening for partner abuse?

Since partner abuse is typically not the presenting issue for couples coming in to treatment, clinicians should consider a multimodal screening process. I recommend that clinicians conduct universal screening, for example using a questionnaire for all couples entering treatment. Secondly, clinicians should approach screening as multimodal, that there be a discussion in the clinical interview process to screen for red flags that may become apparent.

In her master's thesis, Ilene Grosam (2012) surveyed fifty-four clinicians about what were the top five factors that were considered significant in determining the appropriateness for couples therapy: 1) the presence of risk factors such as weapons, past threats to kill, severe abuse, fear level of victim, victim planning to leave or has left in the past, 2) ongoing violence in the relationship, 3) patterns of conflict, 4) controlling behaviors, and 5) severity of conflicts.

Some clinicians will choose a pre-counseling assessment for partner abuse in which the clinician meets briefly with each partner separately to assess for partner abuse, and therapy does not start until after assessment. Since clinicians deem it important to not proceed with couples therapy in the presence of partner abuse, then it warrants an assessment prior to or at the beginning of therapy so that the clinician knows how to proceed.

Global Assessment of Relationship Dimensions

I created the Global Assessment of Relationship Dimensions (GARD, Appendix 4.1) to provide a quick method for the clinician to help the couple assess their relationship on a variety of different dimensions. It is used to identify the level of satisfaction and confidence around sixteen dimensions. When completed, the couple can identify strengths and weaknesses on the dimensions, develop goals based on the scores, and use the GARD as an outcome measure later in the treatment process. Combined with the Excel graphs provided, the couple can have a pictorial view of their relationship in terms of the dimensions, attachment, and trust.

Each partner is given the GARD (client fill-in form, Appendix 4.2) and oriented to the document. The clinician notes the graduated scale on the left and the individual dimensions at the top of the page. Partners are instructed that each dimension will be defined by the clinician, and at that time, the couple will rank either their satisfaction or confidence, depending on the dimension. Each partner will rank their satisfaction or confidence on a scale from one to ten by placing a circle on the intersecting line for each of the dimension. The couple is directed to start all rankings from five. For example, if they are generally satisfied with their emotional closeness (first dimension on the scale), they would draw a circle on the intersecting line at five. If, however, they are more than satisfied with their emotional closeness, they would choose a number above five. Likewise, if they were less than generally satisfied, they would mark a number below five.

Once the directions are given, the clinician then defines each dimension on the scale from left to right and has the partners mark their rankings. Each dimension is narrowly defined by the clinician. It is important that the clinician be the person that defines each dimension before it is ranked. Since everyone will likely define each term differently, the clinician can offer a standard definition. Also, a standardized definition will allow the clinician to use the GARD at another time to assess outcomes of treatment. The following are suggested, brief definitions of each of the dimensions as stated to the couple during the process of the assessment.

Emotional Closeness

Emotional closeness is the perception of closeness that allows each partner to share their feelings accompanied by understanding, affirmation, and caring. How satisfied are you with the closeness in your relationship?

Friendship

True friends make time to do things together, offer unwavering support to one another, and have a willingness to challenge each other and be open to the challenge. Friends are a positive influence in each other's lives. How satisfied are you with the friendship aspect of your relationship?

Intimate Feelings

The communication of feelings is critical for many aspects of intimacy. Sharing of intimate feelings is a two-way street: one partner must be willing to share their feelings and the other must be willing to hear the feelings. How satisfied are you with the expressions of intimate feelings in your relationship?

Couple Time

To be invested in the couple relationship, you must invest time. This is not family time or time with other couples. This is time just dedicated to the two of you. How satisfied are you with the time you spend together as a couple?

Quality of Time

Of the time that you spend together as a couple, how satisfied are you that it is invested in a way that draws you close together?

Sexuality

A healthy sexual relationship includes sensual and sexual experiences with one another, openness to talk about likes and dislikes, respect for sexual boundaries, and sexuality which draws you closer together. How satisfied are you with the sexual aspect of your relationship?

Finance

This is not about how much money you have but more about how successful you are as a couple in discussing and negotiating financial decisions. How confident are you in your ability to make financial decisions together?

Conflict Resolution

Conflict is normal in relationships. To address conflict successfully, couples need to engage one another in a discussion, not avoid for fear of escalation, taking into account each partner's needs. How confident are you that you can resolve conflict successfully?

Affection

Affection can be verbally expressed in a way that will make your partner feel encouraged, loved, or validated. It can also be physical, such as hugging, kissing, and supportive touch. Some couples will express affection through gifts or acts of service. How satisfied are you with the expressions of affection in your relationship?

Positivity

Recent research shows that in healthy relationships there is a ratio of five positive interactions to one negative interaction. Knowing this, how satisfied are you with the positivity in your relationship?

**From this point on, I ask each person to rank their partner on the remaining dimensions.*

Understanding

To create a quality relationship, it is important to fully understand the deeper thoughts and feelings of your partner. It is also important to know your partner's wants, needs, and dreams. How confident are you that your partner understands your thoughts, feelings, wants, and dreams?

Honesty

Honesty, in part, is about telling the truth. It also implies fairness in dealing with others and the refusal to engage in deceit or secrets. How confident are you that your partner is honest?

Personal Presence

Intimate, trusting relationships take effort, and both partners need to have a strong personal presence in the relationship. This means that they need to commit a great deal of their energy to being mentally, physically, and emotionally available to their partner. How confident are you that your partner is personally present?

Advocacy/Repair

An advocate cares and nurtures the relationship. They pay special attention to the state of the relationship and have sensitivity to when things go awry. They quickly attend to repairing when tension occurs in the relationship or conflict arises. How confident are you that your partner is an advocate for this relationship?

Accessibility

An accessible partner is one who will answer the phone when their partner calls or who responds to voicemail and text in a reasonable time. An accessible partner also shares their internal world to their partner, without the need for any prompting. They will openly share their thoughts, feelings, convictions, longings, fears, and doubts. How confident are you that your partner is accessible in your relationship?

Commitment/Exclusivity

Commitment is the mutually agreed-upon promise to one another to be exclusive. It means that partners are "closed" to other options, emotional or physical. Committed couples also create a barrier to all others that might be a risk to the relationship. How confident are you that your partner is committed to your relationship?

Table 4.3 Dimensions of Satisfaction/Confidence, Trust, and Attachment

Satisfaction/Confidence	*Trust*	*Attachment*
Emotional Closeness	Honesty	Emotional Closeness
Friendship	Personal Presence	Intimate Feelings
Intimate Feelings	Advocacy/Repair	Personal Presence
Couple Time	Accessibility	Accessibility
Quality of Time	Commitment/Exclusivity	Commitment/Exclusivity
Sexuality		
Finance		
Conflict Resolution		
Affection		
Positivity		
Understanding		

Once completed, the partners are directed to view their assessment with each other and make some conclusions about the assessment. They are also asked to discuss possible strengths and challenges based on the completed forms and possible goals that might be developed based on the dimensions.

The couple is then instructed to share the number values on their form for the clinician to enter into the GARD (electronic version, Appendix 4.1). This will produce several graphs that the clinician can immediately show to the couple as a means of offering a different perspective based on satisfaction/confidence, trust, and attachment. The electronic version of the GARD includes a graph on general satisfaction/confidence, trust, trust strength (which is an aggregate of each partner's scores), attachment needs from each partner's perspective, and attachment strength (which is an aggregate of each partner's scores). For reference, satisfaction/confidence, trust, and attachment are defined by the following dimensions in Table 4.3.

References

Adams, J. M., & Jones, W. H. (1999). Interpersonal commitment in historical perspective. In J. M. Adams & W. H. Jones (Eds.), *Handbook of interpersonal commitment and relationship stability* (pp. 3–33). New York: Kluwer Academic.

Dytch, A. (2017). *Assessing partner abuse in couples' therapy*. Retrieved March 23, 2017 from www.psychotherapy.net/article/couples-abuse-assessment#section-obligation-to-assess.

Gottman Institute. (2017). *Couples and addiction recovery*. Retrieved March 23, 2017 from www.gottman.com/professionals/training/couples-addiction-recovery/.

Greene, K., & Bogo, M. (2002). The different faces of intimate violence: Implications for assessment and treatment. *Journal of Marital and Family Therapy*, *28*(4), 455–466.

Grosam, I. M. (2012). *Assessment for domestic violence in couples requesting conjoint therapy: Current practice of assessment among licensed therapists*. Submitted May, 2012. Retrieved March 28, 2017 from http://sophia.stkate.edu/cgi/viewcontent.cgi?article=1029&context=msw_papers.

James, R. K., & Gilliland, B. E. (2017). *Crisis intervention strategies* (8th ed.). Boston, MA: Cengage Learning.

Losey, B. (2011). *Bullying, suicide, and homicide: Understanding, assessing, and preventing threats to self and others for victims of bullying.* New York: Routledge.

Shea, S. (2011). *The practical art of suicide assessment: A guide for mental health professionals and substance abuse counselors.* Mental Health Presses.

Shepard, M., & Campbell, J. (1992). The abusive behavior inventory. *Journal of Interpersonal Violence, 7*(3), 291–305.

Sommers-Flanagan, J., & Sommers-Flanagan, R. (2014). *Instructor's manual for clinical interviewing: Intake, assessment, and therapeutic alliance.* Mill Valley, CA: Psychotherapy.net, LLC.

Tomm, K. (1987). Interventive interviewing I. Strategizing as a fourth guideline for the clinician. *Family Process, 26*(1), 314.

Weeks, G. R., Odell, M., & Methven, S. (2005). *If only I had known: Avoiding common mistakes in couples therapy.* New York: W.W. Norton & Company.

Williams, L., Edwards, T. M., Patterson, J. & Chamow, L. (2014). *Essential assessment skills for couple and family therapists.* New York: The Guilford Press.

Appendix 4.1

Global Assessment of Relationship Dimensions (GARD)

Global Assessment of Relationship Dimensions

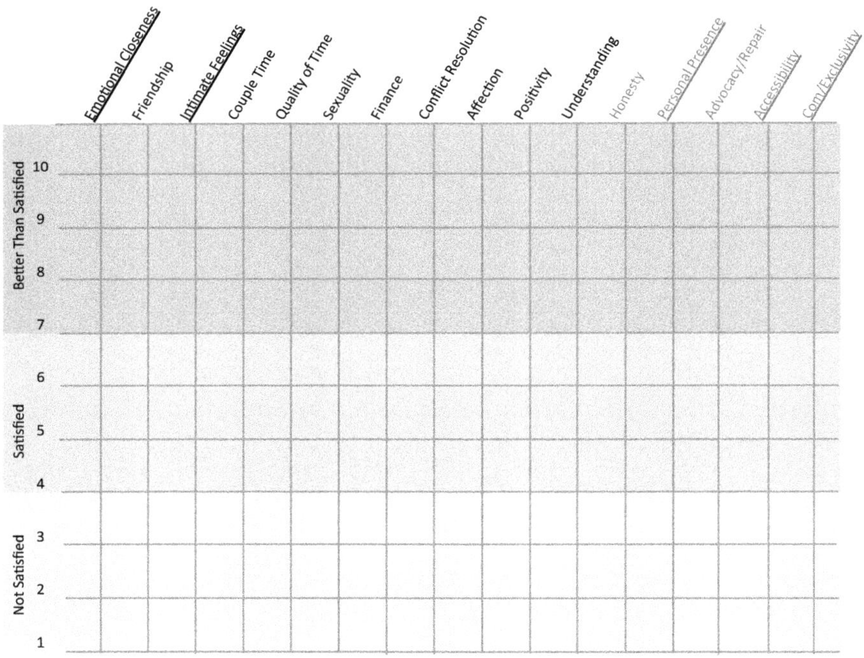

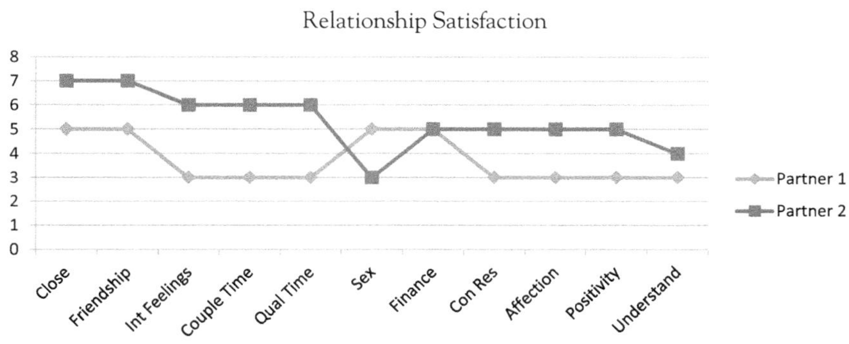
Relationship Satisfaction
8
7
6
5
4
3
2
1
0
Close
Friendship
Int Feelings
Couple Time
Qual Time
Sex
Finance
Con Res
Affection
Positivity
Understand
Partner 1
Partner 2

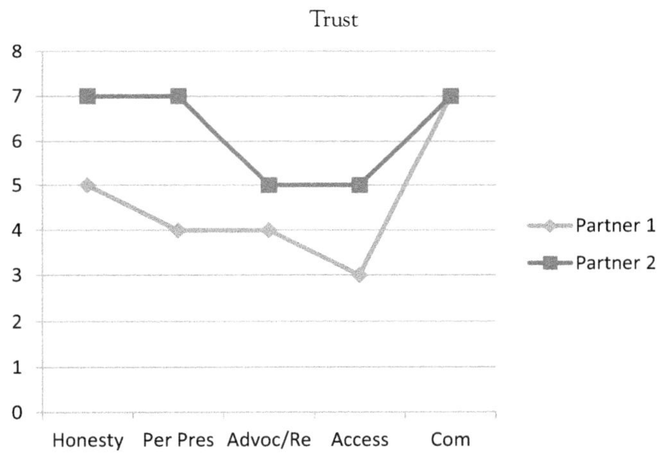
Trust
8
7
6
5
4
3
2
1
0
Honesty
Per Pres
Advoc/Re
Access
Com
Partner 1
Partner 2

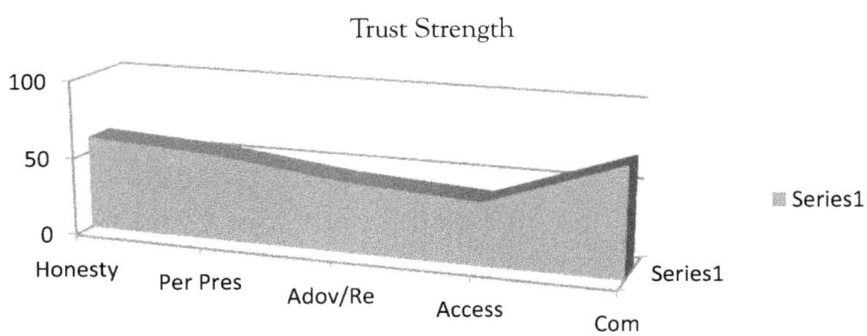
Trust Strength
100
50
0
Honesty
Per Pres
Adov/Re
Access
Com
Series1
Series1

Attachment Needs Partner 1

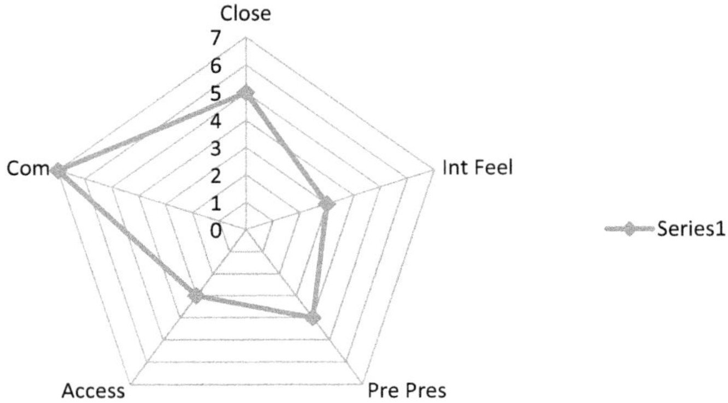

Attachment Needs Partner 2

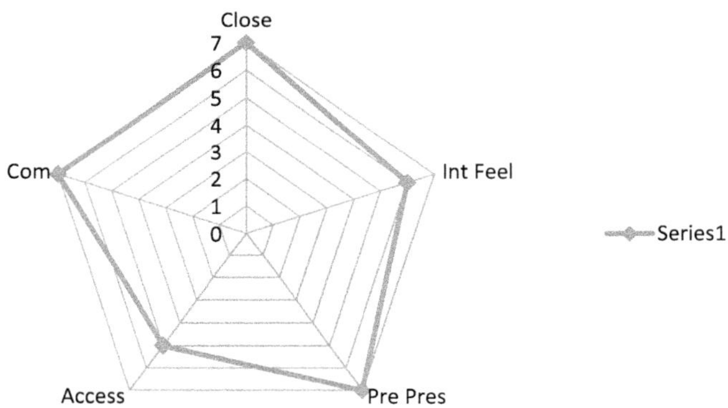

Attachment Strength

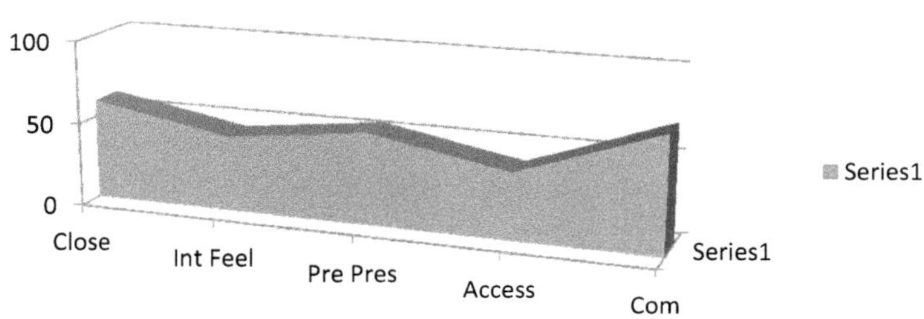

Appendix 4.2

GARD (client fill-in form)

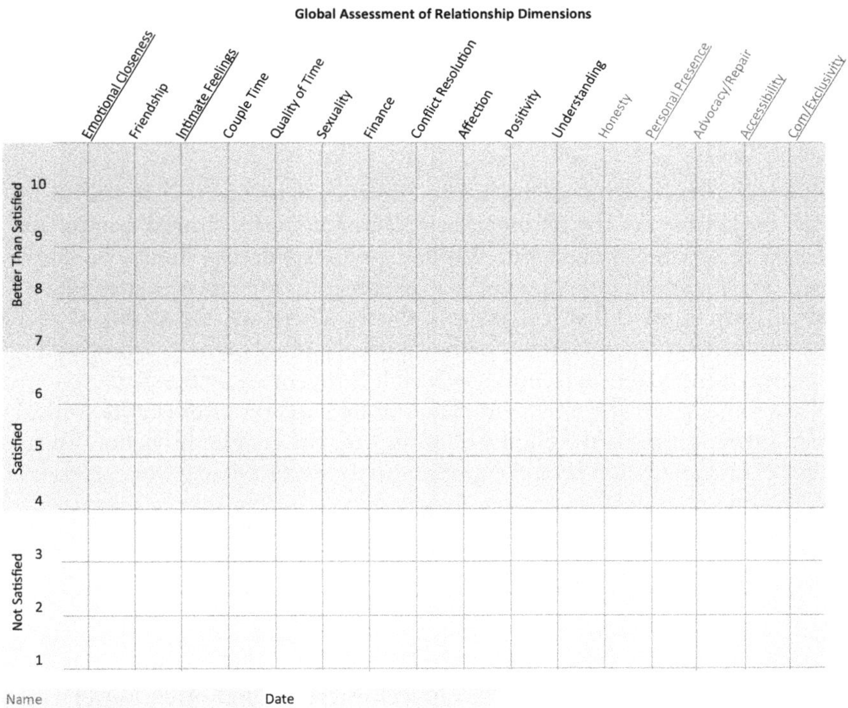

5 Treatment Planning

> *Counselors who impose goals on clients without regard for clients' desires are like salespersons who try to sell products that people do not want.*
>
> —Clifton Mitchel

Following a thorough assessment, the clinician must create a theoretically based explanation of the information obtained from the clinical assessment, referred to as case formulation. While a case formulation should be firmly based on the clinical interview and the assessments/outcome measures administered, keep in mind that it is always a theory. Therefore, the quality of your case formulation depends largely on how logical and coherent it is, how well it integrates all available data, and how well it is supported by the data.

Case formulation and treatment planning are important steps in the clinical process that will guide the clinician's work with the couple throughout treatment. Case formulation should consider three categories: diagnostic, clinical, and treatment formulation.

Diagnostic Formulation

The diagnostic formulation is the theory-based understanding of the client's presenting issue. It is a hypothesis of what happened and the nature and severity of the problem. Data from the clinical interview and other assessments guide the clinician in developing the diagnostic formulation.

Clinical Formulation

The clinical formulation contains both theme and pattern analysis. The hypothesis developed here is the rationale for the development and maintenance of the symptoms or patterns. Pattern analysis looks for the predictable type of behaving, thinking, or feeling the couple utilizes as ways of coping. Pattern analysis considers the following: precipitating factors, such as the triggers or stressors that activate the pattern; the presentation of the pattern, which is the characteristic of the patterned response to the current situation; the perpetuating factors, which include the processes that reinforce the pattern; and the predisposing factors, factors that create vulnerability for the couple.

Treatment Formulation

The treatment formulation includes the treatment goals, plans, and interventions to be used. It also includes the predictions of the outcomes of treatment. Treatment formulation primarily answers the question, "What can be done and how?"

As any seasoned clinician knows, couples are not always aligned in the goals that they have for therapy or for the relationship. Almost half of couples coming to therapy enter with a goal of determining whether the relationship is viable enough to continue. It can be a very challenging situation when one partner wants to improve the relationship and the other is interested only in clarifying whether they want to leave or stay in the relationship.

Research confirms that there is a positive relationship between the initial goals of treatment and the congruence between them, and relationship status post-treatment. Owen et al. (2012) found that when both partners wanted to improve the relationship, the majority of them did. When the initial goal of both partners was to strengthen the relationship, only 7.8% of the couples in the study separated or divorced six months post-treatment. This was markedly different when both partners' goal was to clarify some aspect of the relationship. Over half (56%) separated or divorced within six months post-treatment. When one partner's goal was to clarify and one was to improve the relationship, just under half (45.6%) separated six months post-treatment.

Guidelines for Goal Development

The positive relationship between the initial goals of treatment and the congruence between them creates positive outcomes post-treatment. Another important aspect is the way in which the goals are developed. Clinicians can unknowingly or knowingly advocate too strongly for what they believe to be the best goal for the client and expect the client to adopt it. They may tell the client that this is their goal and then work to implement it. Other clinicians may go into therapy with no agreed-upon goal for the client. It is critical that goals are developed early in treatment and that couples have an active part in the development of the goals.

People do not resist what they want. Therefore, without mutually agreed-upon goals that are aligned with each partner's interest, there will be some amount of resistance to therapy. In addition, when there is

Table 5.1 Guidelines for Goal Development

Assess each partner's preferred outcome for therapy and the relationship.
Develop goals early in the treatment process.
Align treatment goals with each partner's interest.
Develop treatment goals in partnership with the couple.
Develop clinician's process goals to support the couple's outcome goals.

discordance between the goals of the clinician and the goals of the couple, there is even greater opportunity for resistance. Early assessment is key to understanding each partner's preferred outcome for treatment and the relationship. Is the partner interested in improving the relationship or clarifying some aspect of the relationship? Once individual interests are considered, goals can be negotiated, and the clinician can align clinical process goals that best fit the couple goals. Table 5.1 contains a review of guidelines of goal development that can increase potential success in therapy and post-treatment.

The Process of Goal Development

The process of goal development can be viewed as a process in three phases. First, the clinician helps the couple identify each partner's initial relationship goal. This can be done in combination with an initial goal sheet questionnaire upon entry to treatment and a guided discussion in the first session. Second, the clinician facilitates the negotiation of mutually agreed-upon goals between the two partners. Consideration should also be made to incorporate the clinician's ideas as well. This is best done when the clinician works early to establish a strong therapeutic alliance. In addition, the process of negotiating the relationship and counseling goals is an important factor for the developing therapeutic alliance. Third, the clinician identifies process goals that will be integrated based on the clinician's theoretical lens. This will include the approaches and interventions that will be used in the therapeutic process.

Identify Each Partner's Initial Relationship Goal

These goals are the broader-outcome goals that the couple has for the relationship. These are what the couple states they want at the end of treatment. Typically, couples that I work with complete a "goals for counseling" survey which serves as a discussion starter to identify specific goals of each individual partner. I ask the partners to complete the form and to not discuss it with their partner prior to completing it. This helps me understand their individual considerations for the relationship and expectations of treatment. Following is an outline of the main goals for counseling questionnaire.

Main Goals for Counseling Questionnaire

What is the primary goal that you have for your relationship?

Please identify the main problem that has brought you to counseling and rate its severity:

The main problem is: ____

____

On a continuum "None" to "Extreme," how much distress are you experiencing from this problem? (Please circle one):

None Some A Large Amount Extreme

Please identify three main goals that you would like to address in counseling:

1.____
2.____
3.____

What about your present behavior do you want to change?
What feelings do you want to alter (i.e., increase or decrease)?
What benefits do you expect to derive from therapy?
What characteristics should the ideal therapist possess?
How would you describe the ideal therapist's interactions with a client?
What do you think therapy will do for you?
How long do you think your therapy should last?
In a few words, what do you think counseling is all about (in terms of goals, methods, nature of the relationship between therapist and client, etc.)?

Negotiate Mutually Agreed-Upon Goals Between Partners and the Clinician

The second type of goal is outcome goals. Outcome goals are the preferred state at some point in time, usually at the end of therapy. In my practice, I use outcome goals as more of a short-term intervention. I will ask couples to set outcome goals at intervals of every six weeks. These goals are in line with their broader goals for the relationship.

As mentioned in the previous section, an outcome may be to clarify whether the relationship is too damaged to continue. Another may be to re-establish trust after infidelity. Outcome goals are always from the couple's perspective and do not include how they will be achieved in therapy nor the techniques used in the process. When written in the treatment plan, it is in the client's language and free of theoretical jargon. The written outcome goal is defined in a way that allows for verification of whether the goal was attained. Theoretical orientation does not apply to outcome goals; therefore, clinicians from differing perspectives would still agree on what the successful outcome is.

Developing an outcome goal is a process that is facilitated with the couple and is an ongoing negotiation between the couple and the clinicians through three distinct components, resulting in a succinct and measurable goal. The first component is to define the goal-specific behavior. This operationally defines what the couple will *do*. This answers the question of what the couple will do, think, or feel that is different. As an example, the couple may define their goal-related behavior as "We will increase intimate communication."

Next, the clinician will need to help the couple define the goal-related conditions and context. These are the where, when, with, and whom parts of the goal. This includes the particular person(s) that will perform the goal, specifically where and when it will take place, and any specific situations in how the goal will occur. To continue with the example, the couple may define the goal-related condition as "by creating time to talk with each other about personal, non-work related topics."

Lastly, the clinician helps the couple identify a suitable level of change. This can include frequency of behavior or intensity of change, usually expressed in a percentage value. In our example, the couple could say either "every weekday evening for thirty minutes" or "90% of the time." In this example, the outcome goal can be written in two possible ways:

1) We will increase intimate communication by creating time to talk with each other about personal, non-work topics every weekday for thirty minutes.
2) We will increase intimate communication by creating daily time to talk with each other about personal, non-work topics, 90% of the time.

Integrate Clinician Process Goals

Once the outcome goals have been established, the clinician can identify process goals that will support the outcome goals of the couple. Process goals are the clinician's desired in-session experiences. They are based on the clinician's conceptual understanding of the couple and are supported by the clinician's theoretical lens. Considering our example, here are a few process goals that could be considered based on the clinician's theoretical lens:

- The clinician will teach a process of dialogue to assist the couple in creating intimacy in communication.
- The clinician will utilize enactment to facilitate intimate dialogue around gridlocked issues.
- The clinician will utilize guided imagery to help the couple identify attachment needs connected to conflict communication.

References

Mitchell, C. (2007). *Effective techniques for dealing with highly resistant clients* (2nd ed.). Johnson City, TN: Clifton W. Mitchell Publishing.

Owen, J., Duncan, B., Anker, M., & Sparks, J. (2012). Initial relationship goal and couple therapy outcomes at post and six-month follow-up. *Journal of Family Psychology*, *26*(2), 179–186. doi:10.1037/a0026998.

6 Family of Origin

Our family of origin is the primary model for how we will later create our own personal, intimate relationships. Our families provide the first understandings of how partners should treat each other, what is normal in a relationship, what type of relationship we hope to have, and what type of relationship we hope to avoid. These early understandings come from the conversations we hear from our parents and siblings, events and experiences that occur as part of our family history, and observations of the dynamics within our parents' relationship. From the family experience, our attitudes, values, and behaviors are transmitted from our family of origin to our adult relationships.

The messages we receive from our family of origin are correlated to the quality of our future personal and intimate relationships. Researchers from the University of Nevada (Weigel & Weiser, 2014) showed three distinct types of individuals in terms of how they remember the messages from their family of origin. *Optimist* individuals reported receiving messages from the family of origin emphasizing closeness and optimism. These individuals received messages that marriage is enduring, relationships take work, relationships are partnerships, and relationships must have love and happiness. *Structural Optimist* individuals were similar to the Optimist yet had less memory of messages that love and happiness are needed in relationships. Family messages that external pressures influence relationships and that divorce is hard on families were more common with Structural Optimists. *Cautious* individuals had messages that relationships are not permanent, relationships take work, relationships are plagued by lack of trust and fidelity, and it is important to approach relationships with caution. As you can imagine, each of these types of individuals will approach intimate relationships in very different ways.

Early Childhood Experience

Couples come wounded to therapy. They are wounded by their partners during the course of their relationship, and they come with wounds from childhood. To protect these wounds they are defensive. Clinicians can help the couple connect to the wounds and come to an understanding that their patterns of protecting interfere with their relating to one another as a couple. This is the essence of family-of-origin work.

Some couples are triggered back to the past, and some go back with the help of the clinician. Schroder (2015, p. 26) states that a key issue that separates the unhelpful time travel into one's past and focused family-of-origin work is intentionality. When someone is triggered back to the past by a sound, smell, or phrase, the individual needs to manage the emotional state aroused by the trigger, a difficult task for many. This is very different than looking back at the past to consider how a person's past is impacting their choices in the present.

Family of origin is talking with the partners about their parents, their childhood, and the ways in which they dealt with problems in their family of origin. With the clinician as a guide, each partner can uncover the coping patterns that they used as children and how these patterns might be unnecessary in adulthood and ultimately interfering in their relationship. Additionally, each partner could explore the personal resources they used during difficult times in childhood, which I believe are innate personal attributes that they posses, and how they could be utilized with adult relational experiences.

Couple Conflict: The Pain Between Us

A couple's conflict can be seen as a failure to attend to pain in the relationship. The pain can be from early childhood, pain for hurts in past romantic relationships, perpetual hurts in the current relationship, or a specific trauma, such as an affair. Sells and Yarhouse (2011) distinguish between the pain between the couple and the unarticulated pain within the individual. There is an expectation that relief will come, so we seek relief first from our parents, from other important people as we age, and then from our romantic relationships. If the pain persists and is not quenched in the romantic relationship, then the pain moves to occupy a new space: the pain between the couple. Pain can be seen, then, on multiple levels in the couple relationship. Sells and Yarhouse (2011) go on to explain that conflict can be represented as the conflict theme, historical experience with the conflict theme, and respective hurts from family of origin. All of them are operating simultaneously and need to be attended to by the clinician.

The conflict theme is easily recognizable to the clinician. It may come in the form of problems communicating scheduling of the children's activities, who is responsible for making payments for bills, or issues around disciplining the children. Hurts in the relationship can be repetitive, and responses to these hurts can become hardwired in the brain. These are the historical aspects of the conflict. The responses are quick to happen because they are practiced over and over again in the relationship. Lastly, the conflict could have its roots in family of origin. People learn ways to respond to situations, people, and disappointments from their family, and these can be carried into the couple relationship without even the awareness of the couple. When couples are able to step back from the immediacy of the conflict and presenting issue and see the broader aspect of the early life backstories, predictable changes occur. The intensity of the interpersonal conflict diminishes, and a greater understanding of the problematic patterns emerge (Shepard & Harway, 2012, p. 63).

The Initial Family-of-Origin Interview

Clinicians address family of origin differently, and some do not address family of origin at all. For example, a good friend of mine believes that family of origin "is everything," and he dedicates fifteen to twenty sessions specifically to family-of-origin work. In my own practice, I will dedicate two to six sessions for working with family of origin. Regardless of the amount of time allotted, it is important to obtain a comprehensive understanding of the influences of family of origin. In my practice, the family-of-origin interview happens after the assessment session and precedes the family-of-origin work I set out to do. The following is an outline of the primary topics I address in the semi-structured family-of-origin clinical interview.

Primary Caregivers

Please name for me the adult caregivers during your childhood and your relationship with them: for example, mother and father. Close your eyes for a moment and picture yourself in the presence of your (mother/father). Now describe him/her with a noun or adjective. Are there any other important adults other than parents that you would want to identify?

Parents' Relationship

How would you describe your parents' relationship when you were a child? Describe the physical, financial, and emotional situation of your parents. Did you know at the time how your parents felt about your birth? As an adult, what understanding do you have about your parents' feeling about your birth?

Children of Divorce or Separation

How old were you when your parents separated or divorced? How did you find out? What did you feel about it at the time? How do you feel about it now?

Sibling Relationships

Please tell me who your siblings are and if they lived at home with you when you were a child. Describe each sibling using a noun, adjective, or phrase. Where are you in the birth order to these siblings, and does birth order have any significant meaning to you?

Peer Relationships

How easy was it to make friends? In general, how supportive were your friends? Some friends will give nicknames. Did any give you a nickname, either positive or negative? What were they and how did you feel about the nicknames? What problems did you have with peers as a child?

Childhood Memories

Share with me the happiest memory of your (mother/father) when you were a child. Now share with me your worst memory of your (mother/father). What did you want from your (mother/father) that you never received? How do you think that influences you today? How did you go about getting approval from your (mother/father)?

Earliest Memory

What is your earliest memory from childhood? Describe it in detail to me.

Description of Self

How would you describe yourself as a child? Be as descriptive as possible. Describe feelings you had as a child. These may include feelings such as being sad or unhappy or scared, or feelings of shame, guilt, emptiness, and loneliness.

Current Relationship With Caregivers and Family

Describe your current relationship with your (mother/father/another caregiver). If you were to change something about your parents or your relationship with them, how would your life be different today?

Family of Origin

Insights From Practice

Michael Adams, LPCC, CADC

Sophia: "He should just know!" she says angrily to her husband, Josh, as she rolls her eyes once again in the couples therapy session.

> "All he ever does is play on his phone at night, and never shows me any attention! In fact, he's choosing to ignore me!" Her body language is closed off, arms folded, brow bent, as she sits on the other side of the couch.

How many times have we as clinicians experienced similar statements from our clients: "I shouldn't have to tell him/her"; "He/she should just know," and "Will there ever be a time he/she will just get it?"

In order for couples work to be effective, most clinicians agree there has to be a communication component. What do we do after we teach the couple how to communicate and yet they continue to revert to dysfunctional methods? This can be frustrating for the couple and the clinician trying to help them.

I taught her how to communicate using the Feedback Wheel (Real, 2008) several times, but she wasn't using it. At this point, I would encourage all clinicians to ask themselves, "Why? Why is my client stuck?". Instead of teaching it for the third time, I decided to take a break from "Skill Development" and went with the "Root Cause" or "Family-of-Origin" technique I learned from Terry Real.

Try This

Michael: Sophia, being ignored is really painful for you, isn't it?

Sophia: Yes, it is. I hate it.

Michael: Can you describe for me a time when you were ignored, maybe in childhood?

Sophia: Yes. When I was in grade school, I got the lead role in a musical for school. I told my dad about it and the date way ahead of time. I really wanted him to be there. I thought for once maybe he'd show some interest in me. The night of the musical as Mom and I were getting ready I went to Dad. He was in his recliner watching TV, and I said, "Let's go, Daddy."

(Pending childhood wound) He said, "To what?" I said, "My play." He said, "What play?" without ever taking his eyes off the screen." I left crying (she said this very matter-of-factly).

Michael: Oh my goodness, how painful. How old were you?"

Sophia: Six.

Michael: How do you feel right now thinking of that memory?

Sophia: Hurt, rejected, sad, and angry.

Michael: In your mind's eye, can you see yourself as that six-year-old? What does she look like (notice switch to third person in "she")?

Sophia: She's all dressed up: skirt, makeup, hair done, she's beautiful (Terry Real says you usually get something very tender).

Michael: She sounds adorable. Although you didn't have words for this as a six-year-old, I wonder if you wanted to say, "Daddy, please pay me some attention, let me know you love me."

At this point, Sophia began to weep, and her husband began to cry as he held her. I began to tear up. I let her cry; she needed it. I didn't intervene until she was finished. I then said, "How did I know those words would fit for you?" She said, "I don't know." I said, "Because I believe you think those same things of your husband, but you're not willing to bring down the wall and actually ask him. Why would you? Your own father didn't meet your needs (more tears). Sophia, that is not your fault. But now it's your responsibility to learn; would you like me to teach you?"

With this insight and healing, she stated her needs more directly.

"Josh, I need you to snuggle me for ten minutes tonight."

"Josh, I need to have a date night with you this weekend."

"Josh, I need some alone time."

"Josh, will you put your phone down and tell me about your day and ask me about mine?"

Michael Adams, LPCC, CADC has worked in the mental health field since 2006. He received his MS in clinical psychology from Eastern Kentucky University and his bachelors in psychology from Asbury University. He has been in private practice since 2010. In 2012 he opened his own practice in Florence, KY: The Counseling Services of Michael C. Adams and Associates, PSC. He predominantly works with couples and trauma survivors. He enjoys using the works of Terrence Real from the Relational Life Institute and John and Julie Gottman of the Gottman Institute to work with couples. He enjoys using EMDR to help individuals recover from trauma. His practice includes two other associates and works with ages two and up.

Michael can be reached at
859–525–0185
adams.michaelc@gmail.com
www.northernkentuckycounseling.com

Mapping Family Patterns With the Genogram

A genogram is much like a family tree. It is used to map out several generations (usually three) of the family to look at patterns of communication or behavior, experiences, and closeness in the relationships between family members. Clinicians who use the genogram consider it a fast method of assessing a variety of issues within the family. It can be used to help the family see themes and patterns and then begin to explore the reasons that certain issues may have developed and possibly come to understand the reasons behind certain choices, beliefs, and emotions.

I find the genogram extremely helpful as a quick assessment of the couple's family of origin and the couple's nuclear family. Combined with a timeline of the relationship, a comprehensive contextual view emerges of important themes: how the couple relationship formed, spiritual and cultural influences, coalitions and cut-offs among family members, and historical issues such as important milestones, external stressors influencing the couple relationship, and significant transgressions that have occurred.

There are a number of issues that can be explored as the clinician constructs the genogram. Basic information is addressed first, including the names and ages of all family members in three generations. As I add the couple and their parents to the genogram, I ask the couple to identify their occupations and education. Once all family members have been identified, I facilitate a discussion about the relationships between family members, looking for relationship dynamics such as emotional cut-offs, enmeshment, and conflict. I will ask the partners to describe their parents from the perspective of when they were children. I will ask that they give three words that best describe each of their parents. Once identified, I explore each of the words in a bit more detail. When negative words are ascribed to a parent, I work to identify the coping strategies they used to manage life with a parent who is "highly critical" or "unemotional." It is helpful to know how they thought, felt, and behaved during these times and how they might be using these same strategies in their current relationship.

Asking a question about who uses medication can be an inconspicuous way to find out what physical and mental illnesses exist with the family members throughout the generations. Lastly, I ask about spiritual and cultural influences in the family.

Following the creation of the genogram, I create a timeline of the couple relationship. I do so by asking the couple to chronologically identify the positive and negative events for the family. This takes about five to ten minutes and offers quite a bit of information about the nuclear family in terms of formation of the relationship, strengths, relational challenges, and external stressors.

Influence of Attachment on Relational Process

Research on adult attachment suggests that the close emotional bond between parents and their children is responsible for the bond that develops later in life between adults in emotionally intimate relationships. The theory of attachment was originally developed by John Bowlby, a British psychoanalyst who was interested in explaining the intense distress experienced by infants who had been separated from their parents. According to Bowlby, the attachment system essentially "asks" the following fundamental question: Is the attachment figure nearby, accessible, and attentive (Fraley, 2010)?

If the child perceives the answer to this question to be "yes," he or she feels loved, secure, and confident, and will likely explore his or her environment, play with others, and be sociable. If the child perceives the answer to this question to be "no," the child will likely experience anxiety, and if the separation from the primary caregiver is prolonged, he or she is likely to exhibit distress and depression (Fraley, 2010).

Hazan and Shaver (1987) noted that the relationship between infants and caregivers and the relationship between adult romantic partners share certain features. Table 6.1 outlines a number of similarities.

Similarly, Jeffery Young (2017) describes six needs that must be met for a child to thrive. If these needs are not met, he believes that schemas (core beliefs) are developed that later negatively affect adult relationships.

Basic Safety: This need is essential from birth and involves the child's being treated well by his or her family. When the need is not met, maladaptive schemas of abandonment and mistrust can develop.

Connection to Others: Children need love, affection, empathy, and understanding. They also need guidance and understanding from their family and peers. When this does not occur, schemas of emotional deprivation or social exclusion can develop.

Autonomy: A healthy balance of dependence and independence is necessary in childhood. Increasing levels of independence as children get older teaches self-reliance, responsibility, and good judgment. When this need is not met, dependent or vulnerable schemas develop.

Self-Esteem: When children are loved and respected, they develop self-esteem. In the absence of family and peer support, maladaptive schemas of defectiveness and failure can develop.

Self-Expression: In healthy families, children are encouraged to express themselves. When self-expression is discouraged, children learn that their needs and feelings are not important, and maladaptive schemas of suppression can develop.

Again, helping couples understand the schemas that they have developed from early childhood relationships could lead to insights on how their early formation is playing out in their current relationship. In doing so, the couple can come together to consider how they may create a more secure attachment bond.

Table 6.1 Similarities of Infant Caregiver Relationships and Romantic Partners

Both feel safe when the other is nearby and responsive.
Both engage in close, intimate bodily contact.
Both feel insecure when the other is inaccessible.
Both share discoveries with one another.
Both play with one another's facial features and exhibit a mutual fascination and preoccupation with one another.
Both engage in "baby talk."

Couples seek or avoid intimacy along a continuum of secure, anxious, or avoidant attachment styles, and attachment styles for couples tend to predict the long-term outcomes of their relationship. For example, two secure partners have a good chance of staying together, two insecure partners are more likely to split up, and an insecure woman with a secure man will fare better than an insecure man with a secure woman (Carlson & Sperry, 2010).

It makes sense, then, that the preferred attachment style would be secure, and this attachment style has a balance between autonomy and dependence. Intimacy increases when partners have firm and solid self-concepts, which enable them to identify themselves as separate individuals in relationships with their partners (Beyers & Seiffge-Krenke, 2010). In Table 6.2 is a brief outline of the three main attachment orientations.

Cindy Hazan and Phillip Shaver (Hazan & Shaver, 1987; Hazan & Shaver, 1990; Hazan & Shaver, 1994) adapted John Bowlby's research on infant attachment to adult romantic relationships. From their work, they helped define the different attachment styles in adult relationships. These styles are secure, anxious/preoccupied, dismissive-avoidant, and fearful-avoidant.

A *secure* partner will have low anxiety and low avoidance in the relationship. The individual will have a healthy mix of independence and dependence. They tend to have a positive view of themselves, their partner, and their relationship. Both partners will have a strong self-concept; they will feel secure in the relationship and will value each other. Couples will be warm and responsive to one another and take care not to hurt one another.

An *anxious/preoccupied* partner will have high anxiety and low avoidance. The preoccupied partner will seek high levels of intimacy, approval, and responsiveness from their partner, leading to his or her becoming overly dependent. The preoccupied partner will be less trusting and have a more negative view about themselves and their partner. They tend to have high levels of emotional expressiveness, worry, and impulsiveness in their relationships.

The *dismissive-avoidant* partner desires a high level of independence, often appearing to avoid attachment altogether. They view themselves as self-sufficient, invulnerable to attachment feelings, and not needing close relationships. They tend to suppress their feelings and deal with rejection by distancing themselves from their partner.

Table 6.2 Attachment Orientation

Secure	*Anxious*	*Avoidant*
Balance of autonomy and dependence	Fear of losing partner	Fear of losing oneself in partner
	Over-emphasis on comfort and reducing anxiety	Over-emphasis on independence
	Over-emphasis on reducing potential rejection	

The *fearful-avoidant* partner will have mixed feelings about close relationships, both desiring an intimate relationship and also feeling uncomfortable with emotional closeness. They may mistrust their partner and view themselves as unworthy. Like dismissive-avoidant partners, fearful-avoidant adults tend to seek less intimacy and also suppress their feelings.

Treatment With Attachment in Mind

The clinical interventions found to be effective with trauma survivors have direct application to attachment-oriented couples therapy. Drawing from the work of van der Kolk et al. (1996), the new relational experience will require what van der Kolk calls "interpersonal process," a process that positively changes the trauma survivor's relationships with others. To be effective with this interpersonal process in couples therapy requires 1) a safe space to contain emotional outbursts, 2) an opportunity to maintain cognitive awareness in the face of intense feelings, 3) enhancement of the capacity to connect to one's core emotions such as longings and sadness about disconnection, and 4) the challenge to face the fear of true closeness with others. When interpersonal process is in place, a safety zone is created and interactive repair through direct emotional, growth-facilitating communication is possible.

The goal of therapy is to overcome the defensive patterns imprinted in the early attachment experience, break the cycle of mutual hurt, and begin to create the bonding experience that distinguishes successful couples (Solomon, 2009).

The clinician can begin this process by sharing their observations that help each partner understand the pattern of their interaction. Once this is achieved, treatment can focus on how the couple selected each other and coupled, emphasizing that there is an unconscious process that people use to choose intimate relationships to heal the past. The clinician can help the couple understand how their current relationship related to the historical interactions with their family and specifically to their primary caregivers. From there, the clinician can work to restructure the here-and-now psychological and emotional responses of each partner.

It can be helpful to include an educational component in therapy related to the neurological aspects of attachment and its influence in which early relationship struggles or traumas affect the current relationship. Since people have different capacity or interest in understanding research behind the clinician's approach, it can be helpful to simply explain that traumatic experiences are processed in the nonverbal right hemisphere of the brain and that earlier relationship trauma is, in fact, present but can be beyond our awareness. This trauma is now interfering with the current relationship narrative. Bringing this into awareness and connecting the partner to the feelings that have kept them cut off from themselves or their partner, the couple can start their own growth process and reconnect with each other (Solomon, 2009).

Remembering that we develop attachment schemas from our early experiences in childhood, it is important to note that these schemas, or core beliefs, are important to our romantic relationships. Attachment schemas are stable and enduring, are rooted in childhood, and impact every relational experience. Some are certainly healthy schemas. Maladaptive schemas, however, are the result of unmet childhood needs. Bringing these maladaptive schemas to the forefront in therapy will help the couple create growth and change. There are six potential maladaptive schemas to consider when uncovering unmet childhood needs (Skeen, 2011).

I Am Defective

These individuals see themselves as bad, inferior, unwanted and invalidated. They feel shame and fear. They fear that they will be unlovable if their true self is discovered by their partner. Their partners may view them as hyper-critical.

I Am Entitled

Entitled people believe that they are superior and deserve special treatment. Their core emotion is anger. They can be viewed by their partners as controlling, manipulative, and selfish.

People Cannot Be Trusted

These individuals believe that they need to guard themselves in a world of people that cannot be trusted. They experience fear and anxiety and will guard their innermost thoughts and feelings because they believe that others will use the information against them. Their partner may view them as overly sensitive and maybe even abusive as they attempt to control situations or to protect themselves from emotional harm.

I Will Be Abandoned

The core belief for these individuals is that important people will leave them, will behave unpredictably, or will get sick and die. They tend to feel anxious, depressed, or even angry towards people who leave them. Their partner may describe them as clingy, jealous, and possessive, attacking, or withdrawn.

Others Will Not Meet My Emotional Needs

This schema results in people feeling lonely, bitter, disappointed, and anger. Their belief is that others will not be able to meet their emotional needs. They may believe that they are misunderstood, their emotions are not reciprocated, or others are not considerate of their feelings. Their partners may view them as needy and overly demanding and angry when their needs are not met.

Others' Needs Are More Important Than Mine

This individual believes that taking care of other people's needs is more important than their own needs and will allow their partners to control them. They also believe it is bad to express their own needs and desires. They tend to feel fearful, anxious, and depressed. Their partners may view them as unassertive and weak.

Guided Imagery for Identifying Attachment Needs

A creative and fascinating way to work with couples who specifically want to increase intimacy is to use guided imagery. Guided imagery is a meditation technique that, with the help of the clinician, can help the couple imagine a story or a simple progression of images. Guided imagery can be simple or highly specific. Imageries can unlock the conscious and unconscious themes as represented by the images. Paired with the use of enactments, the clinician can coach a discussion of each partner's image and help each partner discover intimate things about themselves and their partner.

Certainly, clinicians can purchase guided imagery downloads and scripts that they can use with couples. Many times, it is helpful to write the script based on client needs and interest. Shepherd (2016) identifies a number of considerations for preparing a specific guided imagery for couples:

- Consider the amount of detail. The imagery can be constructed with specific details or can be a series of images.
- The state of relaxation is important. Sessions start with relaxation techniques and soothing images, such as floating in warm water or rising weightless like a balloon.
- The features of the image are important.
- Consider the identity within the image. The image could take the person to a different age, a different appearance, or different abilities. These can be crafted to suit the storyline.
- The plot can be a peaceful scene with friendly characters or a scene that includes an advisory with whom the person will need to resolve conflict with.
- The location is an ongoing story, so locations change as the story moves forward. Virtually any setting can do, and the people move about through the locations by walking, floating, using a boat, flying through the air, walking across a bridge, or entering through a doorway. Possible places include a meadow, a tunnel, stairs, rooms, an ocean beach, a castle, a forest, a temple, paradise, or a mountainside.
- Using symbolic characters open up the unconscious. Characters can be parts of the self; for example, a dark creature might represent the shadow. A man could portray a woman's animus, a woman could represent a man's

anima. There are also possible archetypal characters, such as the hero, the warrior, the healer, the wizard, the mother, and the father. Characters could also come from myths, fairy tales, and religious stories.
- Consider props within the image: a beloved doll or toy, a blanket that represented security. Consider times that have personal significance.
- For couples, include acceptance and compassion. Within the images, the clinician can direct the client to intentionally direct feelings of warmth, care, love, and acceptance for themselves so that they will experience compassion for themselves and ultimately for their partner.

Use of the Enneagram for Assessment, Exploration, and Change

The enneagram can be a useful assessment tool for helping couples uncover how their personality styles affect how they approach their personal interactions. It can also be used to help couples understand their own and their partner's motivations and habitual patterns in their interactions. The awareness of each partner's personality style can be a positive guide for their day-to-day interactions.

About the Enneagram

The enneagram of personality is a way of describing personality as nine interconnected personality styles. Each style of the nine personality styles are numbered and have a differing point of view, a different emotional response pattern, and a set of behavioral tendencies. Balance is gained when each partner functions from the resourceful, or high side, of their core style while having the resources of all the styles (WEPSS.com, 2017a).

The enneagram also identifies the "wings" of our preferred personality style. These are less dominant than our high side but are still a dominant preference in our personality. A person of the Three personality type, for example, is understood to have points Two and Four as their wing types. The circle of the enneagram figure may indicate that the types or points exist on a spectrum rather than as distinct types or points unrelated to those adjacent to them. A person may be understood, therefore, to have a core type and one or two wing types that influence but do not change the core type. Sometimes you will hear couples or clinicians state, "he is a Three personality with a Nine wing," indicating the two strong aspects of an individual's personality style.

The lines connecting the types (see Figure 6.1) add further meaning to the person's preferred type. There are sometimes called the "growth" and "stress" points in the Enneagram theory, or what clinicians are more likely to call "high side" (growth) or "low side" (stress) of their personality. The theory proposes that people may move away from their dominant type to another type when in a position of security, or alternatively when they are stressed. For

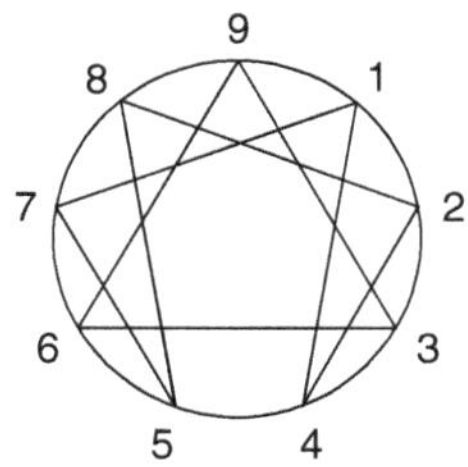

Figure 6.1 The Enneagram Figure

example, a One will likely perform utilizing some of the characteristics of an unhealthy Four when stressed and will at times choose to utilize characteristics of the healthy Seven in times of security.

In summary, individuals have an overall dominate personality type. Along with their dominant personality type, there are at least four other points on the Enneagram that can affect a person's overall personality: the two points connected by the lines to the core type and the two wing points.

The Nine Enneagram Styles

The following descriptions of the enneagram styles are largely based on the descriptions for the Enneagram Institute (2017) but not solely. The Enneagram Institute is a wonderful resource for anyone working with others using the Enneagram or for an individual interested in a deeper understanding of the Enneagram. The following descriptions are also based on personal experience and descriptions shared by other clinicians.

One: "The Reformer"

Ones desire to be good people, seeking to make the world a better place to live in. They seek goodness, integrity, and balance.

A One's primary fear is corruption of themselves or being bad. When moving in the direction of stress, they will become moody and irrational at Four. When moving toward growth, they become more spontaneous and joyful, like a healthy Seven.

Two: "The Helper"

Twos are friendly, generous, and self-sacrificing. They are empathic listeners, sincere, and warm-hearted. They tend to be well meaning and driven to be close to others, but they can fall into doing things for others in order to be needed.

Their primary fear is being unwanted or unworthy of being loved. When moving in their direction of stress, Twos can become aggressive and dominating at Eight. However, when moving in their direction of growth, Twos can become more self-nurturing and emotionally aware, like healthy Fours.

Three: "The Achiever"

Threes are self-confident, attractive, and charming. They tend to be ambitious, competent in what they do, and energetic. They can be driven to be status conscious and highly driven for advancement. They are tactful and poised, but they can also be overly concerned with their image and what others think of them. Others may describe them as workaholic and highly competitive.

Their primary fear of the Three is that they might be worthless. When moving in their direction of stress, Threes can become disengaged and apathetic at Nine. However, when moving in their direction of growth, they can be become more cooperative and committed to others, like healthy Sixes.

Four: "The Individualist"

Fours are self-aware, sensitive, and reserved. They are emotionally honest with others, personal, and creative. Withholding themselves from others due to feeling vulnerable and defective, they can also feel disdainful and exempt from ordinary ways of living. They typically have problems with melancholy, self-indulgence, and self-pity.

The basic fear of the Four is that they will have no identity or that they are insignificant. When moving in their direction of stress, Fours can become over-involved and clinging at Two. When moving in their direction of growth, Fours can become more objective and principled, like healthy Ones.

Five: "The Investigator"

Fives are alert, insightful, and curious. They are able to concentrate and focus on developing complex ideas and skills. They are independent, innovative, and inventive. They can also become preoccupied with their thoughts and imaginary constructs. They become detached, yet high-strung and intense. They typically have problems with eccentricity and isolation.

The basic fear of the Five is being useless, helpless, or incapable. When moving in their direction of stress, Fives can become scattered at Seven. When moving in their direction of growth, Fives can become more self-confident and decisive, like healthy Eights.

Six: "The Loyalist"

Sixes are reliable, hard-working, responsible people. They can foresee problems and foster cooperation. They can be cautious and indecisive, but also reactive, defiant, and rebellious. They typically have problems with self-doubt and suspicion.

The basic fear of Sixes is not having support and guidance. When moving in their direction of stress, Sixes can become competitive and arrogant at Three. However, when moving in their direction of growth, Sixes can become more relaxed and optimistic, like healthy Nines.

Seven: "The Enthusiast"

Sevens are extroverted individuals that are optimistic, versatile, and spontaneous. They are playful, high-spirited, and practical, yet they can also misapply their many talents, becoming over-extended, scattered, and undisciplined. They constantly seek new and exciting experiences but can become distracted and exhausted by staying on the go. They typically have problems with impatience and impulsiveness.

The basic fear of the Seven is being deprived or in pain. When moving in their direction of stress, Sevens can become perfectionistic and critical at One. When moving in their direction of growth, Sevens can become more focused and fascinated by life, like healthy Fives.

Eight: "The Challenger"

Eights are self-confident, strong, and assertive. They are straight talking and decisive but can also be egocentric and domineering. Eights have a strong need to control others and sometimes can become confrontational and intimidating. Eights typically have problems with their tempers and have difficulty with allowing themselves to be vulnerable.

The basic fear of the Eight is being harmed or controlled by others. When moving in their direction of stress, Eights can become secretive and fearful at Five. When moving in their direction of growth, Eights can become more open hearted and caring, like healthy Twos.

Nine: "The Peacemaker"

Nines are accepting, trusting, and stable. They are usually creative, optimistic, and supportive, but they can also be too willing to go along with others to keep the peace. They want everything to go smoothly and be without conflict, but they can also tend to be complacent, simplifying problems and minimizing anything upsetting.

The basic fear of the Nine is loss and separation. When moving in their direction of stress, Nines can become anxious and worried at Six. However, when moving in their direction of growth, Nines can become more self-developing and energetic, like healthy Threes.

The Wagner Enneagram Personality Style Scales

I strongly recommend the Wagner Enneagram Personality Style Scales. The Wagner measures both the positive and negative dimensions of these nine styles. Test takers can see which styles they most identify with and which ones they least identify with. This gives a picture of what resources are available to the person and which strategies might be less accessible. Low scores can be as informative as high scores.

The Wagner acts like a scale with nine plates, weighing how much the individual identifies with each style. The results show which personality styles might be used the most and which styles might be used the least (WEPSS.com, 2017b). The scoring guide for the Wagner describes the nine styles and indicates typical responses of the person that are either resourceful or non-resourceful. The Wagner Scales can be purchased at their website: https://wepss.com/buy.asp.

References

Beyers, W. & Seiffge-Krenke, I. (2010). Does identity precede intimacy? Testing Erikson's theory on romantic development in emerging adults of the 21st century. *Journal of Adolescent Research*, *25*(3), 387–415.

Brooks, L. (2017). *What is family of origin work?* Retrieved January 29, 2017 from http://loveandlifetoolbox.com/what-is-family-of-origin-work/.

Carlson, J., & Sperry, L. (2010). *Recovering intimacy in love relationships: A clinician's guide* (p. 40). New York: Routledge.

Enneagram Institute. (2017). *The nine enneagram type descriptions*. Retrieved January 23, 2017 from www.enneagraminstitute.com/type-1.

Fraley, C. R. (2010). *A brief overview of adult attachment theory and research*. Retrieved January 23, 2017 from https://internal.psychology.illinois.edu/~rcfraley/attachment.htm.

Hasenecz, N. M. (2010). Surviving infidelity: Couples therapists' best practices. *Social Work Today*, *10*(3), 10.

Hazan, C., & Shaver, P. R. (1987). Romantic love conceptualized as an attachment process. *Journal of Personality and Social Psychology*, *52*(3), 511–24. doi:10.1037/0022-3514.52.3.511. PMID 3572722.

Hazan, C., & Shaver, P. R. (1990). Love and work: An attachment theoretical perspective. *Journal of Personality and Social Psychology*, 59(2), 270–80. doi:10.1037/0022-3514.59.2.270.

Hazan, C., & Shaver, P. R. (1994). Attachment as an organisational framework for research on close relationships. *Psychological Inquiry*, 5, 1–22. doi:10.1207/s15327965pli0501_1.

Jacobson, N. S., & Christensen, A. (1996). *Acceptance and change in couple therapy*. New York: Norton.

Real, T. (2008). The new rules of marriage: What you need to know to make love work. *Ballantine Books*, New York, NY.

Relate Institute. (2017). *The relate assessment*. Retrieved February 9, 2017 from https://relateinstitute.com/the-relate-assessment/.

Schroder, D. (2015). *Exploring and developing the use of art-based genograms in family of origin therapy: Sharing the potential for understanding and healing through the art process* (p. 26). Springfield, IL: Charles C. Thomas.

Sells, J. N., & Yarhouse, M. A. (2011). *Counseling couples in conflict: A relational restoration model*. Downers Grove, IL: InterVarsity Press.

Shepard, D. S., & Harway, M. (2012). *Engaging men in couples' therapy*. New York: Taylor and Francis.

Shepherd, P. (2016). *Guided meditation*. Retrieved February 11, 2016 from www.trans-4mind.com/jamesharveystout/guidedme.htm#The technique of guided meditation.

Shoham, V., Rohrbaugh, M. J., & Cleary, A. A. (2008). Brief strategic couple therapy. In A. S. Gurman (Ed.), *Clinical handbook of couple therapy* (pp. 299–322). New York: Guilford Press.

Skeen, M. (2011). *The critical partner*. Oakland, CA: New Harbinger Publications, Inc.

Solomon, M.F. (2009). Attachment repair in couples therapy: A prototype for treatment of intimate relationships. *Clinical Social Work Journal*, 37: 214–223.

Timmons, A. C., Arbel, R., & Margolin, G. (2017). Daily patterns of stress and conflict in couples: Associations with marital aggression and family-of-origin aggression. *Journal of Family Psychology*, *31*(1), 93–104.

van der Kolk, B. A., McFarlane, A., & Weisaeth, L. (Eds.). (1996). *Traumatic stress: The effects of overwhelming experience on mind, body and society*. New York: Guilford Press.

Weigel, D. J., & Weiser, D. A. (2014). Commitment messages communicated in families of origin: Contributions to relationship commitment attitudes. *Communication Quarterly*, 62(5), 536–551.

WEPSS.com. (2017a). *About the enneagram*. Retrieved January 31, 2017 from www.wepss.com/aboutENNEAGRAM.asp

WEPSS.com. (2017b). *About the WPESS*. Retrieved January 31, 2017 from www.wepss.com/aboutWEPSS.asp.

Young, J. (2017). Schema Theory. Retrieved April 11, 2017 from http://www.schematherapy.com/id30.htm

7 Communication

A good majority of couples states that communication is the primary presenting issue when starting therapy. Though most therapists recognize that problematic communication may be a troublesome issue, deeper and more systemic issues tend to be where the problem lies. Barriers in communication begin to develop as partners allow misunderstandings to continue, criticism and defensiveness are used to protect one's emotional or physical safety, partners emotionally disengage with one another, and resentment sets in. By the time couples attend therapy, problematic patterns are entrenched and difficult to change.

Clinicians respond to these difficult communication and behavioral patterns differently based on their theoretical lens. Most clinicians, though, resort to teaching communication skills as part of their practice. Some clinicians may rely solely on teaching communication skills.

Teaching and practicing communication skills may not lead to healthy communication that goes beyond the session. In fact, teaching communication skills in session might not have any lasting effects for the couple. In a comparison study of traditional behavioral couples therapy and integrative behavioral couples therapy, Baucom, Baucom, and Christensen (2015) found that though teaching communication and problem-solving skills created improvements in communication early in treatment, the gains were not maintained after treatment termination. It may be that teaching communication skills helps create structure in the therapy session so that early clinical goals are reached. However, it is the constructive communication between the partners in session that includes the empathic joining with one another, building tolerance to differing perspectives, positive reciprocity, and increasing vulnerability of sharing that are associated with long-term outcomes.

Gottman and DeClaire (2001) suggest that healthy communication is how a couple pays attention to one another. They do not believe that it is the depth of intimacy in the conversation that matters or even whether the couple agrees or disagrees. Gottman proposed that skill-based efforts by the clinician in couples therapy are misplaced and clinicians should instead change the focus in therapy to helping couples continue to engage in dialogue about their "perpetual problems" that are enduring and help them avoid gridlock (Domingue & Mollen, 2009).

In clinical practice, couples report that it is difficult to implement the communication skills that they have learned in session at home after they leave the counseling session. They report that they fall into old patterns of communicating that lead to verbal escalation, limiting their success. Most clinicians understand that once couples are emotionally aroused in their conversation, plagued by ingrained defensiveness and resentment, most skills learned in session are forgotten, and the ongoing, problematic interactional patterns endemic to the relationship take over.

Consider for a moment a child practicing baseball; practice entails rehearsal of movements that mimic situations that will happen in a game. Coaches call this "muscle memory," and it can be called upon during moments in the game without much thought. Couples need this muscle memory to be successful at having conversations during moments of sensitive topics or escalating conversation. Teaching and rehearsing communication skills will be useful in the early sessions of treatment to create therapeutic structure and to help the couple emphasize key communication strategies such as emotional attunement, emotional expression, paraphrasing to demonstrate understanding, and validation. To create positive outcomes for the couple following treatment, the clinician will need to create other communication experiences throughout the therapeutic encounter that go beyond teaching and rehearsing communication skills.

Commitment First

Sheras and Koch-Sheras (2008) make the argument that communication strategies are taught and utilized before they can be maximally therapeutic. From their perspective, the act of commitment has to precede the use of communication training. When the couple is committed to one another and working to make things better, the probability for success with teaching and utilizing communication skills is higher.

Prior to teaching and integrating communication skills, the clinician should help the couple see that a commitment is needed, not just to the partner but to the entity called the relationship. This is a challenging concept because we live in a culture that values individual needs over relational needs. This can be concluded from statements such as "I will not stay in a marriage just for the kids" or "I love him but I am not 'in love' with him." This commitment can start from making a commitment to the therapy process. Successfully creating commitment to the relationship shifts the focus away from the individual needs of each partner to what works best for the relationship. Though the couple may be thinking of breaking up, ending the relationship is not considered one of the options when developing commitment to the relationship or therapy. Commitment to therapy, even for a brief period, is needed (Sheras & Koch-Sheras, 2008).

Another way to support commitment is for the couple to recognize that they are making a commitment to their future relationship. The couple may be rooted firmly in the chaos of the present moment, and it would be beneficial for the couple to have a vision of what the desired future relationship will look like (Sheras & Koch-Sheras, 2008). Having made a commitment to the process of therapy, the entity of the relationship, and the future couple relationship, the couple is better prepared for communication-skill development and the processes of healthy interaction that will be directed by the clinician in session.

Understanding Destructive Communication

John Gottman (2001) discusses a simple and "uninteresting" truth about distressed couples: They are more negative than happy couples, and this negativity comes through in their communication. He also noted that the negativity leaks through in both the verbal and non-verbal communication, though in his lab studies he found it was easier to discern the negativity in the non-verbal communication because it was difficult for the couple to fake being positive as sometimes happens in therapy.

There are four types of negative interactions that Gottman & Silver (2012) called the four horsemen of the apocalypse. He believes that these are lethal elements that can be predictive of divorce and usually rear their ugly heads in the following order: criticism, contempt, defensiveness, and stonewalling.

Complaining about one's partner is normal; however, it becomes a problem when complaints turn into criticism. Gottman distinguishes between criticism and complaints because partners will usually have complaints about each other. The difference between the two is that a complaint focuses on a specific behavior, while a criticism attacks the character of the person.

Contempt is possibly the worst of the four horsemen because it communicates a pervasive disgust to the partner. It is corrosive and enduring. Conflicts tend to escalate in intensity and frequency because it becomes impossible to solve a problem when one partner is disgusted with the other.

As one partner uses contempt, the other partner can become defensive. Defensiveness has a constricting effect for the couple. They are no longer able to be vulnerable with one another, and this limits their ability to examine their own role in conflict and the possible changes that are needed in the relationship. It also constricts intimate communication needed to soften their approach to everyday challenges in the relationship.

Defensiveness can be seen as the product of pain in the relationship. There is a cycle of pain and defense in troubled relationships (Sells & Yarhouse, 2011). This defensiveness should be respected by the clinician, and care should be taken to not challenge the person to reduce the defensiveness. When pain exists and it is not attended to, the person creates a defense in the presence of someone who may hurt them through shame, anger, contempt, or embarrassment. For this reason, asking the person to reduce their defensiveness puts them in an emotionally vulnerable position.

It would be more helpful for the clinician to assist the couple to recognize that people often get stuck in negative communication patterns and help educate them on the circular nature of communication. As couples become aware of the reciprocal or interconnected manner in which they communicate, they might begin to see possible starting points for changes in their patterns of interaction (Fife, Weeks, & Gambescia, 2008) and ultimately reduce the defensiveness in the interaction.

As conflict escalates and limited resolution occurs, one or both partners may emotionally check out of the relationship: what Gottman calls "stonewalling." Stonewalling may be an attempt to reduce emotional flooding that occurs during conflict. However, the unresponsiveness of the stonewalling partner tends to create even more anger in the other partner. Stonewalling usually happens later in the relationship than earlier, when there is a substantial amount of negative sentiment that has developed in the relationship due to the criticism, contempt, and defensiveness the partners may be experiencing.

Understanding Effective Communication

Glasser (1998) talks about seven caring habits that lead to people having satisfying and fulfilling relationships. These habits are the following: supporting, encouraging, listening, trusting, accepting, respecting, and negotiating differences. In contrast, he also identified seven deadly habits: blaming, criticizing, complaining, nagging, threatening, punishing, and bribing or rewarding for control. In Table 7.1, the seven caring and seven deadly habits are contrasted. Couples that show signs of the seven deadly habits can do a 180-degree shift in behavior by integrating more of the opposing caring habit.

Teaching and Rehearsing Listening

People tend to listen for the purpose of responding. I view my clinical role as a facilitator in moving that orientation away from listening to respond, which keeps the focus on the listener's own thought, to listening for the purpose of understanding, which will move the focus to the partner and what he or she is saying.

Table 7.1 The Seven Caring Habits

Seven Caring Habits	*Seven Deadly Habits*
Supporting	Criticizing
Encouraging	Blaming
Listening	Complaining
Accepting	Nagging
Trusting	Threatening
Respecting	Punishing
Negotiating differences	Bribing, rewarding to control

In doing so, couples are directed to consider the listener role as responsible for expanding the conversation and driving it to a deeper level of intimacy. This necessitates that the listener work hard to understand, ask questions, and make statements from a curious perspective. The listener needs to maintain their own emotional regulation, and that of their partner to some degree, and maintain low levels of defensiveness by trying not to create defensiveness in their partner. They need to resist defending their own perspective while in the listening role by focusing on their partner's perspective. Teaching and rehearsing these skills sets the stage for later work in session that will have the couple in conversation with one another with little interference from the clinician.

Teaching Types of Communication

When teaching any skill in session, it is good to have a general framework to teach from. I use a three-step process for teaching any skill: First, I will *teach* the skill and the reason for utilizing it. Next, I will *demonstrate* the successful use of the skill. Lastly, I have the couple *practice* the skill with my coaching in order for the couple to implement the skill successfully.

As a precursor to teaching communication skills, I first discuss the three levels of communication, which are non-verbal, para-verbal, and verbal communication. Knowing these three levels is important because understanding them can lead to accurate attunement to feelings in all three categories. Most couples react to all three categories, yet in their listening with each other, they may stay focused on the verbal communication and not reflect an understanding of the communication that may be coming through non-verbal or para-verbal communication.

The three levels of communication are easily defined. Nonverbal communication is the expressions and actions, such as posture, head movements, closeness or proximity to one another, and facial expressions. I tell couples that para-verbal communication is not what you say but how you say it; it includes the tone, volume, and cadence of the speech. Verbal communication is what you say in words, and, by the way, it is the most direct way to say something.

Interestingly, body language and facial expressions tend to be trusted more than verbal communication. If there is any incongruity in the expression between non-verbal and verbal communication of a given interaction, couples tend to be more trusting of the non-verbal communication.

Imago Dialogue Listening Strategy

The Imago Dialogue, originally created by Dr. Harville Hendrix and his wife, Dr. Helen Hunt, is a simple and unique tool that has been utilized by Imago therapists for over twenty-five years (Imagoworks, 2015). The Imago dialogue strategy is useful for giving a structure to couples that, when used, can be a means of limiting emotional escalation during conversation in session or for use at home. The process clearly identifies the specific task of the sender and receiver roles in intimate communication.

The sender's tasks are less defined than the receiver tasks in this model. The sender's primary task is to communicate in a way that is non-threatening and carefully constructed. The sender does this by communicating with "I" statements, monitoring their tone, and selecting words carefully.

The receiver's role is more emphasized in the Imago process, and this is useful in creating an active listening atmosphere. The instruction for the "receiver" of communication in the Imago model (Imagoworks, 2015) is for the receiver to sequentially 1) *listen* closely to the statements made by the sender of the message, 2) *mirror* or paraphrase back to the person what is said without significantly adding or taking away from the message, 3) *summarize* the content to check for clarity and accuracy, 4) *validate* that the sender's message makes sense from the sender's point of view, and 5) *empathize* by expressing an understanding of what the sender might be feeling about the situation.

The Dialogue Strategy: Teaching Reflection of Content, Thinking, Feeling

In a similar fashion, I teach a dialogue strategy that asks the listener in communication to focus on the important content of the communication, the thinking behind the content, and the feelings associated with the communication. I also put the power and responsibility for guiding the conversation on the listener. In everyday life, people tend to listen to respond, and I challenge couples to first listen to understand. For that reason, it is the listener's responsibility to 1) be good at hearing the perspective of their partner, 2) demonstrate that they understand their partner's communication, and 3) guide the conversation to a deeper level of intimacy.

This is accomplished first by the listener demonstrating to the sender that their message was understood from the sender's perspective. Once understanding is demonstrated, the listener chooses a specific "pathway" to create a deeper understanding of the content that is being delivered.

When teaching the dialogue strategy, I ask couples to listen to their partner using three sequential content areas: content, thinking, and feeling. The receiver is told at the beginning of the session that they are the one in charge of directing the conversation until at some point their partner transfers into the receiver role and they become the sender.

Step 1: Sender Discusses a Mutually Agreed-Upon Topic

The sender is asked to discuss a topic in short messages to the listener. They are encouraged to state what is important to them about the topic, their thinking about the topic, and the feeling associated with it.

Step 2: The Listener Demonstrates Understanding to the Sender

The operative word in this step is *demonstrate*. Many listeners will use the phrase "I understand" as they are responding to the sender. Once the sender has made their statement, the listener repeats back to the sender what they believe is the most important *content* of the communication, the *thinking* or values that underlie this content, and the *feelings* that are expressed verbally and non-verbally in the communication. The listener is reminded to use all of the levels of communication (non-verbal, para-verbal, and verbal) when demonstrating understanding of the sender's feelings.

Step 3: The Listener Selects a "Pathway" to Intimate Conversation

Once understanding is demonstrated, the listener selects a "pathway" to intimate conversation, from the short list in Table 7.2. These are basic strategies that can change the tone and direction of the conversation and are meant as an intentional process of moving the conversation to a greater level of intimacy and understanding of the topic shared by the sender.

Step 4: Repeat the Process

The topic should not be discontinued until at least three conversational rounds have occurred.

Pathways to Intimate Conversation

The pathways to intimate conversation are simple strategies that are couple directed and used by the listener in a conversation to increase the depth of the conversation. Table 7.2 includes a short list of primary pathways.

The Pathway of Curiosity

The pathway of curiosity has a primary goal of "expansion" of the dialogue. This is one of the primary ways to create intimacy in conversation. Consider, for example, a couple in the early stages of dating: they are highly engaged

Table 7.2 Pathways to Intimate Conversation

Curiosity
Underlying message
Validation
Perspective-Taking
Responsibility
Affirmation
Disclosure
Integration

in knowing as much about each other as possible. They have a high level of curiosity, listen intently, and ask many questions. They also have a strong willingness to share of themselves. Asking a curious question after effectively listening drives the conversation to new places.

The listener's orientation is to remain curious and also proportionately non-defensive about the content of the conversation. Remaining non-defensive opens the door to effective passive listening, the ability to listen attentively for the important content of the information, a willingness for the speaker to share more information, and a deeper understanding of the inner thoughts and feelings of their sender.

The Pathway of Underlying Message

Good listening requires attention to both thinking and feeling. Many times, communication is not direct. A person's thoughts can be subtly communicated and mask hidden desires, concerns, potential solutions, or accusations. Emotions play a key part of a couple's communication and can be expressed either verbally (words), non-verbally (gestures), and para-verbally (tone, volume, and cadence). Good listening requires focus on both thinking and feeling, and, in particular, the *underlying* thoughts and feelings. The pathway of underlying message directs the listener to intentionally key in on the expression in all three domains of communication and state any thoughts and feelings that may be just out of awareness of the sender. Attending to the underlying message of the communicator can lead to a stronger level of trust, indicate a stronger understanding, and help each partner to think creatively, identify solutions, and resolve conflict.

The Pathway of Validation

Validation is the reflection of recognition and acceptance of another person's thoughts, feelings, values, and behaviors as understandable from the sender's perspective. This does not mean that the listener agrees with them. It does mean that the listener is trying to understand the sender's perspective and how it may make sense to them.

The Pathway of Perspective-Taking

Perspective-taking in its truest form is only a cognitive process and does not include empathy. To accomplish perspective-taking, couples need to be multi-perspective. They recognize that their personal perspective is one of many perspectives and are open to any of those perspectives, while simultaneously resisting the temptation to fall in love with just their perspective.

The Pathway of Responsibility

Many years ago, I gave up the desire to have my children apologize to each other when they did some egregious act to their brother or sister. I found little benefit in the practice. Couples also hurt each other from time to time. As I watch couples, I notice that apologies tend to be met with skepticism or with challenging questions that seek contrary evidence to the apology.

Two strategies that couples use favorably in dealing with hurts in the relationship are statements of responsibility and impact. In this pathway, the person initially resists the desire to apologize, favoring to identify something they recognize in their behavior that is problematic and take responsibility for this action. They follow this statement with an expansive statement of understanding of the impact it had on their partner, the relationship, or the family.

The Pathway of Affirmation

Affirmation in the couple context is usually defined as emotional support and encouragement. It can also be a confirmation that something is true or logical. The pathway of affirmation can be seen as an add-on to other pathways to create closeness with the partner. For example, one partner may use the pathway of responsibility to say, "I lied frequently when you first discovered the infidelity, and I recognize that this has caused you to question everything I say." This could be followed with the pathway of affirmation by saying, "I love you, and I want you to know that I will not be doing the same thing in this situation. I will do my best to honestly answer all your questions, so keep asking so that I can help you understand what happened."

The Pathway of Disclosure

The pathway of disclosure is a good intimacy builder, and it is also a good trust builder. Transparent dialogue assists the partner in gaining a deeper understanding of thoughts and feelings. The central feature of disclosure is that the information is not solicited but rather voluntarily offered and expansive in its scope. Couples recovering from infidelity can benefit greatly from the pathway of disclosure because it relieves the partner of the burden of interrogation to find the truth. The more expansive the sharing, the more probability that trust can be attained.

The Pathway of Integration

The pathway to integration is used when the partner does not have all the facts or may have misread something, or there is a need to clarify some aspect of the discussion. The key to integration is making sure that the listener has completely demonstrated that there is understanding of the partner's perspective. Once demonstrating understanding, the listener can integrate some element to the discussion from their perspective.

I caution couples to substitute the word "but" with the word *and* because it is more inclusive. The word but tends to take away everything in front of it in a sentence. Imagine the difference between "Honey, you're beautiful *but* . . . "

versus "Honey, you're beautiful, *and* the red skirt you wore last Friday would look great with that top."

The pathway of integration also switches the role of sender and receiver. Once the listener utilizes the pathway of integration, the sender now takes the role of the listener and uses the pathway to develop the dialog in at least three conversational rounds.

"10-10-10" Dialogue Between-Session Task

I learned this strategy from a good friend of mine, Tony Fryer in Cincinnati, Ohio. I believe it is useful to get the couple to use the dialogue strategy with less incendiary topics at home so that they can be more effective when they come back for the next session to talk about a difficult topic.

The process is relatively simple. One partner takes the sender role for ten minutes while the other partner listens using the dialogue strategy and pathways to intimate conversation. The partners then switch roles, with the other partner taking the sender role for ten minutes. The exercise concludes with the partners having an open discussion for the remaining ten minutes. Typically, I will ask the couple to choose a topic that is pleasant to discuss. If they are unable to come up with a topic, I will suggest that they discuss their hopes and dreams for the future relationship.

Teaching Management of Criticism

Criticism can be a difficult aspect of any relationship, and it can take a strong person to manage a consistently critical partner. There are a number of ways that clinicians can help couples manage criticism. Initial efforts could focus on teaching the couple how to accept, manage, deflect, or challenge criticism. This may help the couple create new awareness and strategies with the problem. This may also support the clinician's efforts to systemically address the issue that may take longer-term efforts. The truth is that if the partner is consistently critical, it probably would not matter who was in the relationship with them; they would be critical. In these cases, the couple may benefit from more focus on family-of-origin work.

There are two types of criticism: constructive and destructive. When people offer constructive criticism, they do so with a soft approach and offer feedback that is meant for growth of the other person. Destructive criticism is typically meant to lash out at the other person, expressing a level of unhappiness and contempt that is corrosive, and is usually meant to hurt the other person for some perceived transgression. The focus of destructive criticism is any challenge to one's personality, morality, competency, or ability and the motives of the critical partner can be to punish, get revenge, or shame.

There are several useful strategies for managing criticism. Effective management of criticism requires a number of strategies, including specific efforts from the sender of the criticism, the ability of the receiver to accept constructive criticism, and a method for the receiver for deflecting or declining destructive criticism.

Sending criticism that is constructive indicates that there is a commitment to the well-being and the growth of the other person. Constructive criticism is feedback that may not be in purview of the other person's awareness. The commitment is for both individuals to think reflectively and critically when sending and receiving the feedback.

Accepting constructive criticism then requires a perspective that the other person is offering useful information and it is meant for growth. The receiver of constructive criticism should find a way to pull out the positive information that may be useful to them. They can confirm to the sender that they understand and that they will consider an action to take if possible and then implement some action after thoughtful reflection.

Deflecting destructive criticism takes work because the challenge for the receiver is the necessity to resist possible long-standing automatic responses that can be a part of a negative, circular pattern of criticism and defensiveness. By the time couples get into therapy, the criticized partner has developed unhealthy responses to the situation, usually by adopting one or more of the following responses: flight, fight, or freeze.

An understanding of potential strategies for managing criticism can be helpful for the target of criticism. The following list provides several possible responses to criticism for varying situations.

1) Accept the Feedback (Entirely or in Part)

Accept the feedback when it is expressed in a kind way and it is clear the person is offering the criticism for your benefit. When the feedback is more critical but could be possible, accept the part that could be correct, express gratitude, and then move on. For example, "You might be correct about my reluctance to challenge his opinion. I will give that some thought."

2) Move From the Abstract to the Concrete

At times criticism is hidden in insinuation or veiled in a way that makes the target uncomfortable with the statement, and the target is unsure of how to manage the criticism. In this situation, the target can express a genuine desire to understand the criticism through curious questioning and work to get the critical partner to move towards expressing the feedback in more concrete terms. One way of making these statements concrete is to look for behaviors desired, preferably in terms of the relationship. In doing so, the couple may create a new way of interacting instead of one person's demanding change in the other.

3) Clarify the Real Issue

On some occasions, one partner will carry in hurt feelings or stress to a current conversation and be critical of their partner. In these cases, the target of criticism can clarify the true issue, repeat back what is being stated, discuss what this means to the critic, and empathize and validate the experience. This has the potential to help diffuse the situation so that more effective communication can occur.

4) *Use Agreement to Diffuse*

"Agreeing to disagree" is an overused phrase that people tend to use when they are struggling to resolve an issue. Agreeing to disagree means that the individuals can be emotionally disinterested in the topic, choose not to accept the other person's position, and still work together as usual. This principle may not work well with some couples. Diffusion is a way to limit the escalating effect of criticism so that the couple can move on from the discussion to something else. Diffusion allows the target of criticism to agree in more abstract terms and then move the topic away from the criticism. There are three types of diffusion:

A. *Agree in Part*

Find one small part, however small, and agree with the substance of that part. This can be used as an entry to also sharing what you believe to be true about the criticism.

B. *Agree in Probability*

Make a statement that the criticism is possibly correct, even though the target may believe it to be a slim probability at best.

C. *Agree in Principle*

Make a statement about the general principle and agree that the principle discussed is considered fair and equitable in most relationships.

5) *Delay Discussion*

Simply state that the criticism needs to be considered and reflected upon. Follow up at a later point in time to offer a response, possibly using one of the other techniques listed in this section.

6) *Disagree With the Criticism*

Obviously, sometimes criticism is completely wrong and the criticism is more about the critical partner. In these situations, the target can disagree with the criticism. In doing so, the target can repeat back the perspective of the critic and then add that they disagree with the criticism. This would not be a time to apologize since this is more about the critical partner and the criticism is not meant for growth.

Another possible choice for addressing the critical partner is to choose not to join in when the partner is critical and the criticism is not meant to be helpful. Ongoing debate and defense and attack posture will not be helpful. In any situation in which the target of criticism has disengaged or diffused the criticism in some way, it can be helpful to follow up at a later point to demonstrate that there was continued consideration of the criticism.

Teaching Passive Listening With Self-Restraint

Beyond the need to help a couple develop skills around effective communication, clinicians need to teach the couple to limit their emotional responses to their partner. In doing so, the communication is cleaner and less likely to result in misinterpretation. To help with this, clinicians will focus on the process of active listening, but an even more important process, particularly during escalating conflict, is passive listening. Passive listening in its basic form is staying mostly quiet, attentive, and encouraging of the speaker to continue sharing their perspective. Couples that struggle with this tend to interrupt, talk over one another, or ignore their partner altogether.

The restraint required in passive listening includes non-defensive listening in which the receiver of the communication attends to the message with very limited response. The listener needs to keep their emotional reactions in check and work to attune to their partner's perspective and subtle, non-verbal communication. When the listener cannot maintain passive listening during conflict and is more focused on their own emotional state and defensive reactions, they take in little of what their partner is saying, and the conversation and opportunities for misinterpretation escalate.

Teaching Active Listening With Self-Restraint

Active listening is an intentional process in which the listener attends to specific elements of a sender's communication, verbal and non-verbal, offering feedback to demonstrate that they have understood the communication from the sender's perspective. The restraint required in active listening is also non-defensive, yet there is an additional responsibility to manage one's own defensive responses and the defensive reactions of their partner as they offer feedback while listening. With active listening, the listener manages their partner's defensive reaction through communicating in a way that does not "raise the temperature" of the conversation. Additional features of effective active listening include the ability for the listener to validate the legitimacy of their partner's perspective, to maintain a level of curiosity of that perspective, and to possess an interest in and skill at directing the conversation to a deeper understanding of the sender's perspective.

Sometimes couples believe, in the heat of anger, that their partner needs to know the hard facts of their perspective whether they want to or not. Not everything one thinks should be stated, and couples would be wise to be careful with their words and actions. Statements should be judged and selected based on which will offer the best "good" for the relationship.

Teaching Forgiveness Strategies in Micro-Conflicts

Couples fight; sometimes they get nasty. They hurt each other's feelings, and so forgiveness has to be an essential part of intimate relationships. In the absence of some forgiveness, it is likely that there will be an increasing amount of negative reciprocity in the relationship, and this can overwhelm the positive aspects of the relationship (Fincham & Beach, 2002). Couples that forgive have less psychological aggression toward their partner and increases in engagement with one another (Fincham, 2000; Fincham & Beach, 2002).

When couples have ongoing positive interactions, it makes it easier to address conflicts in the relationship. Offering forgiveness and practicing it on a regular basis, couples can create a positive sentiment in the relationship. Helping couples understand how they approach their "forgiveness episodes" can offer insight into whether they are using forgiveness strategies. If forgiveness strategies are utilized, the likely result is a positive relationship change following the transgression. Framing their forgiveness episodes around forgiveness strategies can give the couple a structure for what to do better the next time they have a fight.

Kelley (1998, 2005) identifies several distinct communication strategies that people use to *grant* and *request* forgiveness. These involve either 1) requesting or granting non-verbal displays of forgiveness, such as hugging or not acting angry, 2) returning to behavior patterns from before the transgression, 3) playing down the offense, such as stating "it was not a big deal," 4) having a meaningful discussion about the transgression, 5) explicitly saying "I'm sorry" or "I forgive you," and 6) giving some form of compensation, such as complying with the hurt partner's wishes or offering a gift.

Many day-to-day conflicts start small, and they can stay small. This requires a culture of forgiveness in the relationship. When transgressions are small, couples can be quick to apologize and take responsibility when they know they are wrong and request forgiveness in these situations, and hurt partners can be willing to accept the apology and offer forgiveness.

Switching From Teaching to Facilitating

A primary modality of work in therapy is communication within the session. This communication, in context to the couple, is central to the therapeutic experience. Therapeutic communication can be one of a number of types, including dyadic interaction between one partner and the clinician, dyadic conversation between each partner, or triadic communication among all three.

In general, dyadic communication refers to communication between two people. Even when there are more than two people, such as in a couples therapy session, it is the two-person interactions of the couple in the session that plays the fundamental role in the long-term change for the couple. Dyadic communication between the partners is powerful because it is the continuous dialogue of the two that offers conditions for intimate, continuous feedback. This interaction, when it occurs in the absence of negative exchanges and with the assistance of a guiding clinician, can help create healthy relationship patterns that extend beyond therapy (Cobb & Bradbury, 2003; Barry & Crant, 2000).

There is a tendency, however, for the couple to construct dialogue with the clinician and not between each other, particularly early in the therapeutic encounter. This is in part due to the couple's attempt to explain the presenting problem, but it is also in part a function of the clinician's need to define the problem from each partner's perspective. This parallel dialogue certainly has its place; however, clinicians should be cognizant of the importance of dyadic communication between the partners and encourage and/or structure opportunities for this as early as appropriate in the therapeutic process.

A number of researchers have weighed in on the dyadic experience in therapy. Murray Bowen, considered to have developed one of the first systemically based approaches for working with families, believed it important to have family members relate personally to each other and about each other. He stated that family members should not talk about others in the family, nor should they talk about impersonal issues. He believed that families members would gain more connection from talking within his therapeutic technique of "person-to-person relationships" and believed that individuals' interacting face-to-face in this manner helps to promote autonomy and intimacy (Gladding, 2015).

Cobb and Bradbury (2003) state that clinicians can help couples as a dyad to shape their behaviors both in conflict and non-conflict situations, which will help the couple revise their view of self and their partner. In doing so, couples will be better able to replicate healthy communication outside the therapy session, provided that the clinician coaches the couple through these difficult conversations and the conversation continues without high levels of defensiveness and escalation.

Barry and Crant (2000) discuss the importance of "expressive attribution" in dyadic communication. Expressive attribution refers to the couple's desire to have emotional satisfaction in the relationship. If each partner has the belief that they can achieve emotional satisfaction, they are going to behave in positive ways toward one another. This expressive attribution can be supported by the clinician through helping couples more deeply understand their partner's logical or positive motivations. Dyadic communication coached by the clinician can lead to deeper insight because emotion-focused attachment communication and processes are supported while problematic patterns are blocked.

Key to a positive dyadic experience, then, is to identify the contextual factors that increase expressive attribution. Barry and Crant (2000) suggest that expressive attribution is associated with partners that have 1) interaction with composure, empathy, affection, and self-disclosure, 2) changes in patterns of communication that signal relationship growth, and 3) favorable relationship perception (dependence, commitment, confidence).

Susan Johnson's (Seid & Johnson, 2009) approach to emotionally focused couples therapy (EFT) emphasizes dyadic communication by supporting the management of interactional patterns designed to expand and reorganize key emotional responses in each partner. New cycles of bonding interactions encourage the couple by replacing negative cycles such as the pursue-withdraw or criticize-defend patterns. Positive cycles then become self-reinforcing and create permanent change. From EFT theory, dyadic experience in therapy fosters the creation of a secure bond between partners, so that the relationship becomes a safe haven and a healing environment for both partners.

Likewise, attachment behaviors increase quality communication between partners. Attachment behaviors linked to quality communication include partners that are responsive, intently engaged, and accessible. For couples who experience relationships as secure, where partners are easily accessed, highly responsive, and intently engaged, communication is likely more positive because the couple connection invites healthy communication. The inverse is likely true as well, with insecurely attached couples experiencing inhibited communication and negative patterns (Knapp et al., 2015).

Couple Enactments

Couple enactment refers to the moments in therapy when the clinician intentionally asks the couple to interact directly with each other. In an enactment, the clinician moves to the periphery of the therapeutic space and the couple moves to the center (Simon, 1995). In a typical enactment, the clinician removes himself or herself from the interactional sequence and ask the couple to face one another to directly discuss a topic, and the clinician coaches the interaction (Brimhall, Gardner, & Henline, 2003).

The hope of the clinician in structuring an enactment is for the couple (and the clinician) to gain access to the issues, understand each partner's emotion and thinking, and discover the couple's dynamics. Negative patterns can be interrupted and positive interaction can be supported so that healthy interaction can be gained through a constructed experience in session (Miller & Aponte, 2010).

Boesky (2000) defines an enactment as a process of communication occurring between the couple that has unknown meaning for a long period of time and then may suddenly become apparent to one or both of the partners. Boesky goes on to state:

> Enactments bridge what is expressible and inexpressible, what is forgotten and what is pressing for revival, what is preconscious and is forced out of awareness, what is past and what is present, what is reality and what is imagined
>
> (Boesky, 2000).

Clinicians commonly facilitate enactments that are either free flowing with limited coaching from the clinician, as when the clinician is making an assessment of communication patterns, or highly structured enactments that are coached by the clinician for a specific intervention. However, empirical research appears to challenge the clinical use of unstructured, unregulated enactments, whether merely for assessment or as an intended intervention (Butler, Davis, & Seedall, 2008). Left unstructured, the clinician becomes a covert, third-party support to the problematic patterns that brought the couple in for therapy. The couple may also question the clinician's capability to manage the session and lose hope that their relationship can improve. When enactment is used as a structured intervention, the clinician elicits the enactment as a means to search for an alternative method of interaction, the clinician stays on the periphery to coach the interaction, and the couple stays central to one another in the communication (Simon, 1995). The clinician becomes a guide who helps the couple navigate difficult territory successfully and helps create possible new ways of interacting.

There is empirical support for the use of enactment with couples. Several studies indicate that enactments are effective for promoting couple self-reliance, healing, and softening (Zitzman & Butler, 2005; Andersson, Butler, & Seedall, 2006; Seedall & Butler, 2006). Butler and Wampler (1999) found that enactments offered superior outcomes compared with those achieved by a clinician-centered approach, which emphasizes interaction that is primarily channeled through the clinician, clinician interpretation, and direct instruction. Considering changes in adult attachment, Butler, Harper, and Mitchell (2011) found that when husbands and wives experienced enactments in early sessions of treatment, they have greater increases in within-session attachment compared to couples who were in treatment with clinicians using a clinician-centered approach. In their study, husbands who received clinician-centered interventions early in treatment showed a consistent decline in within-session change in attachment and a continuation of decline even when enactment sessions were offered later in treatment.

Even though enactments are empirically supported, clinicians may not use enactments frequently. It is possible that clinicians are just more comfortable channeling conversation through the clinician since clinician anxiety may be heightened by the higher level of emotional expression of the couple during the enactment (Woolley, Wampler, & Davis, 2012). The heightened anxiety of the clinician may reduce the likelihood of consistent use of enactment in session. Enactments, however, should be considered a central part of couples therapy and occur as early in the therapeutic process as appropriate.

The Influential Clinician in the Enactment

The therapy session is conversation, but unlike general conversation, the session has specific expectations. The therapeutic conversation is a consensual agreement with the client that the clinician will contribute intentionally towards constructive change in the problematic experiences and behaviors of the client. It would not be therapy without this understanding in addition to the clinician's accepting the responsibility to guide the discussion and persist in this so that change is facilitated (Tomm, 1988; Sutherland, Turner, & Dienhart, 2013). The clinician can assume that listening and empathy reflection may not be sufficient for influencing change, particularly with couples who are entrenched in their problematic patterns (Tomm, 1984). A balance of the authority of the clinician and autonomy of the client may be more helpful. This underscores the inherent need of the clinician to be appropriately influential in session.

Influential does not mean *directive*, since it is possible for the clinician to be influential without being overtly directive. The influential clinician communicates by making linear and circular assumptions, being reflexive to expand clients' understanding, or even being strategic to move the client from one position in thinking to another (Tomm, 1988). Not only can the clinician be influential; they can also be persistently influential by staying the course over several conversational turns despite client responses that could disrupt or distract from the clinician focused on a particular line of inquiry (Sutherland, Turner, & Dinehart, 2013). The art of being persistently influential is a key component to coaching an enactment with a couple in session.

Creating Enactments in Session

Enactments require structure, and a well-crafted enactment will move through clear phases. Butler, Davis, and Seedall (2008) identify three phases: initiation, intervention, and evaluation. A transition phase could also be considered to help limit volatility of the partners. Each of these phases has specific tasks. Table 7.3. defines the phases and task for each phase.

Table 7.3 Phases of a Structured Enactment

Transition to Enactment Phase
Assess readiness for enactment
Buffer with "pass-through" interaction to reduce defensiveness and reactivity
Initiation Phase
Clarify goals of the enactment and the roles
Specify a specific topic
Establish structure

(*Continued*)

Table 7.3 Continued

Intervention Phase
Sustain the interaction
Coach the interaction
Facilitate emotion-focused and/or attachment-focused interaction
Evaluation Phase
Recall goals
Assess/evaluate
Commit to change

Transitions to Enactment Phase

As the clinician plans enactments, early in the treatment process it is also important to gauge when the couple is ready for the increased intensity of an enactment. Some couples will be less successful with the enactment if they have high levels of defensiveness or emotional volatility. In these circumstances, it might be beneficial for the clinician to transition into an enactment using "buffered" enactments, in other words having communication that initially "passes through" the clinician as a means to enter into enactments gradually. This ensures that each partner's story is fully articulated and not threatened by the other partner (Brimhall, Gardner, & Henline, 2003). The focus can then gently be moved to the couple interaction.

There are three possible buffered enactments (gentle entry, creating an audience, side-bar) that when modified as will be described can be used as a segue to gradually move the couple to a facilitated enactment (Butler & Gardner, 2003). With *gentle entry*, the clinician starts with dyadic interaction with each partner to develop an understanding of each partner's perspective, and when the clinician understands each perspective, the clinician directs the couple to turn towards one another and interact on a specific element of the conversation.

Another approach is *creating an audience*. Here the clinician asks an observing partner to sit to the side and assume an attentive, listening position. The partner is encouraged to observe and just listen to the story as the clinician discusses a topic with the other partner. When the perspective is fully developed through the clinician-partner discussion, the clinician can ask the observing partner to paraphrase what they understood from the partner's perspective and then ask any questions that might be useful to create clarity. The clinician can then move to an enactment if appropriate.

After learning something new or hearing something interesting, the clinician can create a *sidebar* and move the chair close to one partner to briefly process the new information (Butler & Gardner, 2003). This strategy helps to ensure that the information can be shared and fully articulated and not threatened by the other partner.

The Initiation Phase

Prior to facilitating a structured enactment, it is important for the couple to understand the goals of using enactment in session. It is helpful for the couple to also be clear on the roles of each partner and the role of the clinician.

Goals of enactment can be either content or process oriented. Content-oriented enactment tends to focus on a specific topic, and the goal is to resolve that particular issue. An example of this would be a couple problem-solving around shared decision-making with financial issues.

Process-oriented enactment goals are to engage the couple in interacting directly with one another so that the clinician can help change the interaction from negative to positive. There are many process goals that are dependent on the context of the couple relationship, including offering a method for containing negativity, diffusing emotional reactivity, regulating interaction, dampening volatility, facilitating soothing and softening for the purpose of producing positive interactional experiences and shifts, and facilitating attachment-oriented emotional disclosure (Andersson, Butler, & Seedall, 2006; Butler & Gardner, 2003). Clinician coaching to facilitate expression of primary underlying emotions through the enactment can lead to the development of greater empathy in the partner and stronger attachment (Woolley, Wampler, & Davis, 2012).

The primary role for each partner is to listen and respond empathically, work to demonstrate understanding of their partner's perspective, and convey attachment needs in a positive way. It is important that the couple receives a direct message from the clinician for each partner to limit defensiveness in their partner through the use of non-critical language. The role of the clinician is interventive, carefully coaching through the enactment and helping the couple express underlying emotions and attachment needs in a positive way.

Structure is developed when the goals of enactment and the roles of the participants are clear. Structure can also be strengthened by the couple's understanding the three primary phases of initiation, intervention, and evaluation.

Intervention Phase

The techniques of this phase, which are identified in what follows, are intended for the clinician facilitating a process-oriented enactment to sustain and coach the interaction while persistently influencing the enactment for the couple to 1) be more intimate in content while staying emotionally in control, 2) open up expansive conversation around a topic that may be closed off to the couple, 3) expand awareness of systemic processes potentially unavailable to the couple and create change in the process as needed, 4) expand understanding of each partner's perspective, 5) encourage positive exchanges, and 6) block problematic communication patterns and processes.

At times, topic selection can be negotiated by identifying several topics to be discussed. It is recommended that the interaction topic be drawn from a number of gridlock subjects that the couple indicates are important but difficult to talk about. These topics can be rank-ordered in terms of their probability for precipitating emotional reactivity (Butler, Davis, & Seedall, 2008). As the client becomes less emotionally volatile in session, the clinician can transition to more difficult topics from the list.

Clinician actions of coaching during the interaction include increasing the intensity; prolonging conversation times; aligning with a partner; directing, teaching, and encouraging positive expressions and challenging negative expressions; suggesting alternate transactions; and making the processes conscious to the couple (Woolley, Wampler, & Davis, 2012). These actions are in balance with the clinician's allowing the couple dialogue without unnecessary interruption. The following are a number of influencing strategies to utilize during the intervention phase of enactment.

Coaching Positive Attending

The clinician promotes each partner's use of basic listening skills: paraphrasing, empathic listening, validation, and de-escalation skills. The clinician can also promote attachment-based processes by reflecting the partner's feelings, validating the partner's feelings, and empathically listening to one partner as they share their story (Butler, Harper, & Mitchell, 2011). These strategies are considered brief clinician interruptions in the conversation meant to prompt these basic listening skills.

Interrupt Negative Interaction

The clinician interrupts negative exchanges as they occur. These interruptions can be followed up with by the clinician's offering an alternative, more softened statement for the partner to repeat, a request for one partner to reframe a statement, or encouragement for the partner to focus on personal feelings.

Persistent Conversational Rounds

One role the clinician plays in the intervention phase of enactment is to be an ally to the couple in facilitating multiple conversation turns with a topic and blocking attempts by the couple to end the conversation prematurely. Clinician persistence in developing multiple conversational rounds of exploration of a topic is important to create new perspectives through the access of new material that may be disclosed. It is equally important for the couple to be persistent during the conversation's turns to experience encouraging, positive interaction with each other.

The clinician can create persistence in conversational rounds by using basic reflexive questioning. Reflexive questioning is an aspect of interventive interviewing (Tomm, 1987; Tomm, 1988) oriented toward creating a persistent line of inquiry that opens up new perspectives, enabling the couple to generate new patterns of thinking and behavior on their own.

Reflexive questioning can be considered categorically. Four broad categories for reflexive questions include 1) backward-looking, 2) inward-looking, 3) outward-looking, and 4) forward-looking (Edutopia, 2016). Backward-looking questions can focus on understanding historical thoughts, problem encounters, and successes. Inward thinking considers feelings, personal values, goals, and judgments. Outward-looking questions include questions of similarity and differences between people, behaviors of self and other. Forward-looking questions include future possibilities and hypothetical questions. A simpler branching structure of questions could include simply past choices, present options, and future possibilities (Tomm, 2016). The success of reflexive questioning is not dependent on the clinician's asking the correct questions (Vee & Barnett, 1994) but more on the creation of opportunity for the couple to reflect and construct their own meaning.

Test a Hypothesis

In this technique, the clinician directs one partner to test the clinician's hypothesis around a content area or a process. To test the hypothesis, the clinician directly describes the hypothesis from a systemic perspective to one partner and asks him or her to explore the hypothesis with the other partner. This is an influencing technique that inserts the hypothesis into the system and creates an alternate perspective for both partners to explore. The clinician can coach the couple to take a curious position in exploration of the hypothesis. As Tom Andersen aptly remarked, two perspectives from the same issue will most likely create new possibilities (Andersen, 1992). Testing the hypothesis can lead the couple to new insights, new ways of experiencing each other, and potentially new solutions.

Positive Connotation with Challenge

Clinician coaching through blocking negative exchanges is part of the process of successful enactments. When positive connotation is used in conjunction with the clinician's challenge of a problematic communication pattern, the message from the clinician can be better assimilated into the couple interaction. The clinical definition of positive connotation is when the clinician attributes a positive motivation to a partner's problematic behavior. For an example of positive connotation with challenge, consider one partner's criticizing the other for being emotionally distant when he or she comes home from work. The clinician could interrupt to say, "Your criticism of Liz shows that it is important for you to connect with her after being apart for the day to feel loved (positive connotation), *and* when you say this as a criticism to her it becomes easy for Liz to be defensive and miss your message of needing this connection (challenge)." The use of *and* instead of *but* also indicates that the clinician is inclusive and that both the criticism and the underlying need may be true, tempering the possibility of rejection of the clinician's idea.

Encouraging Curiosity to Facilitate Intimacy

One central characteristic of intimate relationships is mutual disclosure, which often occurs early in romantic relationships because the couple is highly curious about one another. This is one characteristic in relationship formation that couples describe experiencing when "falling in love." Couples that have higher levels of disclosure tend to have a greater sense of closeness in the relationship (Dibble, Levine, & Park, 2011). The pairing of curiosity in one partner and the willingness to disclose in the other partner can be a good recipe for creating intimacy. During the enactment, the clinician can directly ask one partner to take a curious stance about a topic and maintain openness to hear the responses while directing the other partner to be open to disclosing their thoughts and feelings. The clinician will need to evaluate for the appropriate time in which to utilize this technique based on the couple's guardedness with vulnerability and potential for volatility because a poorly timed intervention can lead to an attack/defense pattern.

Prager and Buhrmester (1998) identify that intimate disclosure has three components: 1) a revelation of something personal or private, 2) an experience of positive feelings about oneself, one's partner, and their interactions, and 3) a belief that that they have advanced or reflected understanding of one another. An enactment is a logical place to create this experience in the context of therapy. Curiosity and a willingness to share will most likely drive any conversation to new places.

Encouraging Responsibility

At times with high-conflict couples or deeply hurt couples, a sincere apology is met by the hurt partner with disbelief in the sincerity, an interpretation that the apology is superficial, a quick, angry response, or even a demand not to apologize. It can be beneficial to coach the apologetic partner to be specific in taking responsibility versus "apologizing." In doing so, the apologetic partner is coached by the clinician to describe his or her own action, describe his or her thoughts and feelings regarding the action, and state to the partner an understanding of the impact to the partner, to the relationship, or to their family.

Creating Insight Through Clinician Interpretation

When the clinician offers an interpretation, the effect is expansion of the perceptual field of the client. The couple can accept the interpretation, accept the interpretation in part, or outright reject the interpretation. Interpretation can include offering insights into the couple's behavior or processes, pointing out the consequences of problematic interaction patterns and problematic ideas about the relationship paired with making suggestions of new ways of looking at things.

Therapeutic Impact Disclosure

Impact disclosures are the objective disclosures by the clinician that occur when the clinician states to the client his or her perception of, and reactions to, the couple's behavior in session (Kiesler & Van Denberg, 1993). Self-disclosure is a controversial topic in the clinical literature, and self-disclosure should certainly be carefully considered before shared in session. When self-disclosure is utilized appropriately during the intervention phase of enactment, it can help couples soften their approach to one another, interrupt a problematic process, or bring a new theme into a current discussion.

In the context of the intervention phase of enactment, impact disclosures can be successfully shared when the clinician recognizes a repetitive pattern in their own thinking or feeling as they experience the couple or one of the partners. It is important to carefully assess that this internal experience is rational, not irrational, unresolved countertransference *and* the clinician believes the self-disclosure can be a therapeutic tool to change the dynamic between the couple. Drawing from the suggestions of Kiesler and Van Denberg (1993), there are several steps in the process of using impact disclosure, which include 1) the clinician recognizes a repetitive pattern in his or her internal reactions of thoughts and feelings; 2) the clinician talks directly to the couple about his or her internal experience and perceptions; 3) the clinician labels the internal experience in the interaction appropriately and connects it to the dynamic of the couple; and 4) the clinician advocates for some change in the process. Since impact disclosures require the clinician to be a good judge of their internal experience over multiple sessions or several transactions to note themes in their internal experience with the couple, impact disclosures are far less frequent than other enactment interventions.

Evaluation Phase

There are three key aspects to the evaluation phase of the enactment. First, the clinician invites the couple to recall and evaluate the level of achievement of the initial goals of the enactment. Second, the couple is invited to reflect with the clinician about the enactment. For a few moments, each partner and the clinician can share a reflection statement, formally or informally, without interruption from the others. For a formal reflection, the couple can be encouraged to write their thoughts down prior to the shared reflection. These new insights may create new perspectives and in turn create possible changes in the relationship dynamics, new understanding of the self, or a new view of the partner. Lastly, the couple is asked to make some commitment to change. Making a commitment can translate the work within the enactment to behavior outside the session.

Measuring Outcomes Related to Communication

There are two primary methods generally used for assessing conflict communication. One is to observe the couple in a short discussion and make conclusions about their interactions. Another method is through questionnaires. In questionnaires, couples report about their own behavior, and each partner reports on the other's behavior.

Keith Sanford created a short inventory that can be given to couples in session to assess the couples' conflict communication during a recent conflict interaction. It is simple and fast and can be useful both for having a method of understanding the couple's communication problem and developing goals around these issues. The survey has five forms: the Couples Emotion Rating Form, Conflict Communication Inventory, Couples Underlying Concerns Inventory, Expectancy Scales, and Conflict Disengagement Inventory. Each inventory is brief and includes statements that the couple answers on a five-point Likert scale. Sanford also has a website dedicated to the questionnaire (www.pairbuilder.com) that is free, gives immediate results, and offers worksheets to develop goals related to the results (see Appendix 7.1 for the paper-and-pencil version).

References

Andersen, T. (1992). Relationship, language and pre-understanding in the reflecting processes. *Australian and New Zealand Journal of Family Therapy*, *13*, 87–91.

Andersson, L. G., Butler, M. H., & Seedall, R. B. (2006). Couple's experience of enactments and softening in marital therapy. *American Journal of Family Therapy*, *34*, 301–315.

Barry, B., & Crant, M. (2000). Dyadic communication relationships in organizations: An attribution/expectancy approach. *Organization Science*, *11*(6), 648–664.

Baucom, K. K. W., Baucom, B. R., & Christensen, A. (2015). Changes in dyadic communication during and after integrative and traditional behavior couple therapy. *Behavior Research and Therapy*, *65*, 18–28.

Boesky, D. (2000). Affect, language and communication. *International Journal of Psychoanalysis*, *81*, 257–262.

Brimhall, A. S., Gardner, B. C., & Henline, B. H. (2003). Enhancing narrative couple therapy with an enactment scaffolding. *Contemporary Family Therapy*, *25*(4), 391–414.

Butler, M. H., Davis, S. D., & Seedall, R. B. (2008). Common pitfalls of beginning therapist utilizing enactments. *Journal of Marital and Family Therapy*, *34*(3), 329–352.

Butler, M. H., & Gardner, B. C. (2003). Adapting enactments to couple reactivity: Five developmental stages. *Journal of Marital and Family Therapy*, *34*, 329–352.

Butler, M. H., Harper, J. M., & Mitchell, C. B. (2011). A comparison of attachment outcomes in enactment-based versus therapist-centered therapy process modalities in couple therapy. *Family Process*, *50*(2), 203–220.

Butler, M. H., & Wampler, K. S. (1999). Couple-responsible therapy process: Positive proximal outcomes. *Family Process*, *38*(1), 27–54.

Crisis Prevention Institute, Inc. (2006). *Instructor manual for the nonviolent crisis intervention training manual*. Brookfield, WI: Crisis Prevention Institute.

Davis, S. D., & Butler, M. H. (2004). Enacting relationships in marriage and family therapy: A conceptual and operational definition of an enactment. *Journal of Marriage and Family Therapy*, *30*, 319–333.

Dibble, J. L., Levine, T. R., & Park, H. S. (2011). The unidimensional relationship closeness scale (URCS): Reliability and validity evidence for a new measure of relationship closeness. *Psychological Assessment*, *24*(3), 565–572. Advance online publication. doi:10.1037/a0026265.

Domingue, R., & Mollen, D. (2009). Attachment and conflict communication in adult romantic relationships. *Journal of Social and Personal Relationships*, *26*(5), 678–696.

Edutopia. (2016). *The forty reflection questions*. Retrieved September 3, 2016 from www.edutopia.org/pdfs/stw/edutopia-stw-replicatingPBL-21stCAcad-reflection-questions.pdf.

Fife, S. T., Weeks, G. R., & Gambescia, N. (2008). Treating infidelity: An integrative approach. *The Family Journal: Counseling and Therapy for Couples and Families*, *16*(4), 316–323.

Fincham, F. D. (2000). The kiss of the porcupines: From attributing responsibility to forgiving. *Personal Relationships*, *7*, 1–23.

Fincham, F. D., & Beach, S. R. H. (2002). Forgiveness in marriage: Implications for psychological aggression and constructive communication. *Personal Relationships*, *9*, 239–251.

Gladding, S. T. (2015). *Family therapy: History, theory, and practice* (6th ed.). Hoboken, NJ: Pearson Education, Inc.

Glasser, W. (1998). Choice theory: A new psychology of personal freedom. *Harper Collins Publishers*. New York, NY.

Gottman, J. M. (2001). What the study of relationships has to say about emotion research. *Social Science Information*, *40*(1), 79–94.

Gottman, J. M., & DeClaire, J. (2001). *The relationship cure*. New York: Three Rivers Press.

Gottman, J. & Silver, N. (2012). What makes love last: How to build trust and avoid betrayal. *Simon and Schuster*, New York, NY.

Imagoworks. (2015). *Instructions for the receiver*. Retrieved January 22, 2015 from http://imagoworks.com/pages/dialogue_instructions.html.

Johnson, S. M. (2003). Attachment theory: A guide for couple therapy. In S. M. Johnson & V. E. Whiffen (Eds.), *Attachment processes in couple and family therapy* (pp. 103–125). New York: Guilford Press.

Kelley, D. (1998). The communication of forgiveness. *Communication Studies*, *49*, 255–271.

Kelley, D. L., & Waldron, V. R. (2005). An investigation of forgiveness-seeking communication and relational outcomes. *Communication Quarterly*, 53, 339–358.

Kiesler, D. J., & Van Denberg, T. F. (1993). Therapeutic impact disclosure: A last taboo of psychoanalytic theory and practice. *Clinical Psychology and Psychotherapy*, *1*(1), 3–13.

Knapp, D., Sandberg, J. G., Novak, J., & Larson, J. H. (2015). The mediating role of attachment behaviors on the relationship between family-of-origin and couple communication: Implications for couples therapy. *Journal of Couple & Relationship Therapy*, *14*, 17–38.

Miller, A., & Aponte, H. (2010). *Instructor's manual for structural family therapy*. Mill Valley, CA: Psychotherapy.net.

Prager, K., & Buhrmester, D. (1998). Intimacy and need fulfillment in couple relationships. *Journal of Social and Personal Relationships, 15*(4), 435–469.

Sanford, K. (2010). Assessing conflict communication in couples: Comparing the validity of self-report, partner-report, and observer ratings. *Journal of Family Psychology, 24*(2), 165–174.

Seedall, R. B. (2009). Enhancing change process in solution-focused brief therapy by utilizing couple enactment. *The American Journal of Family Therapy, 37*, 99–113.

Seedall, R. B., & Butler, M. H. (2006). The effect of proxy voice intervention on couple softening in the context of enactments. *Journal of Marital and Family Therapy, 32*(4), 421–437.

Seid, E. L., & Johnson, S. (2009). *Instructor's manual for emotionally focused couples therapy*. Mill Valley, CA: Psychotherapy.net.

Sheras, P. L., & Koch-Sheras, P. R. (2008). Commitment first, communication later: Dealing with barriers to effective couples therapy. *Journal of Contemporary Psychotherapy*, 38, 109–117.

Simon, G. M. (1995). A revisionist rendering of structural family therapy. *Journal of Marital and Family Therapy, 21*, 17–26.

Sells, J. N., & Yarhouse, M. A. (2011). *Counseling couples in conflict: A relational restoration model.* Downers Grove, IL: InterVarsity Press.

Sutherland, O., Turner, J., & Dinehart, A. (2013). Responsive persistence part 1: Clinician influence and postmodern practice. *Journal of Marital and Family Therapy,* 39(4), 470–487.

Tomm, K. (1984). One perspective on the Milan systemic approach: Part I. Overview of development, theory and practice. *Journal for Marital and Family Therapy*, V.10, N2.

Tomm, K. (1987). Interventive interviewing I. Strategizing as a fourth guideline for the clinician. *Family Process, 26*(1), 314.

Tomm, K. (1988). Interventive interviewing: Part III. Intending to ask lineal, circular, strategic, or reflexive questions? *Family Process, 27*, 1–15.

Tomm, K. (2016). *Reflexive questioning as a means to enable intimacy with couples.* Retrieved September 9, 2016 from www.familytherapy.org/documents/Intimacy-Questioning.pdf.

Vee, G. V., & Barnett, B. G. (1994, Winter). Using reflective questioning to promote collaborative dialogue. *Journal of Staff Development, V15*, N1 16–21.

Woolley, S. R., Wampler, K. S., & Davis, S. D. (2012). Enactments in couple therapy: Identifying therapist interventions associated with positive change. *Journal of Family Therapy, 34*, 284–305.

Zitzman, S. T., & Butler, M. H. (2005). Attachment, addiction, and recovery: Conjoint marital therapy for recovery from a sexual addiction. *Sexual Addiction & Compulsivity: The Journal of Treatment and Prevention, 12*, 311–337.

Appendix 7.1

Couples Emotion Rating Form
Conflict Communication Inventory
Couples Underlying Concern Inventory Expectancies Scale
Conflict Disengagement Inventory

Keith Sanford, Baylor University

This document provides copies of instruments for assessing conflict interactions in couples. Researchers and clinicians are welcome to use these instruments. In addition, couples may visit a free website called the Couple Conflict Consultant, located at www.pairbuilder.com. This site allows couples to take an assessment that includes all the scales previously listed as well as several others, and it provides couples with instant feedback. Couples receive a chart displaying all their scores in the form of T scores.

In most of the original validation studies, these scales were administered via the Internet. This document provides copies of scales formatted as they were in the original studies. In some cases, researchers or clinicians may need to alter this formatting to fit the needs of a current context or situation.

For information on scoring and on the psychometric properties of specific scales, see the following articles:

Couples Emotion Rating Form

Sanford, K. (2007). The Couples Emotion Rating Form: Psychometric properties and theoretical associations. *Psychological Assessment, 19*, 411–421.

Sanford, K. (2007). Hard and soft emotion during conflict: Investigating married couples and other relationships. *Personal Relationships, 14*, 65–90.

Sanford, K. (2012). The communication of emotion during conflict in married couples. *Journal of Family Psychology, 26*, 297–307.

Conflict Communication Inventory

Sanford, K. (2010). Assessing conflict communication in couples: Comparing the validity of self-report, partner-report, and observer ratings. *Journal of Family Psychology, 24*, 165–174.

Couples Underlying Concern Inventory

Sanford, K. (2010). Perceived threat and perceived neglect: Couples' underlying concerns during conflict. *Psychological Assessment*, *22*, 288–297.
Sanford, K., & Grace, A. J. (2011). Emotion and underlying concerns during couples' conflict: An investigation of within-person change. *Personal Relationships*, *18*, 96–109.
Sanford, K., & Wolfe, K. L. (2013). What married couples want from each other during conflicts: An investigation of underlying concerns. *Journal of Social and Clinical Psychology*, *32*, 674–699.

Expectancies Scale

Sanford, K. (2003a). Expectancies and communication behavior in marriage: Distinguishing proximal-level effects from distal-level effects. *Journal of Social and Personal Relationships*, 20, 391–402.
Sanford, K. (2006). Communication during marital conflict: When couples alter their appraisal, they change their behavior. *Journal of Family Psychology*, 20, 256–265.

Conflict Disengagement Inventory

Sanford, K (2014). A latent change score model of conflict resolution in couples: Are negative behaviors bad, benign, or beneficial? *Journal of Social and Personal Relationships*. Published online before print January 10, 2014.

Instructions

Each of the three scales begins with the same set of instructions. Specifically, respondents are told to think of a specific episode of relationship conflict. These instructions may differ slightly depending on the context and purpose of assessment. For example, respondents may be asked to think of a conflict that took place within the last week, or to respond on the basis of a specific conflict discussion that just occurred in a laboratory or clinician's office, or they may be free to think of any conflict that occurred at any time in their relationship. If couples are completing more than one scale in sequence, it is sufficient to provide these instructions only once at the beginning of the sequence.

The instructions currently being used at www.pairbuilder.com are printed in what follows.

> All couples experience conflict from time to time. To complete this survey, you need to think about a single, specific episode of conflict in your relationship. It could be something current or something from the past. The conflict could be anything from a minor disagreement or simple misunderstanding to a big argument. This survey will ask you questions about the single, specific conflict that you select.

Although it is not always necessary, it is sometimes helpful to ensure that respondents have followed the instructions by asking them to answer the two questions provided here (presumably, they could not answer these questions if they had failed to think of a specific episode of conflict).

Approximately how long ago did the specific interaction take place?

- Today
- Yesterday
- Within the last week
- Within the last two weeks
- Within the last month
- Within the last three months
- Within the last six months
- Within the last year
- Longer than a year ago

Where did the interaction take place? (i.e., kitchen, car, etc.)

Couples Emotion Rating Form

At the time of your conflict interaction, how did you perceive your partner's feelings?

Rate the extent to which your partner appeared to be feeling each of the following feelings.

	Disagree Strongly	*Disagree*	*Agree Somewhat*	*Agree*	*Agree Strongly*
My partner appeared to be feeling *angry*.	○	○	○	○	○
My partner appeared to be feeling *sad*.	○	○	○	○	○
My partner appeared to be feeling *bored*.	○	○	○	○	○
My partner appeared to be feeling *annoyed*.	○	○	○	○	○
My partner appeared to be feeling *hurt*.	○	○	○	○	○
My partner appeared to be feeling *uninterested*.	○	○	○	○	○

Rate the extent to which your partner appeared to be feeling each of the following feelings.

	Disagree Strongly	*Disagree*	*Agree Somewhat*	*Agree*	*Agree Strongly*
My partner appeared to be feeling *irritated*.	○	○	○	○	○
My partner appeared to be feeling *concerned*.	○	○	○	○	○

(*Continued*)

Continued

	Disagree Strongly	*Disagree*	*Agree Somewhat*	*Agree*	*Agree Strongly*
My partner appeared to be feeling *indifferent*.	○	○	○	○	○
My partner appeared to be feeling *aggravated*.	○	○	○	○	○
My partner appeared to be feeling *disappointed*.	○	○	○	○	○
My partner appeared to be feeling *disengaged*.	○	○	○	○	○

Rate the extent to which you felt each of the following feelings.

	Disagree Strongly	*Disagree*	*Agree Somewhat*	*Agree*	*Agree Strongly*
I felt *angry*.	○	○	○	○	○
I felt *sad*.	○	○	○	○	○
I felt *bored*.	○	○	○	○	○
I felt *annoyed*.	○	○	○	○	○
I felt *hurt*.	○	○	○	○	○
I felt *uninterested*.	○	○	○	○	○

Rate the extent to which you felt each of the following feelings.

	Disagree Strongly	*Disagree*	*Agree Somewhat*	*Agree*	*Agree Strongly*
I felt *irritated*.	○	○	○	○	○
I felt *concerned*.	○	○	○	○	○
I felt *indifferent*.	○	○	○	○	○
I felt *aggravated*.	○	○	○	○	○
I felt *disappointed*.	○	○	○	○	○
I felt *disengaged*.	○	○	○	○	○

Conflict Communication Inventory

Listed here are things people often do when there is a conflict in a relationship.

To what extent did your partner do these things during the interaction?

	Disagree Strongly	*Disagree*	*Agree Somewhat*	*Agree*	*Agree Strongly*
My partner said something mean.	○	○	○	○	○
My partner made me feel that my viewpoint was valuable.	○	○	○	○	○

	Disagree Strongly	*Disagree*	*Agree Somewhat*	*Agree*	*Agree Strongly*
My partner raised his/her voice.	○	○	○	○	○
My partner was considerate toward me.	○	○	○	○	○
My partner told me I was doing something to cause the problem.	○	○	○	○	○
My partner said something kind.	○	○	○	○	○
My partner argued.	○	○	○	○	○

To what extent did your partner do these things during the interaction?

	Disagree Strongly	*Disagree*	*Agree Somewhat*	*Agree*	*Agree Strongly*
My partner agreed with me.	○	○	○	○	○
My partner defended his/her position.	○	○	○	○	○
My partner politely talked about his/her feelings.	○	○	○	○	○
My partner corrected my statements.	○	○	○	○	○
My partner carefully listened so he/she could understand me.	○	○	○	○	○
My partner criticized me.	○	○	○	○	○
My partner discussed the issue calmly.	○	○	○	○	○

To what extent did you do these things during the interaction?

	Disagree Strongly	*Disagree*	*Agree Somewhat*	*Agree*	*Agree Strongly*
I said something mean.	○	○	○	○	○
I made my partner feel that his/her viewpoint was valuable.	○	○	○	○	○
I raised my voice.	○	○	○	○	○
I was considerate toward my partner.	○	○	○	○	○
I told my partner he/she was doing something to cause the problem.	○	○	○	○	○
I said something kind.	○	○	○	○	○
I argued.	○	○	○	○	○

To what extent did you do these things during the interaction?

	Disagree Strongly	*Disagree*	*Agree Somewhat*	*Agree*	*Agree Strongly*
I agreed with my partner.	○	○	○	○	○
I defended my position.	○	○	○	○	○
I politely talked about my feelings.	○	○	○	○	○
I corrected my partner's statements that were not true.	○	○	○	○	○
I carefully listened so I could understand my partner.	○	○	○	○	○
I criticized my partner.	○	○	○	○	○
I discussed the issue calmly.	○	○	○	○	○

Couples Underlying Concern Inventory

> Note: this header provides a transition from previous scales, but it is not necessary if the preceding scales are not being used

↓

These questions ask about your own experience and about how you perceived your partner.

Rate the extent to which each statement describes your experience during the interaction.

	Disagree Strongly	*Disagree*	*Agree Somewhat*	*Agree*	*Agree Strongly*
I felt *criticized.*	○	○	○	○	○
I felt *neglected.*	○	○	○	○	○

	Disagree Strongly	*Disagree*	*Agree Somewhat*	*Agree*	*Agree Strongly*
I felt *blamed.*	○	○	○	○	○
I felt *forgotten.*	○	○	○	○	○

Rate the extent to which each statement describes how you perceived your partner during the interaction.

	Disagree Strongly	*Disagree*	*Agree Somewhat*	*Agree*	*Agree Strongly*
My partner seemed *judgmental.*	○	○	○	○	○
My partner seemed *uncommitted.*	○	○	○	○	○
My partner seemed *demanding.*	○	○	○	○	○
My partner seemed *unconcerned.*	○	○	○	○	○

Rate the extent to which each statement describes your experience during the interaction.

	Disagree Strongly	*Disagree*	*Agree Somewhat*	*Agree*	*Agree Strongly*
I felt *accused.*	○	○	○	○	○
I felt *invisible.*	○	○	○	○	○
I felt *misjudged.*	○	○	○	○	○
I felt *overlooked.*	○	○	○	○	○

Rate the extent to which each statement describes how you perceived your partner during the interaction.

	Disagree Strongly	*Disagree*	*Agree Somewhat*	*Agree*	*Agree Strongly*
My partner seemed *controlling.*	○	○	○	○	○
My partner seemed *disloyal.*	○	○	○	○	○
My partner seemed *imposing.*	○	○	○	○	○
My partner seemed *inattentive.*	○	○	○	○	○

Expectancies Scale

The next time you discuss this issue, what do you predict your partner will do?

If you do not expect to discuss the issue, just imagine what would happen if you did.

In your next conversation, how many of your **feelings** do you think your partner will understand?

All of them	*Almost all of them*	*More than half of them*	*Half of them*	*Less than half of them*	*A few of them*	*None of them*
○	○	○	○	○	○	○

How many of your **thoughts and opinions** do you think your partner will understand?

All of them	*Almost all of them*	*More than half of them*	*Half of them*	*Less than half of them*	*A few of them*	*None of them*
○	○	○	○	○	○	○

How many of your **wants and desires** do you think your partner will understand?

All of them	*Almost all of them*	*More than half of them*	*Half of them*	*Less than half of them*	*A few of them*	*None of them*
○	○	○	○	○	○	○

How many of your **motives** (the reasons why you do what you do) do you think your partner will understand?

All of them	*Almost all of them*	*More than half of them*	*Half of them*	*Less than half of them*	*A few of them*	*None of them*
○	○	○	○	○	○	○

Conflict Disengagement Inventory

Listed here are common ways that people respond to conflict.

Rate the extent to which you responded in each of the following ways during the interaction.

	Disagree Strongly	*Disagree*	*Agree Somewhat*	*Agree*	*Agree Strongly*
I avoided discussing the conflict.	○	○	○	○	○
I wanted my partner to be faster at recognizing when I am upset.	○	○	○	○	○
I silently refused to say anything.	○	○	○	○	○
I decided it was useless to reply to my partner.	○	○	○	○	○
I quietly waited, hoping my partner would notice I was upset.	○	○	○	○	○
I wanted my partner to drop the issue.	○	○	○	○	○
I decided to remain silent until my partner stopped nagging.	○	○	○	○	○

Rate the extent to which you responded in each of the following ways during the interaction.

	Disagree Strongly	*Disagree*	*Agree Somewhat*	*Agree*	*Agree Strongly*
I wanted my partner to notice my feelings without me having to say anything.	○	○	○	○	○
I withdrew from my partner.	○	○	○	○	○
I wanted my partner to take responsibility for finding out how I felt.	○	○	○	○	○
I wanted my partner to figure something out without me having to say it.	○	○	○	○	○
I chose not to respond to my partner.	○	○	○	○	○
I silently wished my partner would ask about my feelings.	○	○	○	○	○
I wanted my partner to notice something was wrong without me having to point it out.	○	○	○	○	○

8 Managing Conflict in Session

A couple argument in session can challenge the most seasoned clinician. Within just a minute or so, a difficult conversation can move from restrained frustration to attack-and-defend engagement that escalates like a fire fueled with gasoline.

It might be easy to assume that these types of conflict are due to long-ingrained patterns of behavior from couples that have been together for a while. In truth, we see the same pattern in newlywed couples or couples in the early formation of their relationship. There are many possible explanations for why couples fight, for example carry-in from family of origin, long-standing resentment and hurt in the relationship, or skill deficits. The focus of this chapter, however, is to look just at the pragmatic aspect of the conflict in session and how to clinically intervene.

Why Couples Fight

Some couples argue because they are distressed. Some because they are not getting their needs met. Something was said or not said, a disapproving look during a tense exchange, and the list goes on. Underneath what is presented to the clinician in session is some underlying concern that may not be directly stated. This underlying concern has been the focus of a number of research studies.

In a study that included over 3,500 married people, Sanford (2010) identified two basic dimensions of underlying concern. The first type of concern, perceived threat, involves the perception that a partner is being critical or demanding, and thereby threatens one's status. The second type of concern, perceived neglect, involves a perception that a partner is being disloyal or inattentive, and thereby not demonstrating a sufficient level of investment in the relationship.

A research study conducted at Baylor University looked to identify what outcomes couples want when they are in conflict (Sanford & Wolfe, 2013). In the study of 455 married people, the researcher found that couples want their partner to relinquish power, indicating the underlying concern is perceived threat. Secondly, they want their partner to show investment, indicating

Table 8.1 Mean Scores for Desired Resolutions to a Current or Ongoing Conflict

Relinquish power	2.22
Show investment	1.82
Communicate more	.83
Stop adversarial behavior	.82
Give affection	.22
Apologize	.14

the underlying concern is perceived neglect. The lowest-ranked item was to receive an apology. Table 8.1 lists the mean scores of the items in the study.

Based on this study, couples in conflict want disengagement when there is a perceived threat and engagement when there is perceived neglect. When the underlying concern is perceived threat, couples want their partner to relinquish power by showing more respect, being more willing to hear the other partner's perspective, being more understanding, being more willing to compromise, admitting faults, and acknowledging the partner's expertise. When the underlying concern is perceived neglect, couples want their partner to show investment by demonstrating more investment in the relationship, showing more support, showing more appreciation, being more loving, being more honest, and changing the problematic behavior.

Clinicians should consider the underlying concern from the perspective of perceived threat and perceived neglect when they are teaching communication skills or processing conflict in session. I believe most clinicians do a good job at addressing communication skills around perceived threat by helping partners stop blaming, control their negative emotions, show more understanding, take the partner's perspective, and show more respect. When partners are concerned about perceived neglect, clinicians may be less apt to teach a different set of skills that may be needed, a skill set that focuses on behaviors and appraisals pertaining to investment (Sanford & Wolfe, 2013).

The Five Types of Couples

Drawing from over four decades of research data, Dr. John Gottman (The Gottman Institute, 2017) has been able to categorize couples into five types: Conflict-Avoiding, Validating, Volatile, Hostile, and Hostile-Detached. Of these five types, Gottman identifies three to be happy couple types, which are Conflict-Avoiding, Validating, and Volatile. He believes these three couple types are problem-solving approaches in healthy marriages and that they can lead to stable and enduring marriages.

Conflict-Avoiding

These couples avoid conflict, avoid expressing what they need from one another, and congratulate their relationship for being generally happy. An important aspect about Conflict-avoiding couples is in the balance between independence and interdependence. They have clear boundaries and are separate people with separate interests.

Conflict-avoiding couples rarely argue and will avoid conflict at all cost. When they discuss their conflicts, they do so with caution and with limited emotion. From their perspective, there is nothing to be gained out of arguing.

Validating

Validating couples fight politely. They are somewhat expressive, but mostly neutral.

They put a lot of emphasis on supporting and understanding each other's point of view and are often empathetic about their partner's feelings.

In conflict, the Validating couple will value communication and compromise. Even when the discussion gets heated, they validate each other. They do this by expressing empathy for and understanding of each other's point of view.

Volatile

Volatile couples are emotionally expressive. Their conflicts erupt easily and can be explosive. Volatile couples have passionate disputes and fairly frequent passionate arguments.

When they argue, they stick to their point of view and work at persuading their partner. They debate with laughter and humor. They seem to love to debate and argue, but they are not disrespectful and insulting. Their arguments are full of wit and fondness.

There can be a lot of negative affect expressed such as anger and insecurity, but it appears that passion and fighting for the Volatile couple can lead to a better relationship. Despite the level of their argument, they still resolve their differences.

Hostile

Hostile couples frequently argue, and their arguments are hurtful. They use insults, putdowns, sarcasm, and criticism. They fight for their own perspective and offer no support or understanding for each other's point of view. Their fights have too much criticism, defense, withdrawal, and contempt for one another. Their communication is unhealthy and their arguments are dangerous to the relationship. Hostile couples will stay unhappily married.

Hostile-Detached

This couple type is by far the most problematic. Their relationship is a battleground that leads to continual frustration and loneliness. The Hostile-Detached pair usually contains one partner who is the fiery Hostile type and wants to argue and fight and a second who is Conflict-Avoiding, not caring enough to discuss the issues. The primary difference between the Hostile type and the Hostile-Detached type is that the Hostile-Detached comes from very diametrically opposed perspectives with no compromise. Hostile-Detached couples will eventually divorce.

The Stress Spillover Connection to Conflict

Stress of daily life is common for couples. There are many stresses that can intrude on the couple relationship, including job deadlines, pressures from friends and family, and stresses of raising children. This spillover can have a significant effect on the relationship. Alternatively, relationship problems can also spill over into other domains in life, such as work.

There is a link between daily stress and relationship function in daily life. Early spillover research showed that men's stressful workdays were link to their withdrawal in the relationship (Repetti, 1989). In couples with dual-earners, work stress has been associated with combinations of anger, negative mood, and withdrawal during the same evening (Story & Repetti, 2006).

In a study of heterosexual couples (Timmons et al., 2017), relational conflict for women was significantly associated with a number of stressors: having too many things to do, having to make difficult decisions, one's own health, the health of family members, traffic or bad drivers, noise, making mistakes, doing paid work, pressure from unpaid work, feeling overloaded with unpaid work, being criticized doing unpaid work, a child's being irritable, sullen, or angry, and a child's arguing with a parent. For men, daily relationship conflict was significantly associated with many stressors as well: being criticized, doing unpaid work, having conflict with a coworker, a child's being irritable, angry, or sullen, and a child's arguing with a parent. Interestingly, these stressors were only linked to same-day conflict, and there was no correlation with conflict the following day.

Stress spillover can add to the couple's sense that conflict is ever present in their relationship. Spillover is relevant to the daily patterns involving everyday events, as well as the importance of how partners interpret one another's reactions to those events. Increasing awareness of stress-spillover processes and examining each partner's role could be productive directions in therapy.

The Emotional Nature of Conflict

Any worthwhile discussion about couple conflict process has to take into account the role of emotional expression. It is obvious to any clinician that couples respond differently to the different emotions that are expressed by their partner. Anger typically seems to be a difficult emotion for couples to manage, and sadness seems to draw a more compassionate response. If we are willing to admit it, this seems to hold true for clinicians as well.

There is empirical evidence that supports this notion. There is a distinction that can be made between hard emotions and soft emotions (Dimidjian, Martell, & Christensen, 2002). Hard emotions are emotions that include feelings of anger and other negative emotions associated with asserting power and control. Hard emotions, such as anger, contempt, and aggravation, may motivate people to protect themselves against partners who are perceived as harmful or neglectful (Sanford, 2007).

Soft emotions are pro-social emotions that include feelings of sadness, hurt, and other negative emotions associated with experiencing or expressing vulnerability. Since the expression of soft emotion indicates vulnerability rather than attack, it may elicit empathic, caring, and understanding responses from a partner (Sanford, 2007).

This distinction has strong implications for clinical practice. When couples change their expression of emotions, their thinking and behaving will follow suit. Hard emotions lead to more destructive, negative communication and behavior whereas softer emotions will lead to more relationship-oriented behavior and support. Most importantly, when couples engage in conflict communication in session, they are likely to benefit from identifying and expressing soft rather than hard emotions.

Effective Repair Attempts

Couples naturally attempt to repair as conflict begins in their relationship. Some attempts to repair are accepted and some are denied. Some attempts are successful at reducing negative affect, some are successful at increasing positive affect, and some are not.

According to Gottman, Driver, and Tabares (2015), some repair attempts are more successful than others. One assumption that clinicians may have is that a rational, problem-solving approach will be useful when conflict begins in session. However, that is not the case. When Gottman, Driver, and Tabares (2015) evaluated cognitively based repairs that appeal to logic and rational problem solving, they concluded that these repair attempts are quite ineffective at reducing negative affect and/or positive affect. Repair attempts that are based on increasing emotional closeness (agreement, affection, humor, self-disclosure, understanding, and empathy) were the highly effective repairs (Gottman, Driver, & Tabares, 2015).

Another highly effective repair strategy the researcher identified was in moving a conversation from attack/defend mode to self-disclosure mode, in tandem with taking responsibility for even a part of the problem. Even when conflict becomes more escalated, the couple can still turn around the negativity by either partner's taking responsibility for part of the problem and demonstrating some affection toward the other through humor, their self-disclosure, empathy, reassurance, and understanding.

These results on repair suggest that the power in turning around a negative conflict and making it constructive requires creating and maintaining emotional connection. Couples can be effective by moving from attack/defend mode to admitting mode (taking responsibility) and to collaborative mode, in which the couple increases self-disclosure, compassion, and understanding.

Another critical aspect of repair during conflict is to understand the role of accepting a repair attempt initiated by the other partner. As it turns out, when a repair attempt is accepted, the repairing partner had a significant reduction in their negative affect and increase in their positive affect. In addition, the acceptance of a repair attempt was associated with an overall reduction in negative affect and an increase in positive affect during the conflict exchange.

General Principles for Managing Conflict

The clinician needs to have a strong understanding of how they will manage conflict well before it ever happens in a therapy session. The clinician will need to be comfortable with general blocking skills. Blocking skills are polite but firm interruptions of conflict, extraneous conversation, or problematic communication. It is the clinician's primary responsibility to control the level of conflict and to make sure each individual and the relationship is not hurt by nonproductive or harmful communication.

The clinician will need to balance interactions so that each partner has the chance to speak and feel heard. This will require clinicians to continually coach healthy communication and discourage interrupting and other problematic communication patterns.

Lastly, the clinician will need to manage affective intensity. Managing affective intensity means using couple affect therapeutically, assuming that effective therapeutic change can best occur when emotional intensity is present between couples. Thus, this principle reflects how the clinician encourages, redirects, moderates, validates, or rewards affective expression in therapy (Toth, Harnishfeger, & Shea, 2002).

Parking Lot Fights

Common occurrences pertaining to in-session conflict is for the couple to have an argument that they hold to resolve in the therapy session, to have an argument on the way to therapy or to have what I call "parking lot fights," which are prolonged arguments in the parking lot prior to the session. Sometimes it does not take much for the couple to get the argument going, and usually the stress of getting to the appointment combined with an ongoing resentment towards one another can send the couple to a heightened level of conflict.

The clinician can tell immediately from their facial expressions and limited interaction that something just happened prior to session. These parking lot fights can be unnerving for the unprepared clinician, and not taking the time to help the couple work through the conflict will make the session rough at best. Without careful involvement from the clinician, arguments can spiral out of control.

"Did you get into a fight right before coming in?" I ask. When they affirm this, I say, "Let's take a few minutes or a little longer to help you process what happened," knowing that we will come back a bit later to my planned agenda or what the couple had planned for session.

When I have a couple carry in conflict, I find it useful to have a specific crisis conflict structure to follow. Here I draw from my experience from my work as a crisis prevention and intervention trainer. The Crisis Prevention Institute, Inc. (2006) uses the acronym COPING that can be adapted to help the clinician and couple process an argument is session. Using a modified version of this, I facilitate a dialogue between the couple using this acronym. For each of the sections of the acronym, I believe my job is to facilitate a discussion that expands the couple's perception and available information about each topic area. Once the process is completed, I will tell the couple that though the conversation seemed casual, it really had a structure and specific goals. I then teach the couple the acronym and ask them to implement it in a future conflict. Following is an explanation of what the acronym stands for.

Control

This is the starting point for working through the conflict. They must first make sure that they are in emotional control and that they are in a place where they will not escalate the discussion.

Orient

I ask the couple to help orient me to both perspectives of the issue. This requires each partner to sit quietly as the other shares their perspective. This is not a dialogue at this point, so I state to them directly, "please sit quietly as your partner shares their perspective. I will make sure I hear your side in just a minute."

Patterns

Some of what the couple shares to orient the clinician is likely vicious circles, those reoccurring, patterned behaviors that are common in their relationship: for example, one partner's raising their voice to be heard as the other interrupts. Both will admit that this is a pattern that happens with a predictable level of frequency. I will also ask them whether they can identify any triggers that may have gotten the conflict going.

Investigate

"How can you do something differently so that the outcome of this fight is not the same?" I will ask the couple as a starting point to helping them generate alternative ways of behaving.

Negotiate

It is now time to put it all together. "What are you willing to commit to as a couple so that a fight like this will end differently?" The challenge here is for the couple to negotiate and make a commitment to a new response in the future. Once this is completed, I review the outcome of each step of the discussion and reaffirm the new response that the two have agreed upon.

Give

"Now that the two of you have processed this fight, let's do one more thing before we get back to our session," I will say to conclude the conflict-processing session. I then ask each partner to give back to one another, to give some words of encouragement or support to the other. Then we can focus our attention to the session at hand.

The No-Conclusion Intervention for Couples in Conflict

I will regularly tell couples that a primary difference between facilitated conversations in therapy and the difficult conversations that the couple has at home is that in the therapy session, the focus is on dialoguing the topic, not necessarily solving the issue. In this way, I am able to help the couple have an increasingly intimate conversation about the topic that is free of attack/defense interactions.

The No-Conclusion Intervention for Couples in Conflict (Migerode, 2014) comes from the perspective that most conflicts cannot be completely solved. Couples have to decide which differences can be resolved and which issues demand ways of living with "perpetual problems" (Gottman, 2011). The No-Conclusion Intervention is designed to help couples make that decision and handle conflict, and to introduce them to a dialogue that promotes life in the couple, especially in conversations about gridlocked issues.

Migerode (2014) believes in three relationship tensions that are important to the No-Conclusion intervention, which I paraphrase here: 1) opposing perspectives in the relationship is a given, 2) dialogue between opposing perspectives keeps the relationship alive, and 3) tension between the opposing perspectives can never be definitely resolved.

Couples who get stuck discussing oppositions will quite naturally aim for the resolution of the differences. From Migerode's perspective, when therapy follows the same approach by focusing on problem solving or conflict resolution, it might endanger the continuity of the relationship. The No-Conclusion intervention does not promote a dialogue that aims for resolution, agreement, or problem solving, but for ongoing dialogue. Resolution is not rejected, however, but it is definitely not the aim of the intervention.

An open dialogue, in the presence of threatening differences, requires partners to tolerate higher levels of tension. The desire to solve the problem is tempting due to its promise to lower the tension. This is where therapy can be of help because it will be the therapist and the therapeutic context that need to provide for the emotional safety required of the task.

The No-Conclusion intervention was initially developed for a group setting with multiple couples, though I modify it here for couples therapy. The work of the No-Conclusion intervention may take several therapy sessions to complete.

Step 1: Choose and Name a Conflict Issue

First, the couple is asked to identify and write down three issues. They are instructed to come up with the issue without consulting each other. The independent work here is important because it limits the couple from being emotionally reactive to one another.

Step 2: Decide Whether the Issue Is Trivial or Important

Again, without consulting the partner, each partner makes this decision and writes it down next to the three chosen issues. The clinician explains that an issue should be classified "important" only when it is related to 1) their view of themselves, 2) their view of their relationship, or 3) their concept of the world.

Step 3: Exchange Issues and Qualify the Issue Received From the Partner

Partners are asked to exchange issues and to perform the same trivial/important labeling for the issues written down by their partner. The partners are told that this is not a negotiation process, nor are they demanded to criticize the categorization chosen by their partner. Conversely, it is important for each partner to decide on the labeling starting from their own point of view. This step results in couples' placing all of the issues in one of the four following categories on a sheet of paper as follows:

Step 4: Explanation of the Conversations to Follow

Based on the completed table in Table 8.2, the clinician proposes that there are three conversations that need to be addressed and explains that these conversations "automatically" follow from the bringing together of the labeling of the issues. The couple is offered a sheet of paper of the outlines of the three conversations for the couple to follow. The three outlines are discussed in the following explanation of step 5.

Table 8.2 Ranking of Importance of the Issue

	Partner A: Trivial	*Partner A: Important*
Partner B: Trivial	Write here issues that are labeled: Trivial (A)/Trivial (B) Conversation 1	Write here issues that are labeled: Important (A)/Trivial (B) Conversation 2
Partner B: Important	Write here issues that are labeled: Trivial (A)/Important (B) Conversation 2	Write here issues that are labeled: Important(A)/Important (B) Conversation 3

Step 5: Conversations Coached by the Clinician

Conversation 1: Both Partners Identify That the Issue Is Trivial

A brief conversation is suggested for these issues. Couples should only take limited time, something like five minutes, and solve the problem quickly. Life is too short; solve it and move on.

Outline:

- Take a limited amount of time.
- Solve it!
- "Life is too short."

Conversation 2: One Partner Identifies the Issue as Trivial, the Other Partner as Important

This conversation will take time. It is very important that the couple accepts that no agreement or conclusion can be made during this conversation. The conversation starts with partner A explaining his/her qualification of the issue as "trivial." Partner B is invited to listen and try to understand how this can be trivial for the partner. Afterward, Partner B explains his/her qualification of the same issue as "important," and Partner A listens and tries to understand how this is linked to either self, the couple, or their world view.

After both explanations and both attempts to listen, the issue is then put aside for a while. At a later date (next day, next week, next month), the couple restarts the same conversation, again and again, until something happens, such as the qualifications change, possibly indicating that another step can be taken.

The clinician takes time to help the couple discuss each of the steps completely. The role of the clinician is to coach the discussion and limit negative exchanges.

- Take ample time.
- Decide not to come to a conclusion.

- Partner who classified the issue as "trivial" explains classification.
- Other partner takes as much risk of listening as possible and shows understanding.
- Partner who classified issue as "important" explains classification.
- Other partner takes as much risk of listening as possible and shows understanding.
- Put issue aside for another time.
- Start all over.

Conversation 3: Both Partners Identify the Issue as Important

This conversation differs only slightly from the previous conversation. Partners in turn explain and listen to what is important in the issue. The conversation is put aside and restarted over and over again.

The clinician takes time to help the couple discuss each of the steps completely. The role of the clinician is to coach the discussion and limit negative exchanges.

- Take ample time.
- Decide not to come to a conclusion.
- Partner A explains "important" classification.
- Partner B takes as much risk of listening as possible and shows understanding.
- Partner B explains "important" classification.
- Partner A takes as much risk of listening as possible and shows understanding.
- Put issue aside for another time.
- Start all over.

References

Crisis Prevention Institute, Inc. (2006). *Instructor manual for the nonviolent crisis intervention training manual.* Brookfield, WI: Crisis Prevention Institute.

Dimidjian, S., Martell, C. R., & Christensen, A. (2002). Integrative behavioral couple therapy. In A. S. Gurman & N. S. Jacobson (Eds.), *Clinical handbook of couple therapy* (3rd ed., pp. 251–277). New York: Guilford Press.

Gottman, J. M. (2011). *The science of trust: Emotional attunement for couples*. New York: W.W. Norton & Co.

Gottman, J. M., Driver, J., & Tabares, A. (2015). Repair during marital conflict in newlyweds: How couples move from attack—defend to collaboration. *Journal of Family Psychotherapy*, *26*(2), 85–108. doi:10.1080/08975353.2015.1038962

Gottman Institute. (2017). *The five types of couples*. Retrieved April 14, 2017 from https://www.gottman.com/blog/the-5-couple-types/.

Migerode, L. (2014). The no conclusion intervention for couples in conflict. *Journal of Marital and Family Therapy*. V 40, N 3, 391–401.

Repetti, R. L. (1989). Effects of daily workload on subsequent behavior during marital interaction: The roles of social withdrawal and spouse support. *Journal of Personality and Social Psychology*, *57*, N 4, 651–659.
Sanford, K. (2007). Hard and soft emotion during conflict: Investigating married couples and other relationships. *Personal Relationships*, *14*(1), 65–90.
Sanford, K. (2010). Perceived threat and perceived neglect: Couples' underlying concerns during conflict. *Psychological Assessment*, *22*, 288–297.
Sanford, K., & Wolfe, K. (2013). What married couples want from each other during conflicts: An investigation of underlying concerns. *Journal of Social and Clinical Psychology*, *32*(6), 674–699.
Story, L. B., & Repetti, R. (2006). Daily occupational stressors and marital behavior. *Journal of Family Psychology*, *V 20*, N 4, 690 –700.
Timmons, A. C., Arbel, R., & Margolin, G. (2017). Daily patterns of stress and conflict in couples: Associations with marital aggression and family-of-origin aggression. *Journal of Family Psychology*, *31*(1), 93–104.
Toth, P. L., Harnishfeger, B. R., & Shea, A. (2002). Chapter 17: Finding the silver lining: Counseling a couple in conflict. *Journal of College Student Psychotherapy*, *16*(3/4), 269.

9 Intimacy

Clinicians and couples alike see therapy as a way to re-create intimacy. A potential faulty assumption here is that intimacy existed in the relationship at some point in time when in fact maybe it never did. Couples talk about their inability to communicate and view their communication difficulties as a skill deficit that can be fixed by learning the skill from an experienced clinician, resulting in increased intimacy.

By the time the couple enters therapy, a number of relational transgressions have occurred. In all likelihood, the couple has been unable to successfully resolve and forgive each other for the transgressions. Events such as lying, keeping or telling secrets, making threats to end the relations or threats of harm, lacking emotional openness, and causing emotional or sexual infidelity (Khalifian & Barry, 2016) have eroded the couple's confidence in the relationship and put them in a place of self-preservation.

Any intimacy that existed in the relationship has been injured and will definitely need to be recovered (and at some point, increased), and this cannot happen until each partner feels safe with each other to express their thoughts and feelings and also believe that they will be responded to in an appropriate way.

The clinician will need to set the stage for intimacy recovery and development. It begins by creating the intimate environment of therapy: a place of healing, a place of connecting safely around difficult topics.

Fostering a New Relational Experience

Couple intimacy in session, from a clinical perspective, begins with the clinician's structure of the therapeutic space. The clinician needs to help the couple create a "safe relationship" between the two that helps the partners feel safe to share a more vulnerable side of their emotional experience in the relationship. This safe relationship in therapy is different than the one that currently exists between the couple and maybe even what existed in each of the partners' family of origin (Solomon, 1985). The artful clinician nurtures and cares for this safe relationship, knowing that when it is protected, it can foster a new relational experience for the couple.

The primary tasks of the clinician in creating this safety is to help the couple regulate emotions. This is best achieved by the clinician's continual monitoring of distress, volatility, and attachment communication. Sometimes this is achieved by emotional containment through the clinician's buffering the couple interaction by blocking specific communication patterns or making direct requests for a specific communication. When safety is consistent, the couple can more effectively express vulnerable emotions and explore their defensiveness, withdrawal, attacking, blaming, and criticizing (Marmarosh, 2014). The clinician's immediate presence in the intentional regulation of each partner's emotional expression is key to safety.

When the couple is more able to regulate their emotional experience, the work of attaining deeper levels of emotional expression and attunement can occur. The clinician can begin by helping the couple express the emotional content of their experiences. Clinicians will need to move beyond the manifest feelings and help couples attend to the underlying emotional experience and the underlying vulnerability of those emotions. The sheer act of trying to understand (not necessarily complete) successful understanding can create less defensiveness and more disclosure and empathic patterns of relating. It is important to remember that defense-and-attack patterns are protecting the vulnerable emotions that lie beneath them.

Carl Rogers (1958) posed a series of questions in discussing the core characteristics of helping relationships. He asked,

> Can I let myself enter fully into the world of (his or her) feelings and personal meanings and see these as (he or she) does? Can I step into (his or her) private world so completely that I lose all desire to evaluate or judge it? Can I sense it so accurately that I can catch not only the meanings of (his or her) experiences which are obvious to (him or her) but those meanings that are only implicit, which (he or she) sees only dimly or as confusion?

These are beautiful questions that reflect Roger's perspective. Clinicians can create an environment in which one person deeply explores and attempts to understand the other's thoughts and feelings, and it is vital to the therapeutic relationship. Rogers is indicating our potential as clinicians to deeply understand our clients. It is also vital to the couple's intimate experience with one another during the therapeutic encounter. When emotional safety is consistent and guarded in session by the clinician, this deeper understanding can occur and ultimately create the potential for a new relational experience for the couple.

Emotional Regulation/Dysregulation and Intimacy

Emotion regulation is a dimension of emotional intelligence. It refers to a person's ability to shape which emotion they have, when they have the emotion, and how they experience and express the emotion (Gross, 2014, p. 6). This definition puts a strong emphasis on the person's control of the total emotional experience. As mentioned, the skill of emotional regulation is important to the therapeutic process. Emotional regulation is also strongly linked to couple intimacy.

The ability to express and contain one's emotional states is essential for optimal relationship functioning. Dysregulation represents a significant risk factor for the couple's relationship quality due to its dramatic impact on intimacy (Tani, Pascuzzi, & Raffagnino, 2015). Individuals who are not confident in their ability to manage emotions and control their behavior typically avoid close contact with their partner and are less likely to disclose close personal information. Understandably, when one partner is emotionally volatile the other partner is less likely to disclose.

The Pattern of Intimacy

There are a number of processes between the couple that need to be delicately balanced in order to promote intimacy. From a systemic perspective, intimacy requires that the partners prioritize relationship-promoting efforts over self-protection. When this occurs, there is a level of vulnerability and trust that allows for more disclosure (and acceptance of differing opinions) between the couple. Alternatively, emotional dysregulation is destructive to this process. When one partner is unable or unwilling to regulate their emotional experience or expression, the other partner prioritizes self-protection over relationship-promoting behaviors. To be vulnerable and trusting toward someone requires a belief that when one is vulnerable, the other person will respond in a way that is beneficial to the relationship (Khalifian & Barry, 2016).

Defining Relationship Intimacy

Couples tend to begin sessions talking about intimacy in very narrow terms. When asked about intimacy in session, the typical couple response is a quizzical look to one another as if asking, "Is he talking about sex?" Sex is only one piece of the equation. Elizabeth Barrett Browning asked the famous question "How do I love thee?" and then responded, "Let me count the ways." She poetically defined something that has been pondered in poems, paintings, and songs over the centuries. What is love?

Love must surely include intimacy. Psychologist Robert Sternberg (1986) believed that romantic love included components of commitment, passion, and intimacy. He believed that people who have a strong love relationship will have made a *commitment* to love the other person and also to maintain the love and have the *passion* of physical attraction, romance, and a sexual relationship, as well as a level of *intimacy* through a feeling of closeness, connectedness, and a sense of boundedness.

Defining intimacy is a challenging task, so there is no wonder that couples have difficulty with the concept. Most people would describe intimacy as a sense of closeness, both physical and emotional. It certainly requires the ability, and truly the choice, to be close, loving, and vulnerable. Intimacy is not a thing, however; it is an evolving process of increasing self-disclosure and capacity for self-understanding. When intimacy exists, a level of confidentiality is apparent. The relationship becomes private, holding secrets that only the two know, and there is a growing understanding of oneself in the context of knowing the other more deeply. It is critical to understand that the developing process of increasing confidentiality between the partners (Van den Broucke, Vandereycken, & Vertommen, 1995) makes the relationship special.

Consider three primary influencing factors in developing intimacy: 1) mutual disclosure, 2) trust, and 3) vulnerability. Each of these mutually influencing factors (see Appendix 9.1) increases the level of confidentiality in the relationship and therefore the experience of feeling closer to one another. Disclosure, vulnerability, and trust must be operating simultaneously. For this reason, increasing disclosure requires increasing vulnerability to share personal information and also vulnerability to "hear" one's partner's thoughts and feelings. In doing so, ongoing disclosure needs, and increases, trust.

Mutual Disclosure

Once central characteristic of intimate relationships is mutual disclosure. Whether the situation is a couple wanting to increase intimacy in their relationship or someone struggling to rebuild their relationship after infidelity, the level and frequency of disclosure is a key component to wellness for the couple. In fact, the pairing of curiosity in one partner and the willingness to disclose in the other can be a good recipe for creating intimacy. Prager and Buhrmester (1998) identify that intimate disclosure has three components: 1) a revelation of something personal or private, 2) the couple's experience of positive feelings about themselves, their partner, and their interactions, and 3) a belief that that they have advanced or reflected understanding of one another. Unfortunately, couples seeking therapy tend to have blocked intimate disclosure in an attempt to limit escalation, resulting from fear or frustration that they will not be understood or concern that their issues will not be considered. Self-disclosure then needs one partner to risk the vulnerability to reveal something personal and the other partner to be waiting and willing to hear it.

Couples who have higher levels of disclosure tend to have a greater sense of closeness in the relationship. Closeness is generally defined by the strength of the emotional bond and the level of knowledge of the other person. These are strengthened by disclosure (Dibble, Levine, & Park, 2011).

Should clinicians assign couples tasks to have intimate dialogue outside of session, particularly during times of negative sentiment? Prager and Buhrmester (1998) indicate that couples who disclose personal information, even during times of negative interaction, feel more fulfilled in having their needs met. Outside of negative interactions, couples that have at least one intimate interaction per week report more fulfillment in getting needs met.

Trust

Trust is the fruit of a trusting relationship. A trusting relationship will require from each partner consistent truthfulness, accountability for one's time, availability for connections during times when the couple is away from one another, and accessibility (disclosure) of thoughts and feelings. Trust in one's partner also includes the belief that the partner has integrity, in other words that they uphold good moral values and that they follow through with the commitments that they make to their partner, their family, and others. Trust's role in intimacy is that it allows each person to risk being vulnerable.

Vulnerability

Vulnerability is a key to long-lasting relationships. It does not mean weakness. Dr. Brené Brown (2016) states that "vulnerability sounds like truth and feels like courage. Truth and courage aren't always comfortable, but they're never weakness." Vulnerability is increasing emotional exposure.

Vulnerability can only be possible when there is safety. When both partners are vulnerable, there is a need for a mutually protective alliance. This takes a high level of attunement to the emotional experience of the partner and also appropriate responsiveness, such as soothing the partner when they cry. A mutually protective relationship includes a commitment to guarding against hurting the other and a fair amount of compassion and nurturing when the partner is hurting.

Commitment

A common challenge in couples therapy is that upon entry into therapy, there can be varying degrees of commitment to the relationship and to the process of therapy. Intimacy does require a level of commitment to the relationship, and people have different reasons for being committed, or not being committed, to a relationship.

According to Adams and Jones (1999), partners can be committed because of the rewards and satisfactions of the relationship. In these relationships, the couple is bonded in the relationship by love and closeness. Commitment can be a moral obligation. Some people stay in a relationship even when they are unhappy because they see it as a vow, an obligation, or a duty. Sometimes commitment is seen as a constraint. For example, people who stay in a relationship because of the children, because of social consequences of divorce, fear of being alone, or financial limitations.

There are a number of behaviors that if practiced can strengthen commitment. Goddard and Olsen (2004) have described three commitment practices that make a relationship more likely to endure. The first strategy is for each partner to make the relationship a priority over everything else. If couples are not intentional in prioritizing the relationship, demands from work, school, or family can take over with little time left for the relationship. The second strategy is to protect the relationship from external influences. For example, the couple may decide to limit their interactions with friends who are not healthy for the relationship. They may decide not to have intimate conversations about their relationship with friends or family or to go out to dinner with individuals that might be a threat to the relationship. The third is creating rituals or traditions that will sustain the relationship. Some couples will worship together, participate in sports or activities together, or have special holiday traditions. For example, at Christmas my wife and I bring the children together to bless every room in the house with incense and prayer.

Multidimensional View of Intimacy

Intimacy is multidimensional and includes negative and positive elements. Some positive aspects include the ability to maintain closeness, love, care support, good sensuality and sexuality, respect, appreciation, recognition, positive emotions, and sharing of life. Negative aspects include physical and emotional distance between partners, difficulty expressing emotions and identifying their partner's feelings, expression of negative emotions, destructive communication, resentment, and aggression (Tani, Pascuzzi, & Raffagnino, 2015).

Threats to Intimacy

Just as intimacy is multidimensional, so is it that there could be multiple threats to intimacy. Couples face a society that encourages individualism and self-actualization, and without ongoing intentional investment by the couple in the relationship, intimacy can erode to a point where the couple is living parallel lives. Following are some of the common threats to intimacy.

Time Investment

A noticeable threat to intimacy among couples coming into treatment is relationship neglect. These couples have neglected the relationship through focus on career, over-involvement with friends, a drive for personal pursuits, or a difficulty in to balancing the relationship with childcare; triangulation can occur with inappropriate Internet uses, alcohol/drug use, or involvement in relationships outside the relationship. Relationship neglect for some couples entering therapy is so extreme that they have no intimate time together at all or have only a few minutes a day of communication that can be described as intimate. Conversation for these couples is limited to managing the functioning of the family.

Communication

Another significant threat to intimacy is the patterns in which couples communicate. Since disclosure and curiosity are primary avenues to creating intimacy, it is not a surprise, then, that many couples entering therapy list their number one problem as having an ability to communicate.

Communication stymied by fear of how the other partner will react can lead to resentment and inaction in the relationship. No longer are problems identified and discussed; they are left to fester in the heart and mind of the partner to be expressed inappropriately in moments of sheer frustration.

Violations of Trust

Trust is a product of multiple processes in the relationship. A patterned violation of one or several dimensions of trust can thwart intimacy that may be difficult to recover. However, when couples intentionally change the patterns of the dimensions of trust, they can recover intimacy. As mentioned earlier in this chapter, trust comes from consistent truthfulness, accountability for one's time, availability for connections, and accessibility (disclosure) of thoughts and feelings. The need for strengthening these trust dimensions is amplified when couples are recovering from infidelity.

Individual Characteristics

Fear is sometimes the culprit that limits intimacy. A general definition of the fear of intimacy can be defined as an inhibited capacity to be intimate due to anxiety, limiting the revelation of self (Sobral & Costa, 2015)). From a therapeutic perspective, it is important to consider managing the fear associated with intimacy when helping couples recover this aspect of their relationship.

Fife and Weeks (2010) identified a number of common fears experienced by individuals in intimate relationships. These include fear of dependence, fear of the expression of feelings, fear of anger, fear of emotional vulnerability, and fear of abandonment.

Togetherness and Individuality

According to Murray Bowen (Bowen, 1978; Kerr & Bowen, 1988), it is best when couples are connected with one another while still maintaining their sense of self. He called this "differentiation of self" and believed that partners are better relationally when they can separate their own thoughts and feelings and preserve their own individuality while being connected romantically with each other. This can also be described as "knowing of self" in the presence of another (Malone, 1987). Bowen described couples who are unable to do this as poorly differentiated. These couples become emotionally overwhelmed under stress and are more emotionally reactive. Poorly differentiated couples are likely to respond with defensive behaviors of withdrawal or attack.

The level of differentiation for couples has a significant impact on the couple's level of intimacy. Highly intimate partners are able to present themselves more authentically in the relationship and communicate their needs more effectively to the other partner (Patrick et al., 2007). They can agree or disagree on intimacy-related concerns without excessive fear of rejection by their partner and are more able to tolerate relational stress without losing intimacy.

Sexuality

Couple therapists are not likely to prioritize discussions about frequency of sexual intercourse or sexual satisfaction even though it would benefit the couple if more clinicians considered taking an integrated approach and incorporated sexual concepts, assessment, and interventions into couples therapy (McCarthy & Thestrup, 2008). Considering gender differences with clinicians, male clinicians are more likely to encourage discussion of sexual issues. Female clinicians tend to initiate significantly fewer discussions (Heitler, 2017). Since the majority of couple therapists are women, it would stand to reason that most couple therapists do not sufficiently explore this essential aspect of marital functioning.

As I reflect on my writing for this chapter, I realize that this was one of the last inclusions of the chapter, a painfully clear indictor of my inadvertent omission of the priority of the topic. Why do clinicians inadvertently avoid or intentionally choose not to address sexual satisfaction and function in session? There are a number of likely reasons.

One obvious possibility is that the clinician may be uncomfortable talking publicly about a very private matter. It could also be that they sense the discomfort of the couple to broach the topic and relent in their exploration. Yet, we know that as the clinician and the couple talk about the topic, each becomes increasingly comfortable with discussing sexuality and is more capable to create change around sexuality. Another possibility is that the clinician may believe they are inadequately trained on the topic. Ongoing continuing-education training programs post-grad are limited. Lastly, since most clinicians view sex therapy as skill based, they likely believe that they do not have the skill set. They may correctly believe that specific sexual problems lay outside their personal competency.

Distressed couples entering therapy are likely to have issues with sexuality. A paradox exists when considering the treatment of sexual dysfunction and distressed couples. When the sexual aspect of the relationship is functional and satisfying, sexuality plays a small, positive role in the relationship. About 15%–20% of couples indicate that sex enhances vitality and satisfaction. However, when sex is dysfunctional, conflictual, or avoided, resulting in a non-sexual relationship, sex plays an inordinately powerful role, draining the relationship of intimacy and threatening marital stability (Keim & Lappin, 2002).

Discussion regarding sexual satisfaction and performance can begin with routine assessment of satisfaction. There are a number of outcome measures that focus on satisfaction, quality of life, and confidence. Table 9.1 lists a number of these outcome measures (Tabatabaie, 2014) that might be useful for clinicians to consider.

Table. 9.1 Measures of Sexual Satisfaction and Quality of Life

The Index of Sexual Satisfaction
Interpersonal Exchange Model of Sexual Satisfaction
The Global Measure of Sexual Satisfaction
The New Sexual Satisfaction Scale
The Sexual Quality of Life—Female
The Sexual Quality of Life—Male
The Sexual Confidence Scale
Sexual Relationship Scale

Assessment of Intimacy: The Intimacy Inventory

Considering that a romantic relationship can be experienced and evaluated according to different aspects simultaneously, it seems important to consider each partner's views of the relationship as it relates to the different aspects of intimacy. The Intimacy Inventory (see Appendix 9.1) that I developed and describe in this chapter is meant to be a quick assessment for the clinician and couple that offers a pictorial view of each partner's perspective on varying aspects of intimacy in the relationship. Each partner completes the Intimacy Inventory and fills in the form (see Appendix 9.2), and when the form is completed in session, it is reviewed by the clinician and the couple immediately. Following is a description of each section of the Intimacy Inventory.

Items are ranked on a scale of less true, generally true, and mostly true. After the couple completes the Intimacy Inventory form, the clinician enters the raw scores into the Excel database (see Appendix 9.1) to generate a number of graphs related to intimacy. Each graph is meant to be discussed by the clinician as a means to explain different aspects of intimacy and attachment. Used at specific intervals throughout treatment, such as at the beginning, mid-treatment, and termination, it can help the couple monitor progress over time. The Intimacy Inventory is also a useful way for the couple to set treatment goals.

The first section of the Intimacy Inventory is titled Closeness. This section, as shown in Table 9.2, specifically measures the perception of disclosure, vulnerability, and emotional volatility, all key ingredients in creating a sense of closeness in the relationship. For interpretation of the Closeness Graph, couples are encouraged to note where they are on the graph as a couple and are taught that higher levels of disclosure and vulnerability are needed to create a strong sense of closeness.

Trust questions, as shown in Table 9.3, focus on consistency of truth, accessibility of the partner, availability when absent from the partner, and reliability with meeting commitments and moral values. This section is tailored to couples trying to recover intimacy following infidelity, particularly early on in the treatment process.

If you prefer a more general assessment of trust in this section, statements number two and three on the scale can be substituted with My *partner is personally present in this relationship* and My *partner works to resolve issues when they arise*. These substitute questions focus on the commitment to be present consistently

Table 9.2 Closeness

	Less True	*Generally True*	*Mostly True*
Section 1: Closeness			
I believe that we can share private thoughts and feelings with each other.	1 2 3	4 5 6 7	8 9 10
We can talk about things of significant meaning and feeling.	1 2 3	4 5 6 7	8 9 10
I can share private details of my life with my partner that I could with no other.	1 2 3	4 5 6 7	8 9 10
There is a fair amount of emotional volatility in our relationship.	1 2 3	4 5 6 7	8 9 10

Table 9.3 Trust

	Less True	*Generally True*	*Mostly True*
Section 2: Trust			
We are consistently truthful with one another.	1 2 3	4 5 6 7	8 9 10
My partner's whereabouts are known to me and not hidden.	1 2 3	4 5 6 7	8 9 10
My partner is available and responsive to my phone calls and texts when we are not together.	1 2 3	4 5 6 7	8 9 10
My partner follows through with commitments to me.	1 2 3	4 5 6 7	8 9 10
My partner has integrity as seen through strong moral values.	1 2 3	4 5 6 7	8 9 10

in the relationship and work for the common good of the relationship and repair when needed.

Interpretation of the Trust Graph can include a discussion about the importance of accountability and accessibility of each partner during a time when the relationship feels fairly insecure. Though accessibility here is defined in terms of being connected during times of disconnection (when one partner is at work, for example), it is also important to reiterate that accessibility also means that each partner has accessibility to their partner's inner world of thoughts, feelings, and values.

As listed in Table 9.4, these four statements in the Connection section of the Intimacy Inventory were suggested by Bartholomew and Horowitz (1991) to determine the strength of their orientation around the four attachment styles for each partner. The attachment styles and questions are listed as follows:

Secure Attachment: It is easy for me to become emotionally close to others. I am comfortable depending on them and having them depend on me. I don't worry about being alone or having others not accept me.

Table 9.4 Closeness

	Less True	*Generally True*	*Mostly True*
Section 3: Connection			
It is easy for me to become emotionally close to others. I am comfortable depending on them and having them depend on me. I don't worry about being alone or having others not accept me.	1 2 3	4 5 6 7	8 9 10
I am comfortable without close emotional relationships. It's very important to me to feel independent and self-sufficient, and I prefer not to depend on others or have others depend on me.	1 2 3	4 5 6 7	8 9 10
I am uncomfortable getting close to others. I want emotionally close relationships, but I find it difficult to trust others completely, or to depend on them. I worry that I will be hurt if I allow myself to become too close to others.	1 2 3	4 5 6 7	8 9 10
I want to be completely emotionally intimate with others, but I often find that others are reluctant to get as close as I would like. I am uncomfortable being without close relationships, but I sometimes worry that others don't value me as much as I value them.	1 2 3	4 5 6 7	8 9 10

Dismissive-Avoidant: I am comfortable without close emotional relationships. It's very important to me to feel independent and self-sufficient, and I prefer not to depend on others or have others depend on me.

Fearful-Avoidant: I am uncomfortable getting close to others. I want emotionally close relationships, but I find it difficult to trust others completely, or to depend on them. I worry that I will be hurt if I allow myself to become too close to others.

Anxious/Preoccupied: I want to be completely emotionally intimate with others, but I often find that others are reluctant to get as close as I would like. I am uncomfortable being without close relationships, but I sometimes worry that others don't value me as much as I value them.

Interpretation of the Connection section includes a general definition of the attachment styles. Each partner's attachment orientation is pictured on a separate graph. The clinician can ask the couple if the graph is a fair representation of how they approach their relationship with their partner. This can be a new beginning of insight for some couples around their attachment communication and how they are attempting to get their attachment needs met.

Dimensions

The last section of the inventory, illustrated by Table 9.5, reviews the dimensions of intimacy that are commonly thought of when couples define intimacy.

Table 9.5 Dimensions

	Less True	*Generally True*	*Mostly True*
Section 4: Dimensions			
We share enjoyable times with each other.	1 2 3	4 5 6 7	8 9 10
We have common recreational interest.	1 2 3	4 5 6 7	8 9 10
We participate in activities together.	1 2 3	4 5 6 7	8 9 10
We share purpose and meaning in life, including our philosophy and religious experience.	1 2 3	4 5 6 7	8 9 10
As a couple, we enjoy mutual friends.	1 2 3	4 5 6 7	8 9 10
As a couple, we have a good social network.	1 2 3	4 5 6 7	8 9 10
We are sexually close to each other.	1 2 3	4 5 6 7	8 9 10
I feel sensual satisfaction.	1 2 3	4 5 6 7	8 9 10
We have a fair amount of romance in our relationship.	1 2 3	4 5 6 7	8 9 10
We enjoy passionate times together.	1 2 3	4 5 6 7	8 9 10
We face and struggle with differences together.	1 2 3	4 5 6 7	8 9 10
We pursue mutual conflict resolution.	1 2 3	4 5 6 7	8 9 10
We respond together in a united way to pressures of life.	1 2 3	4 5 6 7	8 9 10
We have closeness in coping with problems and pain.	1 2 3	4 5 6 7	8 9 10
We are good with financial decision-making.	1 2 3	4 5 6 7	8 9 10

With most couples, the process of ranking the dimensions of intimacy and discussing their graph in session will fuel goal setting around increasing intimacy.

Treatment Ideas for Recovering or Increasing Intimacy

It should come as no surprise that one of the primary session interventions for intimacy is the strategic influence the clinician has on the discourse in session. The clinician will need to limit hostile exchanges, limit emotional volatility, and thwart efforts by the couple to disengage. As emotional volatility decreases, the clinician increasingly asks the couple to talk to each other while the clinician stays on the periphery to coach the conversation. This is the process of enactment.

Use of Enactments in Session

There are a number of guidelines for helping couples recover intimacy in their relationships. Fife and Weeks (2010) state that the first thing the clinician needs to do is to make sure that they create a safe environment. Since intimacy requires vulnerability, the clinician is a strong influencing factor in creating safety. When emotional safety is established, the primary function of the therapist is to enhance the communication of the couple through enactments that emphasize the speaker/listener role. These enactments should be completed with the couple facing one another and attuning to the meaning and feeling of the content shared. The clinician can also probe with questions and offer reflections to help guide increasing disclosure. I would encourage you to refer back to chapter seven on communication for a detailed review of the enactment process.

Couple Daily Connections for Reactivation of Basic Intimacy

Between-session tasks should be considered when couples are interested in restarting their intimate connection. There are a number of small connections that couples can do throughout the day to make positive connections with each other. Here is a list of just a few:

1) Four points in time: The couple could share with each other how they would like to behave and feel during four important points of time in their day: 1) in the morning when they awake, 2) when they separate for the day to go to work, 3) when they return home in the evening after work, and 4) when they go to bed. Couples that have "nontraditional" schedules would select points of time based on their work schedules.
2) Increasing basic physical connections such as holding hands, offering back rubs, stroking the partner, and hugging more.
3) Creating random acts of kindness for the partner without any expectation for reciprocity.
4) Create fifteen minutes of tenderness with each other in the evening.
5) Have a discussion about each other's passions. Get involved in each other's passions.
6) Do something special for the partner.
7) Celebrate an anniversary or other important event; celebrate some aspect of the relationship.
8) Have fun together.
9) Build a spiritual connection, including going to church or discussing the meaning of life and personal values.
10) Be social together.

Treatment Ideas for Sexual Satisfaction and Functioning

The PLISSIT Model Applied to Couples Therapy

A general model for addressing sexual concerns is the PLISSIT model of sex therapy. This model is useful because it offers a linear approach to the increasing level of interventions that can be used by the clinician. The first level is permission (P), which involves the clinician's giving the client permission to feel comfortable about a topic or permission to change their lifestyle or to get medical assistance. Many couples will need only this level of treatment because creating permission to speak about the topic will move them towards change.

The second level is limited information (LI), in which the clinician offers limited and specific information on the topic. It is important for the clinician to have a number of resources available for the varied issues that might be brought up in therapy. This would also include organizations, support groups, and referral information for specialists.

The third level is specific suggestions (SS). Here the clinician offers suggestions related to the specific problem. These interventions tend to focus on increasing levels of emotional intimacy, increasing the levels of sexual satisfaction and functioning.

The fourth and final level is intensive therapy (IT), which could include a referral for a couple to other mental health or medical professionals who can help the client deal with the deeper, underlying issues and concerns being expressed.

Another general model to consider for the treatment of sexual problems is starting with the "good-enough sex" model by Metz and McCarthy (2004, 2007, 2010). This model is an integrative approach that moves couples away from the perspective of performance as a predictor of sexual quality and satisfaction to "good-enough sex" that is playful instead of perfect. Treatment should acknowledge that performance is variable and related to each partner's emotional and physical state (Tabatabaie, 2014).

Sensate Focus for Sensuality and Sexuality

Some couples have a non-existent sexual relationship, or sexuality is a rare occurrence. Sometimes this is due to performance pressures during sexual intercourse or when performance pressure is a concern in restarting sexuality. Sensate focus is a nice way to activate sensuality and sexuality because it removes performance pressure by setting a clear limit to sexual behavior. With sensate focus, the couple is instructed to create a specific time in the evening where they will explore physical sensual/sexual touch. The couple is told to refrain from having intercourse, focusing instead on the range of physical sensations that can be elicited by touch. Sensate focus is seen as an intervention in itself and not a prelude to sex, so the "goal" of a sexual encounter is removed. The couple learns to heighten their awareness of a broader range of stimuli that includes all of the senses.

There can be a number of guidelines that can be suggested to the couple (Fryer, 2010). The couple is instructed that there is a ban on sexual intercourse and, at the start, also on genital touching. No attempt should be made to involve the partner in intercourse. The couple should try to do the exercises twice weekly for a month. They can start with twenty minutes per session and increase to an hour. There should be no talking during the exercise, with the exception of when touch is uncomfortable. After each session is complete, the couple can share their feelings about the exercise. The point here is that couples should stay focused on the here-and-now of the experience of sensate focus.

Sensate focus moves through stages (Fryer, 2010). Stage 1 involves being naked and touching, but without touching the genitals or breasts and without proceeding to intercourse. This focus is on touching the partner without intending to create pleasure for the partner but to enjoy touching the partner. This stage can be continued for several weeks.

In stage 2 the partners continue the exercises in stage 1, but now include genital touching. They should consider taking time to get comfortable and relaxed at this stage. For the giving partner, it is important that the aim here is about exploration, not pleasing the partner. They should continue to focus on the other's whole body, not just their genitals.

Stage 3 is about entering into the vagina without further movement. There should be no movement, no thrusting. This is a really important step for men with erectile problems or premature ejaculation. For homosexual couples this stage needs to be altered to include intromission of other objects, or entering into the mouth or anus as desired, or holding the genitals against the body of the partner—for example a man may place his penis between the buttocks of his partner. The couple can include oral contact with genitals but with no movement. This focus is not on arousal but exploration. When comfortable, the couple can include slow movement and thrusting, followed by stronger thrusting until the couple can lift the ban on intercourse.

Specific Sex Therapy Interventions

According to the Association of Reproductive Health Professionals (2017), there are a number of common strategies used by sex therapists to help couples reconnect emotionally and sexually:

1) Creating Realistic and Appropriate Goals

In developing goals, the couple needs to have a clear understanding of the problem. Sometimes this requires education or exploration around a specific topic: for example, understanding male and female sexual responses, anxiety or inhibition in sexuality, and physical problems. Education about a sexual problem is often the first step in treatment and goal setting.

2) Exploration of Sexual Fantasies

Clinicians may recommend bibliotherapy, the use of erotic books or videos to spur fantasies. In addition, the sharing of fantasies with a partner can improve relationship communication about what a partner finds arousing and may help a couple revive or develop a new sexual repertoire.

3) Identifying the Context for Initiating Sexual Activity

A clinician can help the couple identify the typical context for initiating sexual behavior. This could include the time of day, the interval between sexual encounters, and how each partner indicates their interest and desire for sexual intimacy. Topics can also include measuring levels of desire for sex and levels of satisfaction, as well as recommendations for increasing desire, arousal, and satisfaction.

4) Cueing Exercises

Cueing exercises are designed to help each partner remember instances in life when they felt healthy and sexy and had a satisfactory level of sexual desire. The partner is instructed to recall their physical appearance, the setting, the smells in the air, the music they were hearing, and the foods he or she was eating at that time and use these as "cues" for feeling sexual in the current relationship.

5) Assigning Sensate Focus Exercises

These behavioral exercises involve a couple taking turns touching one another to heightened awareness of what types of strokes and caresses are most arousing and to remove goal-oriented behavior focus, such as intercourse and climax. Sensate focusing can be both genital and non-genital in nature. It often begins with limited sensual massage of the face, hands, and neck and progresses over time to include sexual intercourse. The exercises are not tied to sexual intercourse, and intercourse is initially discouraged.

6) Exploring Alternative Forms of Sexual Expression

This can include education on sensual massage; fondling and caressing; mutual masturbation; manual, oral, and anal stimulation techniques; use of sexual enhancing toys, such as vibrators; and trying a variety of sexual positions for sexual intercourse.

7) Addressing Sexual Boredom

A couple who has been together for many years can fall into a sexual routine that is unimaginative and boring, reducing sexual desire. A clinician can offer a number of suggestions for reviving a boring sex life, such as changing the venue for sex, as well as sex education books and videos to explore new techniques.

8) Discussing Dilators and EROS Devices

There are a number of tools at the disposal of couples. For a woman suffering from vaginismus, there are vaginal dilators along with a functionalized program that can help reduce anxiety and help facilitate stretching of the vagina. Successful treatment hinges on the partner's being taught how to insert and use dilators appropriately. For a woman with arousal and/or orgasm disorders, sex therapists may recommend the EROS Clitoral Stimulator, a prescription-only device that utilizes suction to draw blood to the clitoral region.

References

Adams, J. M., & Jones, W. H. (1999). Interpersonal commitment in historical perspective. In J. M. Adams & W. H. Jones (Eds.), *Handbook of interpersonal commitment and relationship stability* (pp. 3–33). New York: Kluwer Academic.

Association of Reproductive Health Professionals. (2017). *Sex therapy for non-sex therapists*. Retrieved January 29, 2017 from www.arhp.org/uploadDocs/SHF_Therapy.pdf.

Bartholomew, K., & Horowitz, L. M. (1991). Attachment styles of young adults: A test of a four-category model. *Journal of Personality and Social Psychology, 61*(2), 226–244.

Bowen, M. (1978). *Family therapy in clinical practice*. New York: Jason Aronson.

Brown, B. (2016). *Courage works*. Retrieved January 28, 2016 from http://brenebrown.com/.

Dibble, J. L., Levine, T. R., & Park, H. S. (2011). The unidimensional relationship closeness scale (URCS): Reliability and validity evidence for a new measure of relationship closeness. *Psychological Assessment*, V *24*(3), 565–572. Advance online publication. doi:10.1037/a0026265

Fife, S. T., & Weeks, G. R. (2010). Barriers to recovering intimacy. In J. Carlson & L. Sperry (Eds.), *Recovering intimacy in love relationships: A clinician's guide* (pp. 157–179). New York: Routledge.

Fryer, T. (2010, May 6). *A brief introduction to sensate focus*. Workshop material, Child Focus, Inc.

Goddard, H. W., & Olsen, C. S. (2004). Cooperative extension initiatives in marriage and couples education. *Family Relations*, *53*, 433–439.

Gross, J. J. (2014). Emotion regulation: Conceptual and empirical foundations. In J. J. Gross (Ed.), *Handbook of emotion regulation* (2nd ed.). New York: Guilford.

Heitler, S. (2017). *Why do marriage therapists undertreat sexual problems?* Retrieved January 29, 2017 from www.psychologytoday.com/blog/resolution-not-conflict/201201/why-do-marriage-therapists-undertreat-sexual-problems.

Keim, J., & Lappin, J. (2002). Short term couples treatment: A structural/strategic perspective. In A. Gurman & N. Jacobson (Eds.), *Clinical handbook of couple therapy* (third edition). New York: Guilford Press.

Kerr, M. E., & Bowen, M. (1988). *Family evaluation*. New York: W. W. Norton & Company.

Khalifian, C. E., & Barry, R. A. (2016). Trust, attachment, and mindfulness influence intimacy and disengagement during newlyweds' discussions of relationship transgressions. *Journal of Family Psychology*, V *30*(5), 592–601.

Malone, T. P., & Malone, P. T. (1987). *The art of intimacy*. New York: Simon & Schuster.

Marmarosh, C. L. (2014). Fostering new relational experience: Clinical process in couple therapy. *Psychotherapy, 51*(1), 1–6.

McCarthy, B., & Thestrup, M. (2008). Men, intimacy, and eroticism. *The Journal of Sexual Medicine*, V 6, 588–594.

Metz, M. E., & McCarthy, B. W. (2004). *Coping with erectile dysfunction: How to regain confidence and enjoy great sex* (p. 278). Oakland, CA: New Harbinger Publications, Inc.

Metz, M. E., & McCarthy, B. W. (2007). The 'good-enough sex' model for couple sexual satisfaction. *Sexual and Relationship Therapy*, *22*(3), 351–362. doi:10.1080/14681990601013492

Metz, M. E., & McCarthy, B. W. (2010). *Enduring desire: Your guide to lifelong intimacy*. New York: Routledge.

Patrick, S., Sells, J. N., Giordano, F. G., & Tollerud, T. R. (2007). Intimacy, differentiation, and personality variables as predictors of marital satisfaction. *The Family Journal: Counseling and Therapy for Couples and Families*, *15*(4), 359–367. doi:10.1177/1066480707303754.

Prager, K., & Buhrmester, D. (1998). Intimacy and need fulfillment in couple relationships. *Journal of Social and Personal Relationships*, *15*(4), 435–469.

Rogers, C. R. (1958, September). Characteristics of a helping relationship. *Personnel & Guidance Journal*, *37*, 6–16.

Shepherd, P. (2016). *Guided meditation*. Retrieved February 11, 2016 from www.trans4mind.com/jamesharveystout/guidedme.htm#The technique of guided meditation.

Sobral, M. P., & Costa, M. E. (2015). Development of the fear of intimacy components questionnaire. *European Journal of Psychological Assessment*, *V31*, 302–309.

Solomon, M. (1985). Treatment of narcissistic and borderline disorders in marital therapy: A four-year follow-up study. *Journal of Consulting and Clinical Psychology*, 59, 138–141.

Sternberg, R. J. (1986). A triangular theory of love. *Psychological Review*, *93*(2), 119–135.

Tabatabaiea, A. (2014). "Does sex therapy work? How can we know?": Measuring outcomes in sex therapy. *Sexual and Relationship Therapy*, *29*(3), 269–279. doi:http://dx.doi.org/10.1080/14681994.2014.915705.

Tani, F., Pascuzzi, D., & Raffagnino, R. (2015). Emotion regulation and quality of close relationship: The effects of emotion dysregulation processes on couple intimacy. *Applied Psychology Bulletin* (Bollettino di Psicologia Applicata), *63*(272), 3–15.

Van den Broucke, S., Vandereycken, W., & Vertommen, H. (1995). Marital intimacy: Conceptualization and assessment. *Clinical Psychology Review*, *15*(3), 217–233.

Appendix 9.1

The Intimacy Inventory

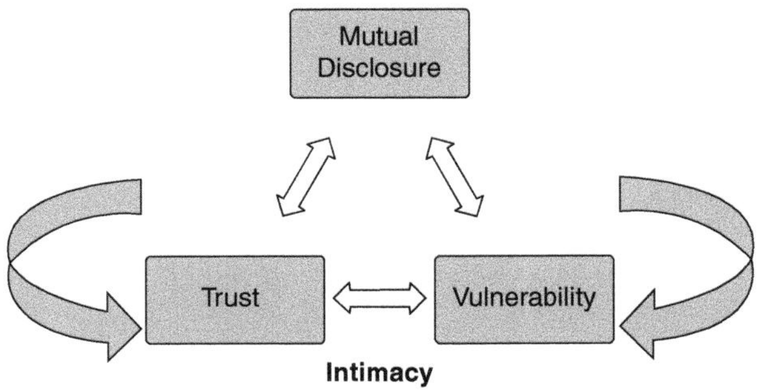

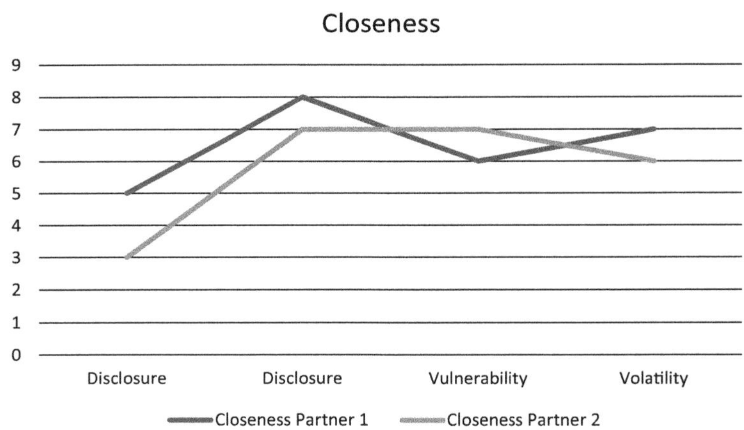

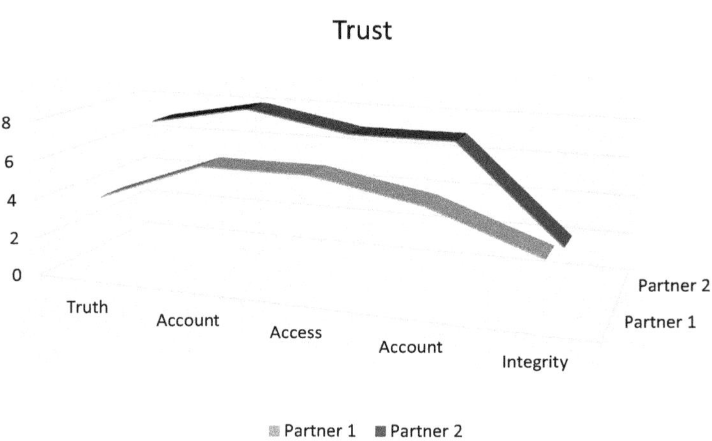

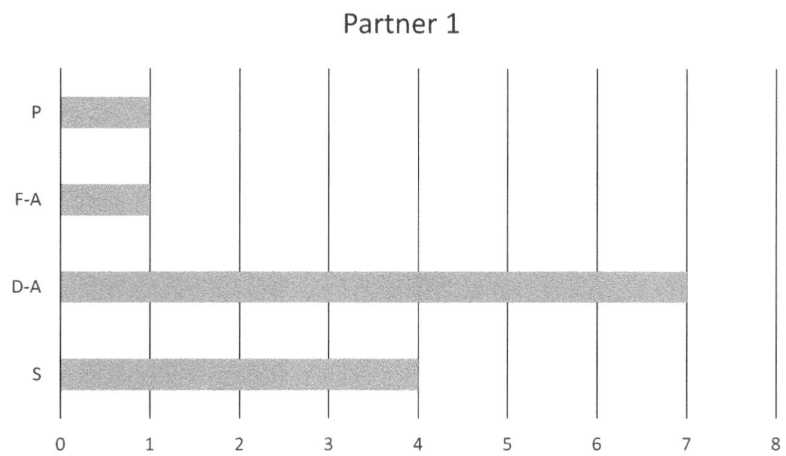

Partner 1
P
F-A
D-A
S
0
1
2
3
4
5
6
7
8

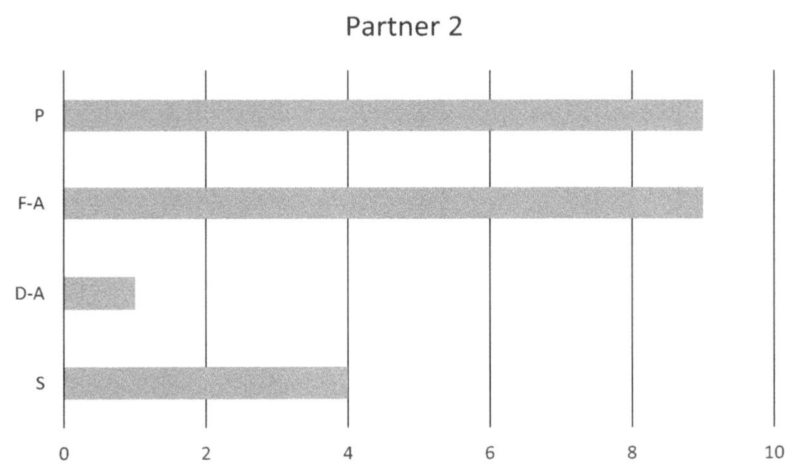

Partner 2
P
F-A
D-A
S
0
2
4
6
8
10

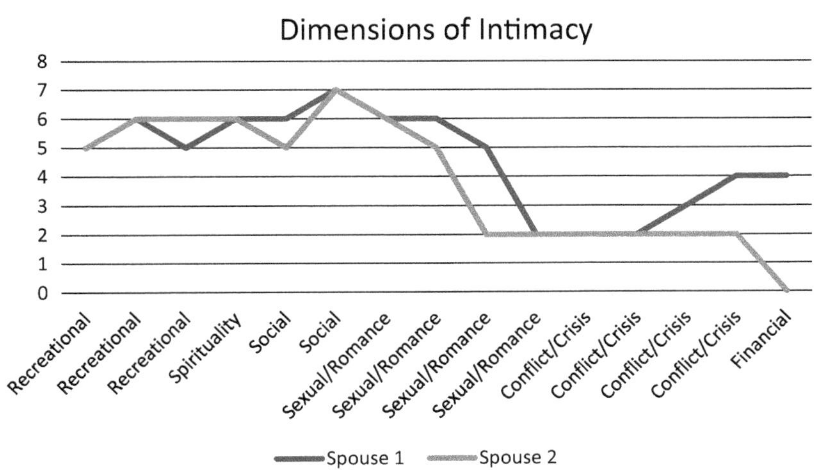

Dimensions of Intimacy
8
7
6
5
4
3
2
1
0
Recreational
Recreational
Recreational
Spirituality
Social
Social
Sexual/Romance
Sexual/Romance
Sexual/Romance
Sexual/Romance
Conflict/Crisis
Conflict/Crisis
Conflict/Crisis
Conflict/Crisis
Financial
Spouse 1
Spouse 2

Appendix 9.2

Intimacy Inventory Form

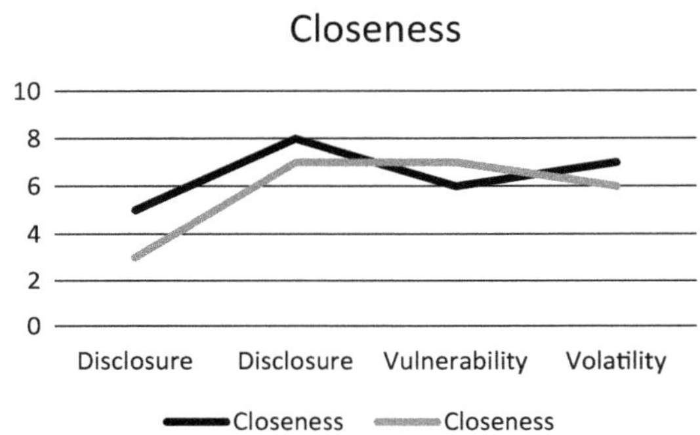

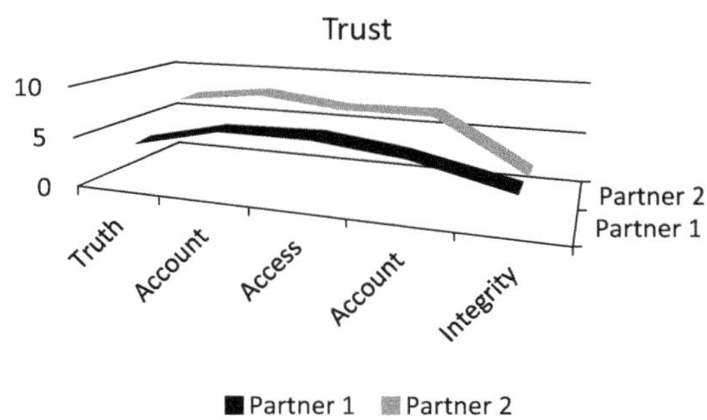

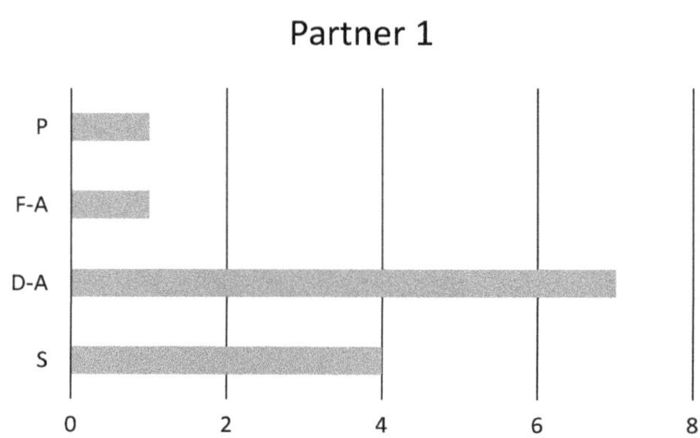

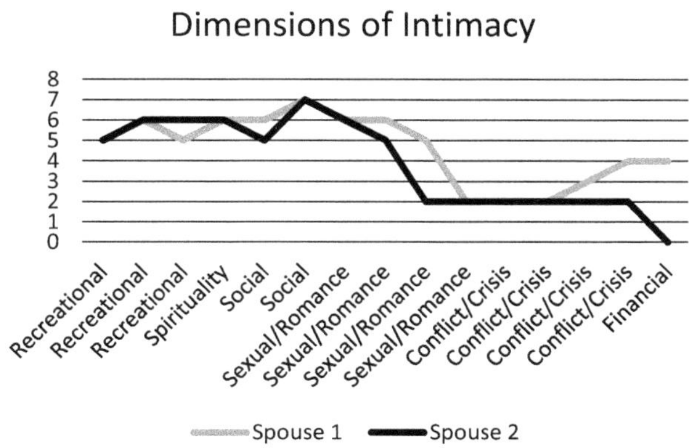
Dimensions of Intimacy
8
7
6
5
4
3
2
1
0
Recreational
Recreational
Recreational
Spirituality
Social
Social
Sexual/Romance
Sexual/Romance
Sexual/Romance
Sexual/Romance
Conflict/Crisis
Conflict/Crisis
Conflict/Crisis
Conflict/Crisis
Financial
Spouse 1
Spouse 2

10 Trust

Trust seems easily defined when you read the definition on any of the online dictionaries. The definition usually only takes one sentence: for example, "Firm belief in the reliability, truth, or ability of someone or something" (Oxford Living Dictionaries, 2017) or "assured reliance on the character, ability, strength, or truth of someone or something" (Merriam-Webster, 2017). Rousseau et al. (1998) offer a nice definition of trust, defining trust as a psychological state comprising the intention to accept vulnerability based upon positive expectations of the intentions or behavior of another.

Ultimately, trust in relationships is a multidimensional construct that when in place results in a trusting relationship. Trust is the fruit of a trusting relationship. Each partner has to have the primary characteristics of trustworthiness and intentionally contribute these characteristics to the relationship through thought and behavior, consistently over time.

The Temporal Aspect of Trust

When couples talk in session about re-establishing trust, they most certainly recognize that it will take substantial time and intentional work. It can be helpful to discuss trust in terms of the mechanisms of temporal change and how this affects the re-establishment of trust. According to Vanneste, Puranam, and Kretschmer (2014), there are several ways in which time affects trust, including initial bias correction, change through contextual experience, and trust-based selection and identification.

Initial Bias Correction

Before entering any relationship, a person may be pessimistic, optimistic, or unbiased in their perspective about the other person's trustworthiness. This orientation comes from past experience in relationships and family of origin. A pessimistic person underestimates trustworthiness, an optimistic person overestimates trustworthiness, and an unbiased person makes an accurate estimation. As the relationship develops, the person gradually moves within the relationship to a more accurate assessment of trustworthiness. This initial bias has an effect on both the willingness to begin the relationship and the evolution of trust within the relationship once it is established. For a person who has an unbiased perspective, trust will remain constant over time.

For couples trying to recover trust, their early formation of trust in the relationship may give a clue to how long the recovery of trust will take. It would make sense that a partner with a pessimistic perspective at the start of the relationship may take a longer period of time to re-establish trust.

Change Through Contextual Experience

Trust is contextual. A person may trust in one context but not another. For example, an individual will describe that he or she is trusting of a partner when that partner is at work but not when at lunch with coworkers. For this reason, if one partner interacts in ways that promote trust in different contexts over time, then trust in the given context can change even when perceived trustworthiness in the relationship remains constant.

Understanding context, then, can be clinically useful. First, trust-building efforts can and may need to be directed at specific contexts, such as demonstrating boundaries when out with coworkers. Second, couples can rebuild trust in specific contexts even when overall trust is either low or high. For example, trust building can take place in a specific context even when the trust in the relationship is vulnerable. This allows for general and targeted interventions.

Trust-Based Selection and Identification

Recovering trust is hard work. Over time, unsuccessful experiences in relationships play a crucial role in the evolution of trust. People prefer to maintain relationships with trustworthy partners. The good news is that consistency in trust-reinforcing behaviors can lead to the decision to stay in the relationship, but trust-eroding behaviors will lead someone to leave the relationship and prefer not to be with someone with similar characteristics.

If trustworthy behaviors continue, the partner also begins to identify with the other person; they will have caring feelings for the other person, increasing trust. For these reasons, it is important for trust-building behaviors to be consistent over time.

Trust as a Function of the Characteristics of the Person

Trust is more than a combination of behaviors. Trustworthiness is also a function of the characteristics of the person. When trust is broken, it is these characteristics that have been breached in the relationship. Recovering trust will require a recommitment to the breached characteristics. Since a trusting relationship requires consistency over time, the feeling of trust may not occur for quite a while, even when one or both partners are demonstrating trustworthy behaviors.

The following material can be useful when exploring the topic of trust with couples. I use the Ten Characteristics of a Trustworthy Partner (see Appendix 10.1) with any couple who is struggling with trust. If infidelity is an issue, I will include the section Strategies for Restoring Trust After Infidelity (see Appendix 10.2). These two topics complement each other.

References

Merriam-Webster. (2017). *Definition of trust*. Retrieved March 10, 2017 from www.merriam-webster.com/dictionary/trust.

Oxford Online Dictionaries. (2017). *Definition of trust in English*. Retrieved March 10, 2017 from https://en.oxforddictionaries.com/definition/trust.

Rousseau, D. M., Sitkin, S. B., Burt, R. S., & Camerer, C. (1998). Not so different after all: A cross-discipline view of trust. *Academy of Management Review*, *23*(3), 393–404.

Vanneste, B. S., Puranam, P., & Kretschmer, T. (2014). Trust over time in exchange relationships: Meta-analysis and theory. *Strategic Management Journal*, *35*, 1891–1902.

Appendix 10.1

Ten Key Characteristics of a Trustworthy Partner

1. Integrity

Integrity means doing the right thing at all times and in all circumstances, whether or not anyone is watching. That means the person with integrity has a strong adherence to their moral and ethical principles, and these principles inform and guide their behavior. Someone with integrity operates beyond basic ethics and lives life by their virtue ethics. Basic ethics tells us right from wrong and answers the question "How should I behave?" However, those operating from virtue ethics concern themselves with the question "What kind of person should I be?" Virtue ethics is embedded in their characters, and they behave consistently with truth, honesty, and compassion, regardless of what others think or do.

2. Honesty

Honesty, in part, is about telling the truth. It also implies fairness in dealing with others and the refusal to engage in deceit or secrets. Honesty is also a demonstration of good character. A person who is consistently honest has integrity, and when you hold the same values in all circumstances, it is easy to be honest.

3. Reliability

A reliable partner is someone that you can depend on to be consistent in character, judgment, and behavior. When they commit to doing something, you can depend on them to keep their commitments. It is easy to predict how they will respond in specific situations because they put their values into practice.

4. Accountability

Partners in trusting relationships openly share how they spend their time and energy throughout the day. They share where they have been, where they intend to be, and who and what gets their attention or does not get their attention.

5. Advocacy

An advocate cares and nurtures the relationship. They pay special attention to the state of the relationship and have sensitivity to when thing go awry. They quickly attend to repairing when tension occurs in the relationship or conflict arises.

6. Vulnerability

It is in risking greater vulnerability in a safe relationship that one can grow in trust. Increased emotional exposure by both partners will create greater intimacy in the relationship. At the deepest level, directly exposing one's pain to another who hears with compassion and understanding creates a confidential relationship that cultivates trust.

7. Accessibility

Pragmatically, an accessible partner is one who will answer the phone when their partner calls or responds to voicemails and texts in a reasonable time. An accessible partner also shares their internal world with their partner, without the need for any prompting. They will openly share their thoughts, feelings, convictions, longings, fears, and doubts. There is a willingness to share these and have open dialogue about them.

8. Presence

Intimate, trusting relationships take effort, and both partners need to have a strong personal presence in the relationship. This means that they need to commit a great deal of their energy to being mentally, physically, and emotionally available to their partner. Spending time together is a priority, and the time together is intellectually and emotionally engaging. In times of crisis, the couple makes their partner a priority over everything else.

9. Transparency

To be transparent is to make intentional choices to allow key information regarding relationship health and fidelity to easily and consistently be available to both parties without requiring a direct request for the information. Nothing in either partner's communications to anyone should need to be so private that it could not be shared openly and willingly with both partners.

10. Commitment

Commitment is the mutually agreed-upon promise to one another to be exclusive. It means that partners are "closed" to other options, emotional or physical. Committed couples also create a barrier to all others that might be a risk to the relationship. This barrier protects the intimacy of the relationship and helps committed partners to be dedicated to the growth, health, passion, and vitality of the relationship.

Appendix 10.2

Strategies for Restoring Trust After Infidelity

Using the same ten characteristics of a trustworthy partner mentioned in the previous section, I find it helpful to give the following information (including the Ten Characteristics of a Trustworthy Person) to couples when they first come into treatment for infidelity. The following outline is set up as a handout and is an excellent complement to a structured discussion with the couple. It is written in language directed to the person who had the affair.

1. Integrity

- Start to think of yourself as someone whom your partner should and can trust. Thinking of yourself this way is the first step toward making it happen.
- Think of the values that you want to demonstrate to your partner. Directly state them to your partner.
- Tell your partner directly that you want him or her to trust you again.

2. Honesty

- Stop lying immediately and strive for honesty. After betraying your partner's trust, you will only hurt your partner more by continuing to lie, change variations of the truth, hide information, or deny aspects of the truth. Do not protect your partner's feelings by hiding parts of the truth: you really are not protecting him or her.
- Today, tell your partner that you want him or her to know all the details of the affair. Provide the complete story up front and do so voluntarily.
- All future statements should be truthful.

3. Reliability

- Today, ask your partner what you can do to make him or her feel safe. Ask him or her to suggest five things that you can do to help.
- Implement the suggestions with tenacity.

- Some suggestions will be harder than others. If you believe that you can't make the commitment for one of the suggestions, be honest and say so.
- Do not commit to anything that you cannot follow through with.

4. Accountability

- Each day, tell your partner your plans for the day and whom you will be with. At the end of the day, review the same. Yes, it may feel like you are seeking permission or that he/ or she is keeping tabs on you. Remember, you kept a part of your world hidden from your partner, and what seemed reality was not. Any secret now will damage the trust you are trying to build.

5. Advocacy

- Triggers are a challenging experience for your partner. Triggers are external or internal cues that lead to distress. External triggers could be any sight, sound, smell, location, date of the year, or scene in a movie or television show. Internal triggers can include passing thoughts, intrusive or reoccurring thoughts, physical sensations, feelings towards you (positive or negative), defensive reactions from you, or comments from other people. You can help your partner with emotional and behavioral experiences when triggered. Notice when your partner is quiet, and offer to talk.
- Today, ask your partner if he or she is eating, sleeping, etc., and whether he or she is doing okay. This may seem basic, but if your partner is in a traumatic state, he or she may not be functioning normally and may be too distraught to convey or even meet personal needs.
- Next, sit together and identify three common triggers that he or she is experiencing.
- Talk about what behavioral signs you see associated with these triggers. This will help your respond with compassion when you see them.
- Ask for specific things to do when he or she is triggered (interventions).
- Daily, notice either the early warning signs or behaviors signs that your partner is triggered and implement the intervention(s). Your goal is to limit or eliminate your partner's triggers.

6. Vulnerability

- Be there to listen, even though you are the person who caused the pain.
- Today, initiate one conversation about some aspect of the pain. Listen with compassion, without defensiveness, and show curiosity by asking questions. Try to get a deeper understanding of what he or she is going through. Your interest will show to your partner that you have not forgotten the pain you caused and that you are a partner in his or her healing.

7. Accessibility

- The more open you are about what you are doing, the less urgency your partner will feel to check in on your activities. Ease his or her insecurities by letting your partner know what you're doing and checking in with messages or quick phone calls when you are not at home.
- Remember that your phone, email, voicemail, and social media account were all in commission of your affair. More than likely, they may feel like sources of secrets and lies to your partner. If you choose to provide voluntary access to these things, your partner may trust you more quickly. You are sending a message that you have nothing to hide. If you cannot offer this access, it would be fair to question what you are indeed hiding.
- Today, invite your partner to go someplace that you typically would go alone, for example, invite him or her to go out with you and your friends or to work out together.

8. Presence

- Your partner needs opportunity to work through things with you, so you need to be spending plenty of time together. At minimum, you need to be emotionally available. However, physical presence is better because it will also counteract your partner's feelings that you don't value him or her.
- If you can't be with your partner physically, keep your phone on whenever possible so that they have access to you. He or she may not even need to call or message you, but knowing where you are and that you are available may help him or her see you in a more positive way. Send text messages of love and that you are thinking of him or her throughout the day.

9. Transparency

- Just because your partner does not bring up the infidelity does not mean it is not on his or her mind. It probably is on his or her mind much of the day. When you are thinking about it, let your partner know. It gives the message that you are still aware of the pain that you have caused and that you have not forgotten and moved on.
- Avoid saying "I don't know," "I can't remember," or "it just happened." Instead, respond with expanded descriptions of how you behaved, what you thought at the time, or how you felt at the time. Any one of these responses is better than "I don't know."
- Don't forget that you are also hurting and maybe feel that you do not have the right to share your feelings. When you are sad, share it. Just make sure that you do not state it in a way that discounts your partner's feelings. For example, don't say, "I am feeling sad too." That would be discounting.

10. Commitment

- The commitment in your relationship feels very fragile for both of you. It is important that what you say and do conveys a new level of commitment.
- If you have not already done so, end the affair openly and immediately. There should be no clandestine meetings with the affair partner to say goodbye. Any message or contact with the affair partner should be in full view of your partner.
- Be patient with the healing and recovery process.
- Make your partner a priority again. Show your appreciation that he or she is willing to stay in the relationship with you.
- Show your partner love: go to new places and try new activities. In essence, you are creating a new relationship with him or her.

11 The Trauma of Infidelity

The thoughts only go away when I sleep,
but they are waiting there for me when I wake up late at night.

—Former client

Infidelity as a presenting problem is not an uncommon occurrence in counseling. It is estimated that 50%–65% of couples in therapy are dealing with infidelity (Atkins et al., 2005). Issues of infidelity in couple relationships present their own brand of difficulty for couples' counselors. In many ways, couples that enter counseling for infidelity are at a high level of crisis, and clinicians should expect to employ methods of crisis response to a higher degree, especially in the early sessions.

Clinicians recognize that counseling for infidelity takes a specific skill set to be effective. There are several reasons why infidelity treatment is different. Couples need to know that the clinician they hire has seen their issue before, has proven strategies specifically to manage the situation, and has had success with it.

When couples enter infidelity treatment, they need direct, active interventions from a clinician who is equipped to offer crisis intervention strategies specific to the experience of infidelity, not merely a clinician who is a "good listener." Early sessions need to focus on creating therapeutic boundaries; setting boundaries with friends, family, and the affair partner; limiting future negative impact; and other stabilizing interventions.

Where Clinicians Go Wrong

One primary mistake that clinicians make when treating infidelity is not recognizing that all affairs are different. How couples respond to infidelity is also different; some affairs will end the relationship while others will create an opportunity for the couple to develop a deeper level of intimacy in the relationship (Peluso & Spina, 2008).

Another common error clinicians make is treating the affair as the sole issue and failing to see how the affair is communicating information about the state of the relationship between the couple (Peluso & Spina, 2008). The affair can be seen as representing an attempt to resolve an existing problem. Clinicians need to recognize this, delve into the context and underlying dynamics of the relationship, and match their approach and interventions to the type of infidelity the couple has experienced. Emily Brown (2001, 2014) categorized affairs into six types based on the underlying issues:

Conflict-Avoidance Affair

The couple expressing this affair is terrified to be anything but nice for fear that conflict will lead to abandonment or losing control. The affair can also be seen as an attempt to get unaddressed issues out in the open.

Intimacy-Avoidant Affair

The couple expressing this affair is frightened of getting too close, so they keep the barriers high between them. Conflict is one barrier; affairs are another. Their emotional connection with each other is through frequent and intense conflict. Often, each partner becomes involved in an affair. These couples are the mirror opposite of the Conflict-Avoidance Affair.

Sexual-Addiction Affair

Sexual addicts use sex over and over again to numb inner pain and emptiness, much like alcoholics use alcohol. Behaviors include going to strip clubs, viewing pornography combined with compulsive masturbation, seeking out prostitutes or escort, and repetitive encounters with sexual partners.

Split-Self Affair

This couple has tried to make the relationship work. Both partner have sacrificed their own feelings and needs to take care of others, and the deprivation has caught up with one of them. The affair is usually serious, long-term, and passionate. The partner who is having the affair focuses on deciding between the marriage and the affair partner and avoids looking at the inner split.

Entitlement Affair

This affair is usually a serious, long-term one in which the straying partner is charming, popular, successful, and powerful. Professional interests become more important than family relationships, and the partners live somewhat separate lives. The third party is attracted to the power and the perks of the straying partner and may have more in common with the straying partner than does the primary partner.

Exit Affair

The couple expressing an exit affair is conflict avoidant at heart, but they take it further. One partner has already decided to leave the marriage, and the affair provides the justification. The other partner usually blames the affair rather than looking at how their marriage got to this point.

Personal Response to Infidelity

There are stages that people go through when experiencing infidelity that are much like a grief response to a loss. Peggy and James Vaughan (1999, p. 6) identify four stages that the hurt partner can go through in response to discovery of infidelity. The first stage is shock. There is such a disruption to what the hurt partner holds as true in the relationship. Everything feels unmanageable, including how to feel, activities of daily living, work, decisions about the relationship, and who to tell. The second phase is holding on. This is the phase where the partner feels stuck, may want to maintain the old relationship, or is in denial. The third phase is acknowledgement. In this stage the couple transitions from being in a stage of crisis to the ability to contain intense emotions and to work toward understanding the root causes of the affair. The final stage is adaption and change. This stage is when the couple adapts to the situation and true recovery begins. This is what the Vaughans would call "establishing a new world and sense of worth" (1999, p. 6). As you might guess, accepted counseling protocol follows these stages pretty closely.

Practice-based evidence indicates that couples who stay in treatment recover from infidelity and enhance their relationship. Carlson and Sperry (2010, p. 20) state that in their practice, they believe there are only a few things that a long-term relationship cannot overcome. From their perspective, three things that will "doom" a relationship are 1) when one or both partners never truly loved one another when they committed to the relationship, 2) when there is too much anger, pain, or damage by one partner or both partners that for one partner love no longer exists, and 3) when one or both partners are unwilling to own their contribution to the problem and will not commit to overcoming those issues.

Common Mistakes Couples Make Early in Recovery

In desperate times, people do desperate things. Following the discovery or disclosure of an affair, couples do things in an attempt to limit damage, make things better, or understand the events of the affair. The participating partner may try to limit the ensuing damage that may occur by disclosing partial information about an affair, or each partner will seek support or understanding from friends and family. In doing so, the couple can inadvertently continue to damage the relationship and limit the process of repair. In my practice, I find it helpful to offer couples a small article that outlines information about what not to do as they prepare to enter treatment. They are asked to read and discuss an article, section by section, and respond to guided discussion questions (see Appendix 11.1). Following is an outline of the ten things to avoid during recovery from infidelity.

Unrestrained Emotions

Emotional regulation for both partners creates the likelihood that there will be less opportunity for escalation, more open and productive discussions, and much better decision-making. A critical strategy here is to practice emotional "attunement." Attunement is the ability to focus on the here-and-now emotions of an experience. Individually, each partner should pay attention to what is going on internally. In situations when one partner is alone and experiencing distress, they should pay attention to what the body and mind are communicating. Couples can be encouraged to take thirty seconds to a couple of minutes to ask these questions: 1) What am I feeling now? 2) What situation or perception is causing me to feel this emotion? and 3) What can I do to take good care of myself? Do this regularly throughout the day.

Attuning to the partner should also be a priority. Couples can do this by paying attention to the partner's cues of distress and responding in a supportive way to the emotions and underlying thinking of the topic expressed. For example, "You are feeling hurt (this is the feeling) because I forgot to call you before I left work (this is the meaning)." Alternatively, couples should try not to ask, "What's wrong?" It is better to express understanding, or even an attempt at understanding, than to ask. Taking a non-defensive approach to this is a key ingredient to being successful with attunement.

Managing emotions can also be as simple as knowing when to take a break from heated discussions or taking care to start conversations in a soft, non-confrontational manner. When couples take breaks during escalating discussions, it can be a good idea to commit to reconnecting to continue the discussion at a specific time, when calmness has returned or a specific relaxing or "distracting" activity has been completed.

Making Emotion-Based Decisions

In the first days of learning about infidelity, emotional experiences for both partners are intense. Sometimes couples make decisions in the context of this emotional intensity and can cause long-lasting consequences. Emotionally charged decisions about separating, moving out, divorcing, and telling the children about the infidelity can have unintended consequences. If couples are planning to enter therapy, couples are asked to postpone major decisions long enough to work through the initial crisis with a trained therapist.

Contacting the Affair Partner, at Least Initially

Contacting the affair partner should be a well-thought-through decision. The hurt partner may want to contact the affair partner to get more information, trap the person into giving previously undisclosed information, or threaten disclosure of the affair as retribution. The participating partner may also want to contact the affair partner for closure of the relationship or to warn of impending contact by their partner. There is limited payoff to any of these scenarios, and a good clinician can guide the couple in understanding the risks and benefits to contacting the affair partner.

Leaking Out Information Over Time

I tell couples in my practice that the participating partner needs to "tell it like it is" as soon as possible. Leaking information when questioned by one partner (by telling only partial information) only makes it look like lying when questions are asked a second time and new information is shared. If the participating partner wants to save their primary relationship, they will need to be willing to offer the facts about the affair and offer a timeline of events, including thoughts and feelings around decision-making before, during, and after the affair.

Not Answering Questions

For the participating partner, when asked a question, answer; when asked the same question again, answer. The rule here would be to show willingness to answer questions and answer them as best as possible. Also, similar or redundant questions should be answered without irritation and as expansive as possible. Make sure responses include information about behaviors, your thoughts, and your feelings.

Creating Opportunities to Defend the Affair Partner

One easy way for the hurt partner to create the opportunity to defend the affair partner is to call the person names in front of the hurt partner. On many occasions, when couples come into treatment the hurt partner is accustomed to calling the affair partner a whole host of filthy names: whore, slut, etc. The participating partner will likely try to quell the name-calling for a variety of reasons, including to reduce their own embarrassment or to demonstrate that the affair partner was not as bad as perceived. Defending this person only creates more hurt. Couples are encouraged to replace name-calling with speaking from their own experience of hurt, discussing the affair's impact to the relationship and expressing personal thoughts and feelings.

Attack-and-Defense Posturing

It is important to successful discussions and ongoing repair of the relationship that each partner is aware of, and manages, the potential dynamic of attack-defense. The hurt partner needs to manage comments and questions so that they are not interpreted as attacking and construct interactions in a way that that will not create defensiveness. The participating partner needs to try to respond in discussions about the affair as non-defensively as possible; in doing so there will be less potential for aggressive questioning, and it will also encourage the expression of hurts.

Creating Triggering Events

What triggers the hurt partner? Is it a scene on a television show? How one partner dresses? Driving by a specific location? It is important that both partners sit down and identify the triggers, the early warning signs of the triggers (anxiety, stomach pains, agitation, shortness of breath), and specific actions for preventing triggers and intervening when early warning signs are present or triggers happen. Couples that create an environment that manages this well ultimately create a supportive environment where triggers are discussed openly and managed with caring behaviors.

Not Being Accountable and Accessible

It is important that the work of re-establishing trust starts immediately. The participating partner will need to work hard so that he or she can account for all of their time when they are away from their partner. When schedules change or irregularities in schedules occur, immediate disclosure will be important. It would also be helpful to predict situations that may be uncomfortable for their partner and avoid these situations.

The participating partner should also be accessible to their partner. Explanations of poor cell phone reception, cell phone batteries that have died, or situations of not answering text and email messages create strong alarm reactions for the hurt partner. Charging up phones, attending to messages, avoiding hot-spot locations, and offering regular contact when away can make all the difference in establishing accountability, accessibility, and ultimately stability and trust.

Not Validating the Partner's Experience

A simple communication strategy used by the participating partner that includes understanding thoughts and feelings and validating the overwhelming experience of infidelity can make a huge difference in the healing process.

Accepted Counseling Protocol for Infidelity

Quite a number of writers have proposed a protocol for addressing infidelity. There seems to be a general consensus on how to approach treatment. Most approaches work through a process of stabilizing the crisis, helping the couple understand the infidelity and what it is telling the couple about the relationship, treating the underlying problematic dynamics of the relationship, facilitating a process of forgiveness, and planning prevention strategies. Following is an outline of a protocol for infidelity treatment and some of the common issues that clinicians will need to address.

Phase 1

Crisis Stabilization and Assessment

Following the discovery or disclosure of an affair, many couples want to get into therapy quickly because of the intensity of the crisis, but which clinician should they choose? Who can the couple trust to help them manage such a difficult situation? The couple fears the unknown of infidelity treatment, including personal confusion and loss for how to react and how to proceed, how and if to share the intimate details of the affair, how their partner will react, whether the therapy will lead to the couple's divorce, whether the clinician will think there is too much damage and recommend divorce, and whether or not the clinician is capable of handling the issue. Paul Peluso (2007, p. 105) states that clinicians should accomplish three tasks in the early sessions of treatment. First, the clinician needs to establish an atmosphere of safety and trust. This happens when the clinician can help the couple control the intense emotions and productively discuss the infidelity. Second, the clinician needs to demonstrate competence. Competent clinicians will demonstrate that they have addressed the issue before and that they have had success in treating it. Third, the clinician needs to prepare the couple for therapy by providing a conceptual model for treatment. This is important to do by the end of the first session. The couple should leave understanding the stages of treatment and the goals and benchmarks for each stage.

Entering counseling for infidelity treatment is overwhelming with many unknowns. Many questions and circumstances will have to be addressed. The couple will want direction on what information, if any, should be shared with others, how to deal with the affair partner, and whether they should continue living together as they work on recovery. The clinician should have well-thought-out plans for addressing the multiplicity of issues that will be presented from the moment the couple enters the office.

Boundary-Setting

Therapeutic Boundaries

Therapeutic boundaries are the rules and strategies the clinician puts in place to create the therapeutic, safe space for the couple to work on recovery. The clinician's priority is to limit hostile exchanges between the couple, such as escalating anger, discounting each other's ideas, blaming, criticizing, or complaining about the other. It would be best if the clinician intervened fairly quickly to these situations to help the couple stay focused and limit further harm to the relationship.

Boundaries With the Affair Partner

I read a blog post some time ago by Brad Hambrick (2012), who was offering strategies for how to end an extramarital affair. Here is an excerpt of his argument that the affair relationship is a very dangerous relationship:

> This relationship should be treated like a poisonous snake in the house with your children. Even if the snake is in another room, you would take every measure possible to destroy the snake because you know the snake is a predator and its presence, even in another room, puts them in mortal danger.

In that vein, most clinicians have an expectation that the participating partner will cut off all contact with the affair partner. This is best to be done quickly with no tapering off. When the participating partner ends the relationship, it also needs to be done in the full view and awareness of their spouse: no clandestine meetings to say goodbye to get closure and no phone calls in secret to apologize privately. There is no such thing as closure when it comes to infidelity; one relationship will end horribly, either the primary relationship or the affair relationship. Believing in closure and acting upon it will only make the recovery process more difficult.

If there is concern that the affair partner is reluctant to end the affair, all requests to end the relationship by the participating partner should be done by email or postal mail. This will make it easier in the future to obtain a protection order to stop contact.

Any contact that occurs following closure of the affair relationship should be disclosed to the hurt partner immediately, including accidental contact, attempted contact by the affair partner, or any probable contact (such as phone call hang-ups). Damage to trust-building will inevitably happen when there is a delay in communicating or the hurt partner learns of the contact without being told (Shelton, 2013).

At times the participating partner is unwilling to end the affair because of the physical or emotional intimacy they are experiencing. In contrast, their current relationship may be shrouded in conflict and uncertainty. It may make sense to the participating partner to take a wait-and-see attitude about both relationships, planning to attend therapy and prolong the affair relationship.

In response to this, it is not an uncommon practice for clinicians to refuse to see the couple that has an active affair. Clinicians do this because of the challenges with managing this triangulation of the relationship. However, refusing to see the couple can create a boundary that can be more destructive than the triangulation they are trying to stop. Clinicians demanding that the participating partner terminate the affair relationship immediately and completely may prematurely cause that partner's decision to end both the therapy and their marriage (Baucom et al., 2006).

Baucom et al. (2006) suggest that for situations involving an ongoing affair, the clinician should work to promote the participating partner's agreement to limit or suspend involvement with the outside person on an intermediate basis. *Intermediate* is the key here; the couple should develop a tentative timeline for reaching a more-permanent decision about whether to end the affair relationship. For those couples that ultimately choose not to end the affair relationship, the discontinuation of therapy may be clinically indicated. If their decision is to limit contact, the clinician should clearly communicate that any continuation of the affair relationship will limit the couple's ability to create stability in their relationship and limit their efforts to restore trust and intimacy in the long term.

Boundaries Around Discussions With Family and Friends

The challenge with seeking support from family and friends is that these individuals tend to support just one person, not the relationship. Unfortunately, this type of support prolongs the personal turmoil the person is experiencing and does not promote stabilization and recovery. Support-seeking is an important feature in the early days following discovery or disclosure, but each partner should consider carefully in selecting someone for support. Though friends and family may have good intentions, they can cause considerable damage by taking sides and blaming one partner. Someone who unbiased and is a support to the relationship can be a more effective and helpful support person.

Boundaries Around Self-Care

Couples in crisis overlook the importance of taking care of their personal needs. The clinician could be helpful to the couple by directing a discussion about including appropriate self-care throughout the week. The couple can be encouraged to monitor physical care, make sure to eat well, get enough sleep, and exercise, if their physical health supports it. Social support can be encouraged, with careful attention paid to what is appropriate to disclose to others and what is not. For couples that are spiritual, meditation, prayer, and talking with spiritual counselors can be extremely helpful.

Establish Commitment

A fair amount of ambivalence about the relationship at the beginning of therapy from one or both partners is relatively common. Some level of commitment is obviously preferred, and it should be noted that there is a relationship between a higher level of commitment to the relationship and a willingness to engage in the emotional risk-taking that therapy requires (Baucom et al., 2006).

Since ambivalence is common, it is important in the first session to assess the couple's commitment to the relationship and also commitment to therapy. For the clinician to ask the couple to commit to the relationship in the first session would be inappropriate, much as it would be to ask them to make decisions about divorce. The emotional strain they are under could make it difficult for the couple to make an informed decision. It would, however, be beneficial for the clinician to ask the couple to commit to the process of therapy. In doing so, the clinician could then support the postponement of any decision about ending the relationship while in the midst of the initial shock and turmoil. This will allow the couple to thoroughly evaluate the relationship and their feelings (Fife, Weeks, & Gambescia, 2008). Ultimately, the decision to postpone could help prevent the couple from making a hasty and uninformed decision about the relationship.

An interesting debate among marriage counselors is to what extent the clinician is committed to the relationship. A majority of clinicians would say that they prefer to stay neutral concerning their clients' relationships. In a national survey of over 1,000 marriage and family therapists, over 60% indicated that they are "neutral" on marriage versus divorce for their clients. Only one third said, "I am committed to preserving marriage and avoiding divorce whenever possible." Even more disturbing, 2.4% said they frequently recommend divorce (National Registry of Marriage Friendly Therapist, 2014).

Create Accountability and Trust

Accountability is accepting responsibility for one's actions, the pain one has inflicted on the other, and the damage done to the relationship (Fife, Weeks, & Gambescia, 2008). The primary and initial way to facilitate accountability and trust in the early sessions is to have the couple develop a specific communication plan in which the partners keep in touch regularly throughout the day to keep each other informed of their schedules and plans. Couples report that simple strategies of sending occasional text messages, making a lunchtime phone call, or calling if schedules change or if they are going to be late influence the feeling of being connected even when they are at work or out of town.

Assess Safety, Mental Health, and Substance Use

Clinicians should not forget that the turmoil of infidelity can be accompanied by mental health concerns such as depression, anxiety, suicide ideation, and homicidal thought. Many of these many health concerns are not uncommon; for example, people experiencing infidelity and other "humiliating marital events" are six times more likely to be diagnosed with a major depressive episode than the general population (Cano & O'Leary, 2000).

Rage and revenge fantasies (toward both the affair partner and the spouse) are also an early experience of the hurt partner, and the client's ability to contain them must be assessed. Couples have reported to me at times that they wish to cause as much pain as they have experienced. Sometimes the pain they want to inflict is meant to disrupt the life of the affair partner by informing their partner. Other times they want to inform the affair partner's partner because they believe it is morally correct to do so. When the clinician assesses that there is a genuine concern for the other person, the clinician should take action to protect this person, following local law and professional ethics.

Alcohol use adds another level of challenge for recovery and can exacerbate existing conditions such as depression and anxiety. Alcohol and substance use increase poor decision-making that can lead to continuation or impulsive connection to the affair partner, higher levels of conflict with their partner, or suicide ideation.

There are a number of free-access measures for depression, anxiety, and substance use. Following is a short list of free-access measures, most presented at the All Ohio Counselor Conference in Columbus Ohio (Erford, 2012):

- The Hamilton Rating Scale for Depression
- The Center for Epidemiologic Studies Depression Scale
- Zung Self-Rating Depression Scale
- Generalized Anxiety Disorder Screener
- Zung Self-Rating Anxiety Scale
- Hamilton Anxiety Screener
- Michigan Alcohol Screening Test (MAST)
- Alcohol Use Disorders Identification Test (AUDIT)

Teach Alternatives to Venting Anger to Partner

The emotion of anger doesn't get a fair shake; anger is usually seen as bad, but anger is truly neither good nor bad. It's perfectly healthy and normal to feel angry in response to infidelity or other personal injuries by others. The feeling of anger is not the problem; how it is expressed makes the difference between harming the relationship further or beginning the healing process.

Studies have consistently revealed over the years that encouraging the expression of anger directly toward another person or even indirectly, such as toward an object, actually increases aggression (Lilienfeld et al., 2009). Considerable harm for the relationship can happen when unbridled anger is expressed, derailing the healing process for the couple.

I am not a proponent of venting anger to your partner. I do believe that using "time-out to time-in," calming strategies, and other alternative to be more effective.

Time-Out to Time-In

Clinicians regularly recommend that couples take a time-out when discussions get heated. I would add to this recommendation by making the strategy "time-out to time-in," in other words having the couple agree on a time-out to calm emotions but also agreeing to a time-in at a specific time later to return to continue the discussion. For example, the couple recognizes that they are escalating in their conversation, so they agree to take a time-out for one hour, returning at 6:30 p.m. During that time, each partner practices a relaxation exercise or some other activity that allows them to return to a non-escalated state. They can also use the time to outline the important topics they want to cover when they return to the discussion. They return at 6:30 p.m., calm and prepared to discuss the issue further.

Cognitive Self-Talk

Effectively managing intense emotions sometimes involves identifying negative thinking and replacing it with realistic and balanced thinking. Because our thoughts have a big impact on the way we feel and behave, changing unhelpful thoughts to helpful ones is key to successful management of emotions. One way to change cognitive self-talk is by identifying cognitive distortions that are being used. Some of the most common distortions are 1) overgeneralization, drawing a broad conclusion based on a single incident or insufficient evidence; 2) jumping to conclusions, assuming we know what others are thinking and feeling; and 3) using shoulds and oughts, using inflexible rules about how we or others should act. Couples can work to identify the use of these cognitive distortions and either modify or replace them.

Calming Self by Using Relaxation

Calm breathing, which involves consciously slowing down the breath, and progressive muscle relaxation, which involves systematically tensing and relaxing different muscle groups, are two primary ways in which couples can take a break and create a sense of calm. Other helpful relaxation strategies include calm music, meditation, guided imagery, and yoga.

Facilitate Discussion Concerning Details of the Affair

A number of clinicians have a strong opinion that discussion about the affair details should be kept to a minimum. They think that details, especially sexual specifics, will cause too much hurt or harm (Shelton, 2013). Couples, though, tell us a very different story. Peggy Vaughan (2002) completed an interesting survey of 1,083 married spouses hurt by infidelity, and her data clearly showed that getting answers to questions and thoroughly discussing the details of the affair increase both the likelihood of maintaining and rebuilding the marriage and the likelihood of recovering from a spouse's affair. For example, when couples were asked, "Did you want to know details about the affair?" 93% of the group wanted information while 62% said they wanted to know everything about the affair, including details. Only 7% said that they did not want to know. There is very little gender difference, by the way, in these findings; in fact, men and women were within only a few percentage points of difference in needing to know the details, both wanting a high level of disclosure. This need to know is driven by the hurt partner's attempt to make sense of what happened.

Most people having affairs are reluctant to disclose information. The common attitude regarding disclosing details is that once the partner is caught they will say as little as possible. In Vaughan's (2002) survey, almost half of those individuals participating in affairs only told the details of the affair after much pressure to do so, and another 28% refused to share any details beyond the mere basics.

An important aspect in recovering from any traumatic event involves telling the story about what occurred (Glass, 2015). From the hurt partner's perspective, then, it is critical in most instances to work to obtain as many details about the affair that feel comfortable for them. It is not warranted for the clinician to work for complete disclosure but for the amount of disclosure that is required from the hurt partner. Another aspect of this disclosure is the willingness of the participating partner to disclose these details. Vaughan (2002) believes that the "willingness to disclose" has a positive impact on recovery and sustaining the marriage because it provides hope for more honesty in the future.

As the work towards disclosure begins, it is also beneficial to discuss the importance of disclosure in the recovery process as mentioned in the previous discussion. The hurt partner should be directed to be careful not to lie or even "lie by omission" because when the omissions are discovered they are perceived as the hurt partner's continuing to be secretive, untrustworthy, and unwilling to share, and this results in perceived setbacks in the healing.

Another disclosure that is useful for the hurt partner answers the question, "How were you able to do this?" Considerable efforts were made to keep the affair hidden, and until the participating partner was caught, they were able to deceive their partner to a large extent. The hurt partner may want to ask questions around what the participating partner did to create this deception.

Knowing the details of the affair is also helpful to the clinician for treatment planning. There are several content areas that the clinician could be listening for and that are facilitative in developing understanding. The following list suggests several areas to assess (Fife, Weeks, & Gambescia, 2008):

- The type of infidelity (whether emotional, sexual, or via the Internet)
- Level of deception
- The time frame or duration in which the infidelity occurred, the frequency of communication and/or sexual contact, and the location of encounters
- History of past infidelity (might include previous affairs and/or sexual addiction)
- Relationship of the affair partner to both partners (friend, coworker, neighbor)
- Degree of collusion by the betrayed partner
- Perceived attractiveness of the affair partner
- Social and cultural context of the infidelity

Facilitate Coping With the Trauma Symptoms

After learning about an affair, the hurt partner may experience a trauma reaction (Glass, 1998) similar to symptoms of post-traumatic stress disorder. Some of the symptoms include flashbacks, nightmares, hyper-vigilance (one couple that I worked with called this symptom "super-sleuthing"), chronic questioning, obsessive rumination, and hyper-arousal symptoms such as being easily startled and having difficulty sleeping. By some estimates, these symptoms can persist for up to two years and maybe longer (Shelton, 2013).

Couples need to understand that these symptoms are common. They can be triggered by a variety of things and are considered a re-experience of the trauma. These symptoms will fade over time starting with the frequency, then the duration, and finally the intensity of flashbacks (Shelton, 2013).

Emotion-focused strategies are the most commonly used strategies when a painful, unchangeable situation such as infidelity has caused distress and problem-solving can't improve the outcome (Folkman & Lazarus, 1991). Working for healthy expressions of feelings of anger, fear, confusion, resentment, and the like can help reduce the symptoms and heal the relationship. Later in this chapter, a more detailed look at strategies based on a trauma-informed approach will be explained, which I have found to be very helpful for couples as a between-session task.

Use of Intensive Sessions

I offer intensive sessions at my practice for couples responding to infidelity during the first few days after discovery. These sessions are three hours long and have specific tasks that are meant to help manage the crisis and limit the destructive impact of an affair. Many couples will choose to do intensive sessions because they believe the crisis demands an immediate response and they recognize that they need help organizing their thoughts and feelings to create an organized and productive response. One primary benefit is that couples can accomplish the same level of work in two intensive sessions that would take six weeks or more of traditional weekly sessions. One downside of intensive sessions is that the clinician needs to be careful not to move too quickly. With the consolidated time frame of each session, there can be less time for individual processing of thoughts, feelings, and the concepts discussed in session.

Phase 2

Exploring Context

The focus in phase 2 transitions from managing the impact of the affair to understanding the underlying personal, relational, and external factors that could have potentially contributed to it. This is an important component of treatment that can be rushed by the clinician, so I offer a cautionary note here:

Exploring context should only start when the crisis aspect of the relationship is stabilized. Concentrating on underlying issues before the crisis phase has passed will usually cause the hurt partner to feel unsupported or even scapegoated by the therapist (Shelton, 2013).

When considering contextual factors, there is a clear distinction between potential factors that may have contributed to the affair and the decision by the participating partner to have the affair. As the work in this phase begins, it is important to be careful to make it clear that the participating partner is responsible for their decision to have the affair even though there are relational and external factors that may have contributed to it.

There are three primary areas to explore: relationship aspects, individual characteristics, and external influences. This can be a two-stage process, first assigned as a between-session task in which the couple prepares for the next session by thinking through these factors that may have created vulnerability for an affair, and second as an honest discussion with the clinician at the next session. The couple is asked to identify 1) the aspects of the relationship, such as difficulty communicating or finding time for each other, which have left the relationship vulnerable, 2) issues specific to either the participating partner or the hurt partner, such as developmental history, relationship skills, substance use, mental health issues, and beliefs about marriage, and 3) external issues that may have had impact on the relationship, such as conflicts with in-laws, the influence of single friends, job stress, and financial difficulties.

Family of Origin for Infidelity

Conor and Meave married just out of college and had been great friends before becoming lovers. They were both happy Catholics and had lots of similar interests. Their sex life had been mutually satisfying. It was agreed that Conor could do full time study for a Graduate Degree and Meave would provide income. It was tough and then they had their first child and relocated for an excellent job that Conor was offered in a corporate position. When (super responsible) Meave annunciated her resignation, her co-worker expressed love for her and they became sexual. She was overwhelmed with feelings of love and wanted a divorce. Conor was traumatized and pleaded for them to enter therapy in their new town.

Meave had feelings like she'd never had before and felt that indicated that she was not really in love with her husband. Also, she felt that Conor had been so critical of her since they had their child and had lost his sense of fun. Conor was not aware of the level of Meave's discontent because she always seemed fine.

The second paragraph is where we often put our focus, and changing some behaviors and structures can help a couple to feel reconnected and hopeful. It also helps us to understand some of the reasons why Meave was unfaithful. We need to be clear that the other spouse did NOT cause the infidelity. My experience would suggest it is preferable to go a little further and this involves doing some work on the Family of Origin.

Having completed the work, they were clearer on how Meave had to constantly take care of the needs of her parents when in her developmental years. She was, as a result, often oblivious to her own needs wants and desires. She felt she SHOULD just 'get on with it' and as long as she was pleasant and responsible then she would be loved. Conor had come from a very strict and rigid family. He could never be good enough for his father and he did not see a need to compliment and show appreciation. Although constantly striving to become the Breadwinner, he never felt good enough. With this new awareness of their past they could change some beliefs about themselves and become more connected to their feelings. Now they could ask more clearly for what they wanted.

Clinicians should consider looking at Mom, Dad and Self. Ask for three adjectives to describe each person, as the client would have said up to the age of ten years old. Take each word and ask the client to elaborate so that 'I get the picture'. Then try to tease out the interrelationships of the three people. The clinician should be hypothesizing as they listen. When the client has described each person then the clinician should share some of her/his hypotheses with the client. About what the impact of the relationship may have been on the child and how that could be adding to some of the problematic communication between the couple. Focus should be on what partial impact the childhood experiences have been on limiting the ability of the person who had the affair to more healthily deal with life stresses and how to be aware of her/his feelings/needs/wants and desires. The other spouse will also develop more understanding of her/his part in some poor relationship tendencies. Lack of this awareness is part of the reason that the person concerned has made poor choices and violated the couple's boundaries. The idea of this work is so that the clients are more able to identify unhealthy life style approaches and see what changes need to be implemented. They alter some beliefs about life and self. The partner, who did not have the infidelity, is present to hear the new information and this helps her/him to build more trust that infidelity is less likely to occur again. Empathy is developed. Both can see that the person who had the affair is more likely to be able to 'catch herself' from perpetuating poor behavior in the future. Both partners are more aware of the impact of childhood relationships on their present behaviors and this enables more choice, rather than habitual reactions or reenactions.

Tony Fryer, LIMFT is a private practitioner in Cincinnati Ohio. The bulk of his clients are couples. He works with a range of issues including enhancing communication, infidelity, sexual dysfunction, and blended family issues. His sessions are very focused on clearly established client goals. Homework is given to couples every session. He helps clients to tap into their own reserves to find better ways to live. Tony is from Ireland and is a married man and father of two. He has lived in England and Taiwan and came to Cincinnati from Ireland in 2001.

Tony can be reached at:
513-631-3131
tonyfryer@tonyfryer.com
tonyfryer.com

Phase 3

Treating Factors that Contributed to the Infidelity

Now that the relational aspects, external influences, and personal characteristics have been identified, a picture will have emerged of the negative cycles and other aspects that were perpetuating or maintaining the relationship distress prior to the infidelity. As an example, treatment may include addressing the wellness of one of the partners, disrupting negative communication patterns between the couple, establishing emotional closeness of both partners, reducing stressors that are impacting the relationship, or all of the above.

Phase 4

Rebuilding a Post-Affair Relationship

The fourth phase of treatment is to work toward a new, post-affair relationship, and this includes the process of forgiveness. In truth, forgiveness is a process that started at the beginning of treatment. The couple can be told that forgiveness is a natural response to trauma. To start this process, Gordon et al. (2005) suggest that the process of forgiveness be presented to the couple and that the clinician draw parallels between the forgiveness process and the work the couple just completed. This highlights for the couple that first, there is a response to the initial impact and that second, there is an attempt to give the affair some kind of meaning, or put it into context; finally, the person begins to move forward and readjust. In the next chapter I will discuss the process for forgiveness in more detail.

Prevention Planning

As the couple progresses through the phases of treatment, one common statement made by the hurt partner is something similar to "tell me how to make sure this doesn't happen again." However, much of the work that the couple has already completed at this point will help prevent a reoccurrence. Even so, couples regularly ask for a concrete plan of action. I ask couples to make a concrete plan around four important areas: 1) prevention efforts, 2) current risk and mitigating strategies, and 3) old patterns. The couple's work during the earlier context phase of treatment provides the information that they will need to develop this plan.

Prevention Efforts

The couple's prevention efforts begin with maintaining the gains they made in therapy and staying committed to their treatment goals beyond the therapy experience. Shirley Glass (2003, p. 13) uses the metaphor of "walls and windows" to communicate the importance of boundaries that need to be strengthened in therapy and maintained post-therapy. As the metaphor goes, couples need to keep the window to each other open to nurture an intimate and secure relationship and to put up the privacy wall to protect from others who may threaten the relationship. According to Dr. Glass (2003, p. 13):

> To reestablish a marriage that is intimate and trusting after an affair, the walls and windows must be reconstructed to conform to the safety code and keep the structure of the marriage sound so that it can withstand the test of time. You install a picture window between you and your marriage partner and construct a solid or opaque wall to block out contact with the affair partner. This arrangement of walls and windows nurtures your marriage and protects it from outside elements and interference.

Applying the metaphor to prevention planning, prevention efforts can focus on keeping the window open and the wall closed. To keep the window open to each other, couples should work to be romantic and affectionate, participate in shared activities with each other, have regular discussions that are open and honest about the relationship, stay emotionally connected, reframe criticism and blame to the request of needs, and have sex regularly, just to name a few.

Closing the wall to potential threats to the relationship could include limiting social interactions that may increase the likelihood of infidelity, such as avoiding starting emotional relationships with attractive alternatives to the primary relationship or sharing intimate personal details about one's personal life with them; carefully monitoring interactions at business socials; refraining from hanging out with single friends late at night or with peers that tend to "fool around" with multiple partners; fostering relationships with other healthy couples; avoiding pornography, online dating, escort sites, and other problematic Internet use; resisting avoidance of conflict and dealing with the conflict effectively; and always considering the consequences of one's thoughts and actions.

Current Risk and Mitigating Strategies

I also ask the couple to identify what they believe to be the risk areas for the relationship. Generally by this late in treatment, the couple has a strong understanding of the current risk. These are restated, and post-treatment goals can be created so that strategies can be put in place to mitigate the risk.

Old Patterns

Couples fear that at the end of treatment there is a risk that they will go back to old patterns in the relationship, such as coming home from work and not talking to one another, not doing couple activities, or being hyper-critical. In preparation for termination, these old patterns are restated and plans are put into place to monitor for the pattern and intervene if activated.

The Trauma Model of Infidelity Treatment

One of the challenges that I have had in the past in clinical practice is feeling limited in managing the distress of the hurt partner. Discovery of infidelity can leave a person struggling with intrusive memories, hyper-vigilant behavior, obsessive thinking, numbing, and avoidance. These are also some of the same symptoms of post-traumatic stress disorder. They can experience stages of shock, denial, and confusion. They may be driven to ask questions of the offender repeatedly and may have obsessive thoughts of acts of revenge or punishment.

It makes sense, then, to consider how the post-traumatic stress of the discovery or disclosure of infidelity can be addressed in therapy. The remainder of this chapter will focus on how to assess the level of trauma symptoms and how to create a treatment approach to help manage the symptoms.

Post-traumatic Stress Disorder Symptoms

Following a traumatic event such as infidelity, it is a common experience for the hurt partner to have some of the symptoms similar to post-traumatic stress disorder. It is also common to find it difficult to stop thinking about the affair, to have nightmares, or feel insecure or numb.

Post-traumatic stress disorder symptoms are grouped into four groups: 1) intrusive symptoms, 2) avoidance, 3) negative changes in mood or thinking, and 4) changes in emotional reactions. Many of these symptoms can be present as someone struggles with the discovery of infidelity. Table 11.1 lists a number of common symptoms of PTSD that couples struggle with following discovery or disclosure of infidelity.

There are two common ways that the intrusive symptoms of post-traumatic stress disorder manifest in response to infidelity. Chronic questioning is an intrusive symptom that is a method the hurt partner utilizes to gather evidence about events, whereabouts, behaviors, and intent associated with their partner's affair. Couples report that they feel like they have limited control of the need for questioning. Intrusive thoughts and obsessive rumination are also a common intrusive symptom and a serious source of distress for the hurt partner as they are experiencing disorientation about the discovery.

Measuring Trauma and Associated Symptoms

I developed the Trauma Response to Infidelity Scale (TRIS, Appendix 11.2) as a means to helping couples gauge the level of distress during the early part of treatment. The TRIS is a brief self-report questionnaire containing thirty-four items and is, I believe, an appropriate tool to measure the subjective response to the impact of infidelity. I have used other questionnaires for post-traumatic stress, but I also wanted to get a good picture of the level of depression, anxiety, and panic that is also associated with the infidelity. Combining these into

Table 11.1 Post-traumatic Stress Disorder Symptoms Relative to Infidelity

Intrusive Symptoms
Recurrent, unwanted, distressing memories of the disclosure or discovery
Reliving the discovery or disclosure as if it were happening again (flashbacks)
Upsetting dreams
Severe distress or physical reactions to something that reminds one of the infidelity
Avoidance Symptoms
Trying to avoid thinking or talking about the infidelity
Avoiding places, activities, or people that remind one of the infidelity
Negative changes in thinking and mood
Negative feelings about self or other people
Inability to experience positive emotions
Feeling emotionally numb
Lack of interest in activities once enjoyed
Hopelessness about the future
Changes in emotional reactions (arousal symptoms)
Irritability, angry outbursts, or aggressive behavior
Always being on guard for danger
Self-destructive behavior, such as drinking too much or driving too fast
Being easily startled or frightened

one screening measure helped considerably to view a broader array of symptoms and subsequently eliminated the initial need for three screening tools. If high levels of anxiety or depression were indicated, I could follow up by administering a more specific screening tool.

The TRIS is useful in a variety of ways: it is helpful for the couple to recognize the associated "fallout" resulting from infidelity, in which the participating partner may be limited in their understanding of the true impact of the trauma. Once the symptoms are identified, the clinician can facilitate the development of short-term goals to address the symptoms. The TRIS is also a useful outcome measure to monitor the reduction of symptoms over time, and any reduction in symptoms can indicate that the couple relationship is more stable and possibly ready to move to the second phase of infidelity treatment.

Table 11.2 shows the TRIS in its entirety. The items are listed in three categories, based on type of symptom. Category A includes symptoms that

Table 11.2 Trauma Response to Infidelity Scale (TRIS)

				Level of Distress	
CATEGORY A	Obsessively thinking about your partner's actions	NE	LOW	MED	HIGH
	Chronic questioning for evidence about events, whereabouts, behavior, intent	NE	LOW	MED	HIGH
	Flashbacks: Reliving some aspect of the experience as if it were happening again	NE	LOW	MED	HIGH
	Recurrent, involuntary, unwanted, distressing memories	NE	LOW	MED	HIGH
	Upsetting dreams or nightmares about the infidelity	NE	LOW	MED	HIGH
	Severe emotional distress or physical reaction to something that reminds you of disclosure or discovery of infidelity	NE	LOW	MED	HIGH
	Strong effort to avoid thoughts or feelings	NE	LOW	MED	HIGH
	Feeling numb or detached	NE	LOW	MED	HIGH
	Difficulty feeling positive emotions	NE	LOW	MED	HIGH
	Persistent, strong, negative beliefs about self	NE	LOW	MED	HIGH

			Level of Distress		
	Hyper-vigilance: Searching phone bills, text messages, and email to find evidence of potential affair behavior	NE	LOW	MED	HIGH
	Irritability concerning typically trivial issues	NE	LOW	MED	HIGH
	Problems concentrating	NE	LOW	MED	HIGH
	Strong startle response	NE	LOW	MED	HIGH
	Strong feeling of retribution toward spouse or affair partner	NE	LOW	MED	HIGH
		SUBTOTAL:			
CATEGORY B	Rapid heart rate or pounding heart	NE	LOW	MED	HIGH
	Elevated blood pressure	NE	LOW	MED	HIGH
	Difficulty breathing or shortness of breath	NE	LOW	MED	HIGH
	Chest pains	NE	LOW	MED	HIGH
	Dizziness or light-headedness	NE	LOW	MED	HIGH
	Muscle tension and pains	NE	LOW	MED	HIGH
	Increased sweating	NE	LOW	MED	HIGH
	Chills or heat	NE	LOW	MED	HIGH
	Hyperventilation	NE	LOW	MED	HIGH
	Headaches	NE	LOW	MED	HIGH
	Stomach upset	NE	LOW	MED	HIGH
		SUBTOTAL:			
CATEGORY C	Depressed mood most of the day, nearly every day	NE	LOW	MED	HIGH
	Diminished interest or pleasure in all, or almost all, activities most of the day	NE	LOW	MED	HIGH
	Inability to sleep or sleeping too much	NE	LOW	MED	HIGH
	Significant weight loss when not dieting, or weight gain	NE	LOW	MED	HIGH
	Fatigue or loss of energy nearly every day	NE	LOW	MED	HIGH
	Feelings of worthlessness or guilt	NE	LOW	MED	HIGH
	Diminished ability to think or concentrate	NE	LOW	MED	HIGH
	Thoughts of death or suicide	NE	LOW	MED	HIGH
		SUBTOTAL:			

Category A Total: Category B Total: Category C Total:

TOTAL TRIS SCORE:

are post-traumatic-related symptoms, category B includes anxiety- and panic-related symptoms, and category C includes depression-related symptoms. The items on the TRIS are based on the DSM-5 criteria for post-traumatic stress, anxiety and panic, and depression and are adapted to fit the circumstance of infidelity. Though the categories are based on the DSM-5, the TRIS is not intended to diagnose any disorder.

To administer the TRIS, the client is asked to read each statement on the questionnaire and select the level of distress that best describes how they have been feeling over the past two weeks, on a continuum of Not Experiencing (NE), Low Distress (LOW), Moderate Distress (MED), or High Distress (HIGH). The TRIS take a little over five minutes to complete.

To score the TRIS, each item is scored as follows: NE=0, LOW=1, MED=2, HIGH=3. Each category is subtotaled to get a score on each of the three categories. These categories are totaled together to get a total TRIS score. Please see Appendix 11.2 for a ready-to-use copy of the TRIS.

Treatment Approach for Emotional Dysregulation

The emotional experience following discovery or disclosure of infidelity poses challenges for the clinician. The hurt partner will likely have deficits in managing environmental triggers, reminders of the discovery, and the distress of their own thoughts. Helping the hurt partner with the emotional turmoil, and the problematic behaviors that come from it, is a precursor to a deeper level of therapy.

Applying trauma-informed principles can be a useful model for managing this distress. Glenn Saxe (2002) recommends that trauma protocol take into account two primary issues: 1) a dysregulated nervous system and 2) a social-environment that cannot contain the dysregulation.

Dr. Saxe (2015) is the chair of the Department of Child and Adolescent Psychiatry at the Child Study. His work has a focus on the psychiatric consequences of traumatic events in children. Dr. Saxe and his team have developed Trauma Systems Therapy (TST), a community-based intervention for traumatized children. Though he primarily works with children and treatment programs, these two concepts translate to our work with adults around the emotional dysregulation that is commonly a product of infidelity.

Regulating a Dysregulated Nervous System

The hurt partner must learn how to control their emotional and behavioral experiences when they are triggered. In regards to trauma, one of the most important concepts to understand is what happens when that experience is triggered and there is a transition from "calm and continuous states" to "discrete states of emergency" (Saxe, 2002). Triggering events can lead to dramatic change from calm to a perceived state of emergency in a variety of areas of functioning, including affect, thought, behavior, and sense-of-self (Saxe, 2002), much as if it were happening all over again. Interventions directed to the hurt partner, then, are to help the hurt partner to maintain calm and engaged states, to prevent emotional and behavioral disengaged states, and to build cognitive structures that allow choices.

One of the primary ways to help regulate the system is by creating a social environment of support. The social environment, in this case the couple relationship, can be a healing place for infidelity. When the hurt partner starts to emotionally escalate or display inappropriate behavior, a healing response can be provided by the participating partner's offering calm, caring, nurturing, and empathic responses. Interventions directed to the participating partner then would be to adjust the environmental conditions at home to provide this nurturing environment.

I have to admit that considering the work related to reducing the trauma symptoms, I place a large part of the responsibility for reducing the dysregulated symptoms and creating a supportive environment on the one who was unfaithful. This is primarily because the unfaithful partner made the choice to have the affair and is the one who created this particular crisis. The expectation is that they will work hard to stabilize the relationship. That is not to say that the hurt partner has no work in the process, but the emphasis is greater on the unfaithful partner, particularly early on in the process.

There has to be willingness to listen and respond from the hurt partner to establish the environment for healing. As a clinician it is easy to recognize which partners will succeed at reducing the trauma symptoms of the hurt partner by noticing the level of openness of the participating partner to listen caringly to expressions of feelings and to respond to questions. If the participating partner continues to withhold information, dismisses or denies the destruction of the affair, or does not take actions to help restore safety in the relationship, the hurt partner remains in a situation of perpetual threat until he or she finds ways to develop self-protection skills and adaptive ways of managing the anxiety and stress (Steffens & Renee, 2006).

The ability to listen without defensiveness is a critical element in a healing dialogue. In doing so, they can connect at a deeper level to the emotional experience of the hurt partner. There are several other key aspects of communication for creating a healing environment. The participating partner should take the time to quietly *listen* and reflect to their partner what is being said by addressing both the content of the message but also the underlying meaning that may not directly be stated. They should *observe* the nonverbal and paraverbal communication of their partner and reflect the feelings that are being expressed. Para-verbal communication comes in the form of tone, volume, and cadence of the message and is useful for keying in on unexpressed verbal expressions of emotions. They should *respond* to the emotions by reflecting the feelings of the partner and *be curious* by asking questions to create a greater understanding of the partner's experiences.

Examine Early Warning Signs, Triggers, and Pair Interventions

A trigger in its basic form is simply a cue that leads to a dramatic change in behavior, mood, or thinking. Triggers can be viewed as external or internal cues that lead to distress. External triggers could be any sight, sound, smell, location, date of the year, scene in a movie or television show, or yes, even therapy. Internal triggers can include passing thoughts, intrusive, reoccurring thoughts, physical sensations, feelings towards a partner (positive or negative), defensive reactions from a partner, or comments from other people.

Triggered flashbacks are a common occurrence in treatment, and it is important that couples learn to manage them. An important tool for clinicians in aiding couples in trigger management is mindfulness of early warning signs and potential triggers in their clinical practice. Clinician mindfulness can help couples identify triggers that can potentially ignite trauma responses and incorporate this understanding in treatment (Gillece, 2014).

To help the couple, it is important that the therapist have a plan to manage the trigger and the arousal state that follows it. Gillece (2014) identifies a three-step process for managing triggers:

1) Identify triggers
2) Identify the early warning signs
3) Develop strategies

Once the couple has identified the triggers, early warning signs are identified so that the couple can benefit from early intervention. I ask couples to think of the physical sensations that might occur just prior to losing control and may even be out of their awareness at the time. I also ask the participating partner to consider what they observe in their partner that might indicate an early warning sign. Many times the participating partner will identify behaviors they see in their partner. This process typically leads to a short list of fairly important early warning signs and triggers.

Having identified the triggers and early warning signs, strategies are developed that interrupt the escalating loss of control to create calm and manage or minimize stress. Couples choose a wide variety of strategies for calming, and these include taking time out from the situation, going for a walk, journaling, taking a hot bath, listening to music, or practicing meditation or mindfulness, to name just a few.

Other couples will develop partner-assisted strategies. For example, the participating partner will notice an early warning sign and make a statement to acknowledge it, such as, "You seem sad, would you like to take a break and talk?" Some couples will pair calming strategies with cognitive strategies, such as challenging, modifying, or replacing unhelpful thoughts.

The Importance of Compassionate Response

As a couples therapist working with couples recovering from infidelity, I regularly encounter situations in which the hurt partner desperately needs compassion from the partner who had the affair. At times, though, couples are unable or unwilling to offer a compassionate response when it seems so obvious that this is the one thing their partner most needs.

In the context of infidelity treatment, compassionate response, even when the partners have limited interest or ability in doing so, can be a therapeutic tool used as a soft, supportive way to handle triggering events and situations that have the potential to escalate to high levels of emotional intensity.

At home, couples report to me that they struggle to manage the trauma responses that are associated with the discovery or disclosure of infidelity. These responses include obsessive and intrusive thinking, frequent questioning, investigating, emotional instability, and feelings of negative self-worth.

If one partner is struggling with some of these behaviors, I will ask the partner to consider a few of the following strategies:

1) Begin by allowing yourself to hear the message without judgment. In doing so, you can more effectively take your partner's perspective and help him/her process difficult emotions.
2) Respond with empathy. It is better to demonstrate that you understand than it is to say you understand. So resist the temptation to say, "I understand," and demonstrate that you understand both the feeling and the meaning of what your partner is telling you. Later you can integrate your ideas about the situation.
3) Resist apologizing when confronted on your behavior in favor of accepting responsibility. Too often, an apology for the hurt partner feels empty and overused. To take responsibility, acknowledge the behavior and then discuss the impact of this behavior on the hurt partner and on the relationship. For example: "Yes, lying to you about the text messages that I sent to her was wrong, and it makes it very difficult now for you to trust most things that I say to you."
4) Respond to the mood state instead of asking, "What's wrong?" I am sure that you can relate to this if you are struggling to put the pieces together after your infidelity. You come home and you see the look on your partner's face and you become concerned. You ask, "What's wrong?" A better approach would be to state the feeling that you believe is associated with the facial expression you are observing and invite discussion with your partner. For example, instead of asking, "What's wrong?" state, "You look frustrated. Would you like to take a walk and talk?" Another possible response would be to state, "You look hurt; maybe you are thinking about what I said earlier." The second strategy attaches both feeling and meaning to the facial expression. Both statements invite discussion.

Infidelity recovery is a slow process. Small moments of compassion can make a big difference in the stabilization of the relationship immediately following the discovery of infidelity. It can also increase intimacy, even during difficult times.

Managing Obsessive Thoughts

Couples have told me that they may have sixty to seventy thoughts a day about the affair. Some couples believe that they are completely without control of their thought process and are merely victims to this obsessive thinking. It is important to recognize that obsessive thinking is a process that moves like a river to emotional distress and that the individual can take control by disrupting the process in some way, even if it is momentarily.

Couples seem unprepared for managing this problem and will ask for concrete strategies to reduce or eliminate the obsessive thoughts. Though it may seem logical to work with the person to stop the thoughts or force the thoughts out of their mind, my guess is that stopping rarely works in this situation. In fact, research suggests that attempts to stop obsessive thoughts may only intensify obsessive thinking (Hubbard, 2015). A better strategy is for the clinician to help the person minimize engagement in the obsessive process, but can this be done? Here are a few strategies to minimize the engagement with the process.

Moving From the Internal World to the External Experience

Obsessive thinking is an internal process. Maintaining the internal process allows for rumination and disengagement from real-world experiences. It is helpful for the person to get out of their head and to be more engaged in the real world around them. Mindfully focusing on a behavior can be beneficial. Refocusing on what is happening now in the moment or even taking the time to practice mindfulness can be useful.

Shifting to a Predetermined Thought

This strategy encourages the person to shift from the negative, obsessive thought to a more reasonable alternative thought. Rather than attempting to "stop" the obsessive process, it works by shifting the attention to a predetermined thought. For example, state, "These are just thoughts and they are not helpful" or "I am okay and I will now refocus on my work," and then move on to the task at hand.

Practicing Distraction

Many couples find success by simply distracting the thought by doing some alternative activity, even if it is only ten minutes. The simpler the better;

activities such as going for a brisk walk, playing with their child or pet, or playing a video game can help disengage from the obsessive process.

Cataloging and Moving on

With this strategy, the hurt partner is asked to notice the intrusive thought, catalogue it and then move on to the task at hand. From the catalogue list, the hurt partner is asked to share one or two of the cataloged thoughts with their partner at the end of the day. They are also encouraged to ask any questions related to the thoughts. Their partner should listen to and validate these feelings and answer any questions as thoroughly as possible. One couple stated the benefits of this (Losey, 2014):

- Did not feel so isolated with their thoughts
- Helped reduce her own curiosity about facts and events
- Gave permission to ask multiple questions and to ask the same question more than once
- Allowed her to write the questions down and filter out the ones that were just angry questions

I have had a number of couples talk about the emotional breakdowns they experience as a result of a trigger. As they describe a breakdown, there are several negative aspects that they indicate, including feeling like they are unable to maintain control, feeling guilty for the breakdown, or saying hurtful things to their partner. However, couples will also identify positive aspects of an emotional breakdown. For example, the breakdown is an opportunity to vent feelings and share thoughts that have been repressed, there is a period of emotional calm following the breakdown, distressing dreams are less vivid, obsessive thinking is reduced, it is more difficult to be triggered, it gives the participating partner opportunity to apologize, and there is a reduction in overall energy for the hurt partner.

Interestingly, it may be beneficial to construct structured emotional experiences for the couple that allow for some of the positive aspect of breakdowns. Couples that have been successful with this in my practice use this technique for a short period of time each day. The hurt partner is encouraged, and sometimes expected, to deeply experience his or her feelings. The structure would need to include short and clear start and end time frames for the discussions, passive listening of the participating partner without defensiveness, limits around escalation, and reflection through journaling each experience.

Reclaiming Space and Events

Couples talk about the difficulty and distress of going to certain places, hearing certain songs, and encountering other experiences that are strong reminders of the infidelity. The process of managing avoidance is addressed in counseling both through imaginal and in-vivo experiences. Imaginal experiences are the discussion and interventions that occur in the therapy session to address the avoidance about the places and events related to the infidelity. In-vivo experiences are the experience in which the couple "avoids the avoidance" by re-experiencing the place, song, or other experience. They take back the power they feel they lost. They "reclaim the space."

People will feel powerless with triggering events and places. Rita, a thirty-two-year-old mother of two, knew that her husband regularly gave flowers to his affair partner, shopped at a certain store for her, met regularly at specific restaurants, and took a "business trip" with the affair partner to New Hampshire the weekend after Valentine's Day. Rita felt powerless to listen to certain songs, drive by an Applebee's restaurant, receive flowers from anyone, or shop at Bed Bath & Beyond. Driving by Applebee's or noticing the smell of a specific store in the mall would be enough to activate great anxiety for her, crying and what she would describe as an emotional breakdown. She had written off ever visiting the state of New Hampshire.

I suggested that she reclaim the songs, the events, and places. This was a novel concept to her. She assumed that she would have to avoid these things forever. Reclaiming space and events functioned as a way for her to take back control of the things that are triggering. She created a list of triggering spaces and events and then ranked them according to the level of anxiety they produced. Starting with the least anxiety-producing item on the list, she and her husband set out to experience each of these items in a different way. The result was a strong sense of empowerment for both Rita and her husband and a reduction in Rita's trauma responses to the triggering events and places.

References

Atkins, D. C., Baucom, D. H., Eldridge, K., & Christensen, A. (2005). Infidelity and behavior couple therapy: Optimism in the face of betrayal. *Journal of Consulting and Clinical Psychology*, *73*(1), 144–150.

Baucom, D. H., Gordon, K. C., Snyder, D. K., Atkins, D. C., & Christensen, A. (2006). Treating affair couples: Clinical considerations and initial findings. *Journal of Cognitive Psychotherapy: An International Quarterly*, *20*(4), 375–392.

Brown, E. M. (2001). *Patterns of infidelity and their treatment* (2nd ed.). Philadelphia, PA: Brunner-Routledge.

Brown, E. M. (2014). *Types of affairs*. Retrieved December 24, 2014 from www.affairs-help.com.

Cano, A., & O'Leary, K. D. (2000). Infidelity and separations precipitate major depressive episodes and symptoms of nonspecific depression and anxiety. *Journal of Consulting and Clinical Psychology*, *68*(5), 774–781.

Carlson, J., & Sperry, L. (2010). *Recovering intimacy in love relationships*. New York: Routledge.

Erford, B. (2012). *Free access assessment instruments for depression, anxiety, eating disorders, disruptive behavior and substance use*. All Ohio Counselor Conference, Columbus Ohio.

Fife, S. T., Weeks, G. R., & Gambescia, N. (2008). Treating infidelity: An integrative approach. *The Family Journal: Counseling and Therapy for Couples and Families*, *16*(4), 316–323.

Folkman, S., & Lazarus, R. S. (1991). Coping and emotion. In A. Monat & R. S. Lazarus (Eds.), *Stress and coping: An anthology* (3rd ed., pp. 207–227). New York: Columbia University Press.

Gillece, J. (2014). *Understanding and addressing trauma in the lives of those we serve*. Retrieved September 19, 2014 from www.nasmhpd.org/docs/NCTIC/Joan_Gillece_SAMHSA_2012_updated_Trauma_PPT.pdf

Glass, S. (1998, August). Shattered vows. *Psychology Today*, p. 34ff.

Glass, S. (2003). *Not just friends: Rebuilding trust and recovering your sanity after infidelity*. New York: Free Press.

Glass, S. (2015). *Reflections by glass: The trauma of infidelity*. Retrieved January 16, 2015 from www.shirleyglass.com/reflect_infidelity.htm

Gordon, K., Baucom, D. H., & Snyder, D. K. (2005). Forgiveness in couples: Divorce, infidelity, and couples therapy. In E. L. Worthington (Ed.), *Handbook of forgiveness* (pp. 407–421). New York: Routledge.

Hambrick, B. (2012). *How to end an extra-marital relationship*. Retrieved December 29, 2014 from www.bradhambrick.com/how-to-end-an-extra-marital-relationship

Hubbard, B. (2015). *Obsessive thinking, worry and cognitive-behavior therapy*. Retrieved July 30, 2015 from http://cognitive-behavior-therapy.com/cognitive-behavior-therapy-for-obsessive-thinking-worry-rumination/.

Lilienfeld, S. O., Lynn, S. J., Ruscio, J., & Beyerstein, B. L. (2009). *50 great myths of popular psychology: Shattering widespread misconceptions about human behavior*. Hoboken, NJ: Wiley-Blackwell.

Losey, B. (2014, October 26). Session with Client.

National Registry of Marriage Friendly Therapist. (2014). Retrieved December 24, 2014 from www.marriagefriendlytherapists.com/cfaq.

Peluso, P. R. (2007). *Infidelity: A practitioner's guide to working with couples in crisis* (p. 105). New York: Routledge.

Peluso, P. R., & Spina, P. (2008). Understanding infidelity: Pitfalls and lessons for couples counselors. *The Family Journal: Counseling and Therapy for Couples and Families*, *16*(4), 324–327.

Saxe, G. (2002). *Treating traumatized individuals: Neurobiological & psychological effects of trauma*. Retrieved September 20, 2014 from www.hogg.utexas.edu/uploads/documents/neurobio_psych.ppt.

Saxe, G. (2015). *Website biography of Glen Saxe*. Retrieved January 14, 2015 from www.aboutourkids.org/about_us/staff/clinical_faculty/glenn_saxe

Shelton, P. (2013, May/June). Helping couples recover from affairs. *The Therapist*.

Steffens, B. A., & Renee, R. L. (2006). The traumatic nature of disclosure for wives of sexual addicts. *Sexual Addiction & Compulsivity*, *13*, 247–267.

Vaughan, P. (2002). *Help for therapists and their clients in dealing with affairs*. San Diego, CA: Dialog Press.

Vaughan, P., & Vaughan, J. (1999). *Recovery from affairs: A handbook for couples* (p. 6). La Jolla, CA: Dialog Press.

Appendix 11.1

10 Things to Avoid During Recovery from Infidelity

By Dr. Butch Losey

Dr. Butch Losey is a couple's counselor in private practice in Cincinnati, Ohio. He is the author of the book "Creating an Effective Couple's Therapy Practice" that teaches clinicians methods of using outcomes to guide treatment and create successes in couple's therapy. He is also an associate professor at Xavier University in the Department of Counseling.

A discussion guide for couples

1. *Not managing your emotions*

Emotional regulation for both partners creates the likelihood that there will be less opportunity for escalation, more open and productive discussions and much better decision making. A critical strategy here is to practice emotional "attunement". Attunement is the ability to focus on the here and now emotions of an experience. Individually, each partner should pay attention to what is going on internally. In situations when one partner is alone and experiencing distress, pay attention to what your body and mind are telling you. Take 30 seconds to a couple of minutes to ask yourself these questions 1) What am I feeling now? 2) What situation or perception is causing me to feel this emotion? and 3) What can I do to take good care of myself? Do this regularly throughout the day.

Attuning to your partner should also be a priority. Do this by paying attention to the partner's cues of distress and responding in a supportive way to the emotions and underlying thinking of the topic expressed. For example, "You are feeling hurt (this is the feeling) because I forgot to call you before I left work (this is the meaning)". Alternatively, try not to ask "what's wrong?" It is better to express understanding, or even an attempt at understanding, than to ask. Taking a nondefensive approach to this is a key ingredient to being successful with attunement.

Managing emotions can also be as simple as knowing when to take a break from heated discussions or taking care to start conversations in a soft, non-confrontational manner. When couples take breaks during escalating discussions, it can be a good idea to commit to reconnecting to continue the discussion at a specific time, when calmness has returned or a specific relaxing or "distraction" activity has been completed.

2. *Making hasty, emotion-filled decisions*

In the first days of learning about infidelity, emotional experiences for both partners are intense. Sometimes couples make decisions in the context of this emotional intensity and can cause long-lasting consequences. Emotionally charged decisions about separating, moving out, divorce, and telling the children about the infidelity can have unintended consequences. If couples are planning to enter therapy, couples are asked to postpone major decisions long enough to work through the initial crisis with a trained therapist.

3. *Contacting the affair partner, at least initially*

Contacting the affair partner should be a well thought through decision. The hurt partner may want to contact the affair partner to get more information, trap the person into giving previously undisclosed information or to threaten disclosure of the affair as retribution. The participating partner may also want to contact the affair partner for closure of the relationship or to warn of impending contact by their spouse. There is limited payoff to any of these scenarios and a good therapist can guide the couple in understanding the risk and benefits to contacting the affair partner.

4. *Leaking out information over time*

I tell couples in my practice that the participating partner needs to "tell it like it is" as soon as possible. Leaking information when questioned by your spouse (by telling only partial information) only makes it look like lying when questions are asked a second time and new information is shared. If the participating partner wants to save their primary relationship, they will need to be willing to offer the facts about the affair and offer a timeline of events, including thoughts and feeling around decision-making before, during and after the affair.

5. *Not answering questions*

For the participating partner, when asked a question, answer; when asked the same question again, answer. The rule here would be to show your willingness to answer questions and answer them as best you can. Also answer similar or redundant questions without irritation and to be expansive as possible in your responses. Make sure your responses include information about your behaviors, your thoughts and your feelings.

6. *Creating opportunities to defend the affair partner*

One fantastic way for the hurt partner to create the opportunity to defend the affair partner is to call the person names in front of your spouse. On many occasions when couples come in to treatment, the hurt partner is accustomed to calling the affair partner a whole host of filthy names, whore, slut, etc. The participating partner will likely try to quell the name calling for a variety of reasons, including to reduce their own embarrassment or to demonstrate that the affair partner was not as bad as perceived. Defending this person only creates more hurt. Couples are encouraged to replace name-calling with speaking from their own experience of hurt, discussing the affair's impact to the relationship and expression of personal thoughts and feelings.

7. *Attack and defense posturing*

It is important to successful discussions and ongoing repair of the relationship that each partner is aware of, and manages, the potential dynamic of attack-defense. The hurt partner needs to manage comments and questions so that they are not interpreted as attacking and construct interactions in a way that that will not create defensiveness. The participating partner needs to try to respond in discussions about the affair as non-defensively as possible, in doing so there will be less potential for aggressive questioning and will also encourage the expression of hurts.

8. *Creating triggering events*

What triggers the hurt partner? Is it a scene on a television show? How your spouse dresses? Driving by a specific location? It is important that both of you sit down and identify the triggers, what are the early warning signs of the triggers (anxiety, stomach pains, agitation, shortness of breath) and identify specific actions for preventing triggers and intervening when early warning signs are present or triggers happen.

9. *Not being accountable and accessible*

It is important that the work of reestablishing trust start immediately. The participating partner will need to work hard so that he or she can account for all of their time when they are away from their spouse. When schedules change or irregularities in schedules occur, immediate disclosure will be important. It would also be helpful to predict situations that may be uncomfortable for their spouse and avoid these situations.

The participating partner should also be accessible to their spouse. Explanations of poor cell phone reception, cell phone batteries that have died, or situations of not answering text and email messages create strong alarm reactions for the hurt partner. Charging up phones, attending to messages, avoiding hotspot locations, and offering regular contact when away can make all the difference in establishing *accountability* and *accessibility* and ultimately stability and trust.

10. Not validating your partner's experience

A simple communication strategy used by the participating partner that includes the understanding of thoughts, feeling and validates the overwhelming experience of infidelity can make a huge difference in the healing process.

Discussion Questions

Couples are encouraged to read this article and discuss each of these items one at a time. Answer the following questions and discuss your responses with your spouse for each item:

1. What do I think about Dr. Losey's perspective on this item? Agree/disagree?
2. How do I evaluate us as a couple on this item?
3. What change would I like us to make concerning this item that would increase stability and trust in the relationship?

Appendix 11.2

Trauma Response to Infidelity Scale (L-TRIS)

		Level of Distress			
CATEGORY A	Obsessively thinking about your partner's actions	NE	LOW	MED	HIGH
	Chronic questioning for evidence about events, whereabouts, behavior, intent	NE	LOW	MED	HIGH
	Flashbacks: Reliving some aspect of the experience as if it were happening again	NE	LOW	MED	HIGH
	Recurrent, involuntary, unwanted distressing memories	NE	LOW	MED	HIGH
	Upsetting dreams or nightmares about the infidelity	NE	LOW	MED	HIGH
	Severe emotional distress or physical reaction to something that reminds you of disclosure or discovery of infidelity	NE	LOW	MED	HIGH
	Strong effort to avoid thoughts or feelings	NE	LOW	MED	HIGH
	Feeling numb or detached	NE	LOW	MED	HIGH
	Difficulty feeling positive emotions	NE	LOW	MED	HIGH
	Persistent, strong negative beliefs about self	NE	LOW	MED	HIGH
	Hyper-vigilance: Searching phone bills, text messages, email to find evidence of potential affair behavior	NE	LOW	MED	HIGH
	Irritability concerning typically trivial issues	NE	LOW	MED	HIGH
	Problems concentrating	NE	LOW	MED	HIGH
	Strong startle response	NE	LOW	MED	HIGH
	Strong feeling of retribution toward spouse or affair partner	NE	LOW	MED	HIGH
	SUBTOTAL:				
CATEGORY B	Rapid heart rate or pounding heart	NE	LOW	MED	HIGH
	Elevated blood pressure	NE	LOW	MED	HIGH
	Difficulty breathing or shortness of breath	NE	LOW	MED	HIGH
	Chest pains	NE	LOW	MED	HIGH
	Dizziness or light-headedness	NE	LOW	MED	HIGH
	Muscle tension and pains	NE	LOW	MED	HIGH
	Increased sweating	NE	LOW	MED	HIGH
	Chills or heat	NE	LOW	MED	HIGH
	Hyperventilation	NE	LOW	MED	HIGH
	Headaches	NE	LOW	MED	HIGH
	Stomach upset	NE	LOW	MED	HIGH
	SUBTOTAL:				

		Level of Distress			
CATEGORY C	Depressed mood most of the day, nearly every day	NE	LOW	MED	HIGH
	Diminished interest or pleasure in all, or almost all, activities most of the day	NE	LOW	MED	HIGH
	Inability to sleep or sleeping too much	NE	LOW	MED	HIGH
	Significant weight loss when not dieting or weight gain	NE	LOW	MED	HIGH
	Fatigue or loss of energy nearly every day	NE	LOW	MED	HIGH
	Feelings of worthlessness or guilty	NE	LOW	MED	HIGH
	Diminished ability to think or concentrate	NE	LOW	MED	HIGH
	Thoughts of death or suicide	NE	LOW	MED	HIGH

SUBTOTAL:

Category A Total: Category B Total: Category C Total:

TOTAL TRIS SCORE:

Name________________________________ Date____________________

12 Forgiveness

Probably one of the most challenging tasks when talking about forgiveness is defining the concept. Researchers, theologians, and clinicians alike debate the definition. Though most couples in therapy may have a definition of forgiveness, their definitions rarely are the same as the clinician's definition. Some couples are reluctant to forgive, for example a wife whose husband had an affair with a neighbor, because they believe that forgiveness will in some way let the other partner "get away with" their transgression. In some way, the hurt partner sees forgiving as a way of absolving their partner of responsibility and risking the future relationship.

However, *forgiveness* is not synonymous with verbs such as *pardoning*, *condoning*, *excusing*, *forgetting*, or even *reconciling*, although it is possible that these actions may result. The clinician has to be sensitive to the couple's understanding of the difference and be aware that if forgiveness is addressed too early in the therapeutic process it may unintentionally translate to the partner as pardoning or condoning. The paradox is that forgiveness begins when a couple comes to therapy to heal their relationship, yet some elements of therapy need to take place before the discussion of forgiveness can take place without risking one partner feeling invalidated.

I believe a common view of forgiveness includes the notion that forgiveness can occur in the absence of reconciliation with the transgressor. It is not uncommon to hear a person on the news or in a movie state that they have forgiven the stranger who attacked them. This common view indicates that forgiveness is an intrapersonal process, one that primarily resides within the self. In other words, when victims forgive an offender, they have completed the process of internally changing for the better how they view the offender (and possibly the offense), without necessarily reconciling the relationship.

Defining the Multiplicity of Forgiveness

One common characteristic of forgiveness that I regularly hear couples talk about in therapy is the concept of letting go of the hard feelings. They believe that they have completed forgiveness when they no longer feel anger, sadness, and anxiety. This is only partially true; the response to transgressions falls into three different domains: cognitive, affective, and motivational. Cognitive responses include attributions of blame and ruminative thoughts; affective responses include feelings such as hostility, sadness, or fear; and motivational responses include desires for revenge or avoidance. From this viewpoint, the letting go will require a release in all three domains.

Forgiveness can be viewed as being one of two types, either emotional forgiveness, which indicates some difference in feelings toward the transgressor or the situation, or decisional forgiveness, which has to do more with behavioral changes. Decisional forgiveness lacks the emotional component and could be stated as, "I forgive you for what you've done, but it will take more time for me to get over this emotionally."

Emotional forgiveness, then, is transformative. It is the displacement of negative attitudes, such as anger and revenge towards damaging situations or people, with positive attitudes such as compassion and tolerance. Emotional forgiveness is seen as a healthy attempt to cope with the negative outcomes which are caused by the maltreatment of others or wrong behaviors by oneself (Reed & Enright, 2006; Maltby, Macaskil & Day, 2001). As this definition suggests, forgiveness has a function that transforms negative feelings into positive feelings.

Traditional definitions of forgiveness have differed on whether the process involved only a reduction in the victim's negative emotions, motivations, behaviors, and cognition or whether it also led to a corresponding movement toward a positive experience toward the offender. The question is whether forgiveness is solely intrapersonal or interpersonal, or is a combination of the two.

An intrapersonal model of forgiveness states that forgiveness is an internal process of either the injured party or the transgressor. The injured party copes through reduction of the negative affective, cognitive, behavioral, and motivational experiences and forgives the transgressor without the transgressor's involvement in the process or acknowledgement of responsibility. According to the intrapersonal model, the offender forgives themselves for their role in the transgression without involvement with the victim. Alternately, the interpersonal model of forgiveness would focus on an expression of forgiveness toward the offender in a personal way. As such, forgiveness is an interaction between the forgiving person, the offending person, and the relationship between the two of them.

How does the transgressor fit into the equation from the perspective of interpersonal forgiveness? There are multiple factors related to the transgressor, including beliefs both partners hold about the relationship, the degree of empathy the hurt partner has for the transgressor, the perceived severity of the offense by both partners, and the transgressor's efforts to seek forgiveness (McCullough et al., 1998). In the therapeutic context, the offender would acknowledge responsibility and convey remorse.

Janis Abrahms Spring (2004, pp. 9–10), in her book *How Can I Forgive You*, compares four different approaches to forgiveness based on two key concepts of interpersonal forgiveness: whether or not the hurt partner comes to terms with the injury and whether or not the offender participates in the healing process.

She begins with the concept of *cheap forgiveness*. This type of forgiveness is given too early; it is superficial and underserved. The offender ignores the pain. The person may offer cheap forgiveness to preserve a relationship or to reduce relational tension, but they are likely to suffer and carry resentment. The hurt person will not come to terms with the injury and the offender is not involved in the healing process, yet reconciliation can occur.

Another approach is *refusal to forgive*, which happens when the person wants to punish the offender or that the person associates forgiveness with reconciliation or compassion, each of which the person is willing to offer. The hurt person does not come to terms with the injury, the offender is not involved in the healing process, and refusing to forgive will not lead to reconciliation.

Acceptance is a choice to take control of the pain and make sense of the injury when the offender is unavailable or unrepentant (p. 53). The hurt person does come to terms with the injury, the offender is not involved in the healing process, and it may lead to reconciliation.

The last approach is *genuine forgiveness*. Genuine forgiveness requires the heartfelt participation of both the hurt person and the offender (p. 123). The hurt person comes to terms with the injury, the offender is involved in the healing process, and it could lead to reconciliation.

As you can see, defining forgiveness is multifaceted, and the clinician needs a strong understanding to approach forgiveness effectively in therapy. Forgiveness encompasses cognitive, affective, and motivational responses. It is transformative in that it is the displacement of negative attitudes, such as anger and revenge towards damaging situations or people, with positive attitudes such as compassion and tolerance. Interpersonal forgiveness results in the hurt person's coming to terms with the injury through a dedicated healing process with the offender, which may lead to reconciliation.

Forgiveness and Well-being

Forgiveness contributes to the wellness of the individual and the wellness of relationships. Some researchers view the act of forgiving as indicative of a more enlightened and desirable personality, particularly if the alternative is the polar opposite, which is holding grudges and carrying unresolved anger.

Many studies have highlighted the productive advantages and pro-social function of forgiveness (Chung & Lee, 2014), and the benefits of replacing anger with forgiveness for individuals, relationships, and societies (Burnette et al., 2009). Benefits of forgiveness include general well-being in the relationship, relationship longevity, and relationship satisfaction (Gordon, Baucom, & Snyder, 2005; McNulty, 2008).

There is also a cost associated with not forgiving. The lack of forgiveness is related to maintaining negative feelings, grudges, desires for retribution, and depressive symptoms, which indicate that not forgiving creates psychological maladjustment (Myung-Sun, 2016). Forgiveness not only contributes to the reduction of negative feelings but also to the frequency of positive feelings (Enright & Fitzgibbons, 2000).

There is a benefit/cost consideration. In some circumstances, the cost of forgiveness could be too high, particularly related to behavior change of the transgressor. There is less likelihood for change when there are multiple transgressions, which indicate that there is a low level of accountability in the relationship that is necessary for behavior change and less probability of forgiveness (McNulty, 2008). It is hard to forgive when there is high probability that there will be additional harm in the relationship.

How Do Clinicians Address Forgiveness in Session?

There is not much written in the research about what clinicians do to facilitate forgiveness in their sessions. So, what do they do? Researchers from Florida State University (Olmstead, Blick, & Mills, 2009) interviewed marriage and family therapists about how they approach forgiveness in session, and several themes emerged.

First, the clinicians in the study emphasized the importance of understanding the couple's view of forgiveness and using their language in the discussion. Using the couple's language can show respect and sensitivity to the topic and make it easier to address misunderstandings about forgiveness.

The clinicians believed that psychoeducation was an important component of the treatment process. Two critical aspects of psychoeducation were identified: 1) helping clients understand that forgiveness is a process, and 2) facilitating client understanding of misconceptions regarding forgiveness.

Another theme was clarity. The clinicians reported that it is important to understand what the couple wants and needs. This includes an assessment of the couple's desire for the future of the relationship. Some couples may want to work towards forgiveness and reconciliation while other may want to forgive and separate.

The strongest theme of the study was the concept of time. The clinicians believed that couples should understand that forgiveness is a process and that it takes time. Since two people are working for forgiveness in couples therapy, and each may be in a different place in healing and forgiveness, the length of the process may be longer than what the couple expects. Clinicians should also be careful in their timing of forgiveness interventions. It is important for the clinician to recognize the clients' readiness for forgiveness and wait until the clients are ready before suggesting the option of forgiveness. There is the possibility that the clinician can broach the subject of forgiveness too early in the therapeutic process. One circumstance where timing can be too early is when there is not sufficient evidence from the hurt partner's perspective that further hurt will not occur, for example, a couple recovering from infidelity in which the participating partner has had multiple affairs. In truth, forgiving could be considered a questionable endeavor when there is a likelihood of further transgressions. Therefore, encouraging someone to forgive a wrong without an assessment of the relationship may be inviting further injury.

Effective, Evidenced-Based Forgiveness Intervention for Couples

Effective facilitation of forgiveness in the therapeutic context is not solely the responsibility of the clinician. Forgiveness is a multifaceted experience for the couple. The clinician can only create the context for interpersonal forgiveness for the couple who has a desire and willingness to experience the process. Effective interventions take into account both the clinician and the couple.

Intentionality of the Couple

Forgiveness is an intentional and effortful behavior (Younger et al., 2004). It takes hard work on the part of the hurt individual. It will also take hard work and patience for the transgressor. As with any intentional behavior, individuals need a compelling reason for their behavior (Ajzen, 2011).

The Couple's Belief There Is a Benefit to Forgiveness

One compelling reason is the person's belief about the outcome of forgiveness, and this belief has a strong influence on their intention to forgive. People are more likely to forgive if they consider that forgiveness will better their relationship or will increase their own personal wellness in some way (Jeter & Brannon, 2015). It may seem very obvious to mention this, but research also indicates that couples respond more negatively (i.e., with anger and avoidance) when victims responded unforgivingly, and they respond more positively (i.e., with benevolence and empathy) when victims responded forgivingly (Jennings et al., 2016).

Understand and Clarify Beliefs About Forgiveness

Effective interventions also incorporate the beliefs and attitudes of forgiveness that the couple endorses to help them accomplish tasks that they believe necessary to forgive (Thoresen, Luskin, & Harris, 2008). In addition, when the clinician is sensitive to the couple's language and understanding of their definition of forgiveness, it becomes easier to modify the couple's definition if they ascribe to any myths of forgiveness.

Facilitate Exploration of Risk and Benefits of Forgiveness

Effective interventions will also help people see the benefits of forgiveness for both their relationship and themselves (Thoresen, Luskin, & Harris, 2008). Benefits of forgiveness include general well-being in the relationship, marital longevity, and marital satisfaction (Gordon, Baucom, & Snyder, 2005; McNulty,

2008). On the other hand, the cost of forgiveness should be considered, particularly related to behavior change of the transgressor. The hurt partner needs significant confidence that the risk to the relationship has been removed.

Assess Commitment to the Relationship

It is helpful to assess the couple's commitment to the relationship in regards to forgiveness. Some couples may want to work towards forgiveness and reconcile, while other may want to forgive and separate. It is not uncommon for couples to want to forgive and separate, some for their own well-being and meaning-making of events and others because forgiveness may let them function better as parents in a shared custody arrangement.

Planned Clinician Timing

Clinician timing of the discussion of forgiveness is crucial. If the topic is broached too early, the risk increases that the hurt partner will feel invalidated. This could stall treatment or, worse, could increase the likelihood that the couple will drop out of treatment.

Reduce Negative Emotional, Cognitive, Behavioral, and Motivational Experiences

People also need a compelling emotional reason to change. Effective interventions for couples tend to target pro-social change within the relationship and generally encourage the reduction of negative emotions, such as anger, hostility, and blame (Thoresen, Luskin, & Harris, 2008).

Encourage Empathy and Patience

The clinician can encourage the transgressor to practice empathy for the hurt partner. This takes effort and patience. Since oftentimes both partners are on different timelines for healing, forgiveness and healing will be a slow process. The timeline can be explained this way: The hurt partner is working through a slow process of making sense of things, and the transgressor is moving a bit more quickly to move the relationship to a new place of relationship functioning. Patience is needed to allow for this process.

Approaches to Forgiveness in Couples Therapy

Psychoeducation

Educating clients about forgiveness may be an important part of treatment. Many couples that come to treatment will understand that forgiveness includes cognitive, emotional, and behavioral aspects, yet some will also include concepts of condoning, excusing, and other components that are not included in the definition of forgiveness. To increase the likelihood of forgiveness, clinicians should discuss the differences between forgiveness and other similar concepts (Kearns & Fincham, 2004).

Another part of psychoeducation is providing resources for the couple. Some couples may want faith-based resources, and others may want resources specific to a particular situation, such as infidelity. Couples may also need to be educated about the timing of forgiveness, mainly that forgiveness is a process, not a product, and that the process of forgiveness can take time to go through. In addition, the clinician will need to be careful on their timing of discussions about forgiveness and may need to explain to couples that the decision to forgive typically happens in the latter part of therapy.

Decision-Based Forgiveness Approach

The focus of decision-based forgiveness is on the decision to forgive, which involves steps that allow for a reduction of negative emotional, cognitive, and behavioral experiences. Decision-based forgiveness is defined as letting go of the need for vengeance and releasing negative thoughts of bitterness and resentment. It involves a willful decision to restructure feeling, behavior, and cognitions regarding the offender and the offense (DiBlasio & Brenda, 2008).

The Decision-Based Forgiveness Model was developed by Frederick DiBlasio (DiBlasio, 2000). It includes thirteen steps for the treatment process. The steps are categorized into three sections. DiBlasio states that the process takes work. For example, the forgiveness session is from two to three hours (steps 4–12). It also requires time and emotional readiness.

The model offers each partner an opportunity to disclose and focus on his or her own hurtful behaviors through a step-by-step session in which the behaviors are thoroughly stated and explained and where there is a full hearing of the hurt and pain involved. The three-hour session includes the creation of plans to stop and/or prevent the behaviors of the past, and it gives the couple an opportunity to seek formal forgiveness. The structure of the therapy session is outlined in the steps that follow:

Steps 1–3 Definition and Benefits of Forgiveness Therapy

1. Definition and benefits of forgiveness therapy provided
2. Seek forgiveness for wrongdoing
3. Forgiveness treatment introduced

The couple is asked about their definition of forgiveness; the clinician shares that there are many definitions of forgiveness but that the common thread is "letting go" of bitterness towards the other person (not to be confused with reconciliation). Therefore, in the first three steps, the couple is introduced to the forgiveness treatment process and the steps involved, and they are asked whether they would like to participate. In the process, both individuals will seek forgiveness and offer forgiveness.

Steps 4–12 Seek Forgiveness for Wrongdoing

4. The offense is stated
5. The offender provides explanation
6. Questions are raised and answers given
7. The offended gives emotional reaction
8. The offender provides empathy
9. The offender develops a plan to stop/prevent behavior
10. The victim identifies with offender's hurt
11. Choice and commitment provided for letting go
12. Formal request made for forgiveness

The offender should detail the offense and summarize the reasons for their behavior, while being careful not to excuse the behavior. The injured partner is then encouraged to ask questions of the offender and receive honest and comprehensive answers. An exchange is then encouraged for the hurt partner to give an emotional reaction; the offending partner is to provide an empathic response, demonstrating understanding for the hurt partner's feelings.

The offending partner formulates a detailed plan and shares it with their partner. The clinician should work with the couple to identify the strengths of the plan and any barriers that might make it difficult to implement, adjusting the plan accordingly.

The session ends with a formal request for forgiveness.

Step 13 Ceremonial Act

13. Ceremonial Act

This is a symbolic act that the offense has been forgiven. The couple is encouraged to take their time in creating this act. Though it may be very private, DiBlasio suggests that they should give a definite signal to family and community that this transition has been made.

Gordon & Baucom's Forgiveness Process Model

Gordon and Baucom (2003) developed a cognitive model of forgiveness that proposes that forgiveness of major betrayals, such as infidelity, closely parallels recovery from traumatic events as both partners deal with the impact of the event, make meaning from the event, and move on.

Forgiveness can aid in reconstructing individuals' beliefs about their partner and their relationship and help them regain the sense of safety, control, and predictability in the relationship that is necessary to move on from the transgression.

The three stages of forgiveness from Gordon and Baucom's point of view are impact, meaning, and moving on. These stages are not necessarily strictly linear, as there can be movement between the stages as issues and feelings can resurface. Tasks for each stage include 1) recognizing and assessing the need to forgive and doubt about all relational assumptions, 2) discovering why the offense occurred and how it impacts the relationship, and 3) attending to both positive and negative qualities of the offender, as well as creating new, realistic expectations, standards, and assumptions regarding the offender, self, and relationship (Gordon & Baucom, 2003).

Couples will know that they have reached a level of forgiveness when they have attained 1) a realistic, non-distorted, balanced view of the relationship; 2) a release from being controlled by negative affect toward the participating partner; and 3) a lessened desire to punish the participating partner (Gordon & Baucom, 1998).

Facilitating Forgiveness in the Treatment of Infidelity

Stephen Fife and Gerald Weeks have written extensively on facilitating forgiveness within the context of infidelity. They do not regard their model of forgiveness as a comprehensive approach to treating infidelity but rather as a central part of the treatment process. Following is a brief description of these important steps that may help clients prepare to work through forgiveness when recovering from infidelity (Fife, Weeks, & Stellberg-Filbert, 2013).

Precursors to Forgiveness

Couples dealing with infidelity come to therapy in crisis. In the initial sessions, the hurt partner often expresses a strong need to know. Yet an excessive preoccupation with the details of the affair can hinder the process of healing for the hurt partner and ultimately for the couple. In order to help the hurt partner move from obsessive fact-finding to more healing behavior, the clinician may need to monitor and limit obsessive questioning. I will usually ask partners to consider what is helpful versus what information could create additional harm for the hurt partner.

To establish the context of the relationship prior to the affair, an assessment should be made in order to identify individual, relational, and environmental factors that may have been associated with the betrayal. Most cases of infidelity occur in a relational context in which the primary relationship is suffering. The affair may be a symptom of the relationship problems.

Clinicians should encourage the hurt partner to define the boundaries they would like to have for interactions between the couple as well as with others, such as family members, friends, and "potentially attractive others." Additionally, any intervention for forgiveness and healing will be thwarted if there is an ongoing affair. The participating partner must commit to cease all contact with the affair partner in order for trust to be rebuilt and healing to begin.

As in other approaches to forgiveness, understanding the couple's definition of forgiveness is important to the process. The clinician should facilitate discussion between partners so that they can understand the way in which each of them defines forgiveness. When the couple struggles with the idea of forgiveness, the clinician can assist by clarifying what forgiveness is and offering more helpful definitions for them to consider.

The goals of this phase include the following:

- Encourage a commitment to treatment.
- Help the couple manage the initial crisis.
- Examine the relationship context prior to the infidelity.
- Help couples establish appropriate relationship boundaries.
- Define forgiveness: clarify clients' definitions and clear up misunderstandings.

Facilitating Forgiveness: Four Unifying Factors

This next phase is not considered as sequential steps, but rather it is advantageous if these four factors are operating simultaneously, depending on the couple's readiness. These factors can create a soothing effect between the couple and help the process of forgiveness.

1. Empathy

Having empathy is difficult when one has experienced infidelity. Each partner can be overwhelmed with emotions and may find it difficult to express empathy toward the other. The clinician can help the couple by addressing defensiveness early in session and helping the couple communicate with nondefensive, empathic listening with the goal of developing a mutual understanding of each other's experience.

2. Humility

In many cases, the participating partner may attempt to rationalize their behavior and avoid taking responsibility for their actions. They may become defensive when questioned about what they did, what they were thinking, or the damage they have caused, creating a barrier to healing. However, through humility, the participating partner can learn to accept responsibility for the affair and express sorrow for the hurt they have caused.

3. Commitment and Hope

Forgiveness is most likely to occur when both partners desire reconciliation and when the couple is willing to put forth a shared effort to facilitate healing.

Commitment to the relationship is highly significant for the success of the forgiveness process because the partners' level of commitment and hope for the future will influence their current behavior and the decision to forgive. Hope can come from reviewing good memories, creating closeness and connection with one another as they work toward healing and reconnect with shared goals and dreams.

4. *Apology*

Apologizing is a critical step for healing the relationship after an affair. Specifically, an apology can help soothe the hurts caused by infidelity, increase trust, and establish a sense of safety and control for the hurt partner. A genuine apology requires significant effort and preparation. Numerous apologies may have already been offered and may feel insincere. For that reason, the clinician and couple may plan for a specific session in which partners come prepared to apologize and ask for forgiveness. Prior to facilitating an apology, the clinician must be clear that unfaithful partners understand the damage caused by their behavior, are truly sorry, and are committed to remain faithful. At the conclusion of this phase, the partner can offer an apology and request forgiveness.

References

Abrahms Spring, J. (2004). *How can I forgive you?* New York: Harper Collins Publishers.

Ajzen, I. (2011). The theory of planned behavior: Reactions and reflections. *Psychology & Health*, *26*, 1113–1127.

Burnette, J. L., Davis, D. E., Green, J. D., Worthington, E. L. Jr, & Bradfield, E. (2009). Insecure attachment and depressive symptoms: The mediating role of rumination, empathy, and forgiveness. *Personality and Individual Differences*, *46*, 276–280.

Chung, M. S., & Lee, K. J. (2014). A path-analytic study of associations between attachment, rumination, empathy, and forgiveness. *Journal of Special Education and Rehabilitation Science*, *53*, 193–209.

DiBlasio, F. A. (2000). Decision-based forgiveness treatment in cases of marital infidelity. *Psychotherapy*, *V37*(2), 149–158.

DiBlasio, F. A., & Brenda, B. B. (2008). Forgiveness intervention with married couples: Two empirical analysis. *Journal of Psychology and Christianity*, *27*(2), 150–158.

Enright, R. D., & Fitzgibbons, R. P. (2000). *Helping clients forgive: An empirical guide for resolving anger and restoring hope*. Washington, DC: APA Books. doi:10.1037/10381-000.

Fife, S., Weeks, G., & Stellberg-Filbert, J. (2013). Facilitating forgiveness in the treatment of infidelity: An interpersonal model. *Journal of Family Therapy*, *35*(4), 343–367.

Gordon, K., Baucom, D. H., & Snyder, D. K. (2005). Forgiveness in couples: Divorce, infidelity, and couples therapy. In E. L. Worthington (Ed.), *Handbook of forgiveness* (pp. 407–421). New York: Routledge.

Gordon, K. C., & Baucom, D. H. (1998). Understanding betrayals in marriage: A synthesized model of forgiveness. *Family Process*, *37*, 425–449.

Gordon, K. C., & Baucom, D. H. (2003). Forgiveness and marriage: Preliminary support for a measure based on a model of recovery from a marital betrayal. *The American Journal of Family Therapy*, *31*, 179–199.

Jennings II, D. J., Worthington Jr., E. L., Van Tongeren, D. R., Hook, J. N., Davis, D. E., Gartner, A. L., . . . Mosher, D. K. (2016). The transgressor's response to denied forgiveness. *Journal of Psychology & Theology*, *44*(1), 16–27.

Jeter, W. K., & Brannon, L. A. (2015). Increasing awareness of potentially helpful motivations and techniques for forgiveness. *Counseling and Values*, 60, 186–200.

Kearns, J. N., & Fincham, F. D. (2004). A prototype analysis of forgiveness. *Personality and Social Psychology Bulletin*, *30*, 838–855.

Maltby, J., Macaskill, A., & Day, L. (2001). Failure to forgive self and others: A replication and extension of the relationship between forgiveness, personality, social desirability and general health. *Personality and Individual Differences*, *30*, 881–885. doi:10.1016/S0191-8869(00)00080-5.

McCullough, M. E., Rachal, K. C., Sandage, S. J., Worthington, E. L. Jr., Brown, S. W., & Hight, T. L. (1998). Interpersonal forgiving in close relationships II: Theoretical elaboration and measurement. *Journal of Personality and Social Psychology*, *75*, 1586–1603.

McNulty, J. K. (2008). Forgiveness in marriage: Putting the benefits into context. *Journal of Family Psychology*, *22*, 171–175. doi:http://doi.org/c8tmt8.

Myung-Sun, C. (2016). Relation between lack of forgiveness and depression: The moderating effect of self-compassion. *Psychological Reports*, *119*(3), 573–585. doi:10.1177/0033294116663520.

Olmstead, S. B., Blick, R. W., & Mills, L. I. (2009). Helping couples work toward the forgiveness of marital infidelity: Therapists' perspectives. *The American Journal of Family Therapy*, *37*, 48–66. doi:10.1080/01926180801960575.

Reed, G. L., & Enright, R. D. (2006). The effects of forgiveness therapy on depression, anxiety, and posttraumatic stress for women after spousal emotional abuse. *Journal of Consultation in Clinical Psychology*, October; *74*(5), 920–929.

Thoresen, C. E., Luskin, F., & Harris, A. H. (2008). Science and forgiveness interventions: Reflections and recommendations. *Dimensions of Forgiveness: A Research Approach*, *1*, 163–190.

Younger, J. W., Piferi, R. L., Jobe, R. L., & Lawler, K. A. (2004). Dimensions of forgiveness: The views of laypersons. *Journal of Social and Personal Relationships*, *21*, 837–855.

13 Documenting the Session

Necessary Evil or Clinical Tool?

Usefulness requires specificity.

—Robert Mitchell (2007), *Documentation in Counseling Records*

Unfortunately, the view of many clinicians is that clinical documentation, and in particular the session note, has become the necessary evil. We spend much of our day planning how we are going to find the time to write the session note. Maybe we are so overwhelmed with our utilization that we hope for a "no show" so that it frees up an hour to write our notes. Later in the day, we decide that tomorrow morning will be a good time to finish up our notes.

When busy, we shortcut our notes and document less information, and certainly quality suffers. Yet we trudge along and do it because we have to. Funders will not pay us without it, quality-assurance committees will punish us if we do it incorrectly, and no one holds up a spotlight on a fantastically written session notes. It's just paperwork anyway, correct?

Users of the Client Chart

The complete client chart serves many different functions for quite a few different entities. Knowing the users of the chart helps direct the clinician in their writing so that they can match the needs of the potential users. It is also important to demonstrate ethical behavior, professional behavior, and competent service in the chart. Table 13.1 provides some specific examples of by whom the clinical record may be used:

Functions of the Clinical Record

Reamer (2005) identified that the clinical chart serves six primary functions. These functions serve to increase quality of care, provide interdisciplinary communication and coordination, support the supervision and development of the clinician, and protect the clinician and supervisor from liability.

1) *Assessment and planning* is a primary function. All related facts and circumstances should be clearly and comprehensively documented. Incomplete

Table 13.1 Users of the Clinical Record

The clinician will need it to develop a comprehensive treatment plan.
Insurance companies will want to identify the billable service.
The clinical supervisor will want to ensure that clients are getting appropriate care.
The agency quality-assurance committee will review the record to make sure that the documentation meets specific standards.
A colleague may review the chart to cover the clinician's absence due to illness or extended leave.
A court may require it for review at a lawsuit.
The professions board may want to review the record to investigate the clinician.
The client might want to read some or all of it.

records could lead to inadequate planning and interventions, judgment errors, and poor outcomes for clients.

2) To offer competent, high-quality *service delivery*, thorough documentation is necessary. Good progress notes indicate competent treatment. Documentation should be the best representation of the service the clinician provides.
3) *Continuity and coordination of service* facilitates professional interdisciplinary collaboration and is considered a necessary standard of practice by most insurance panels.
4) Clinical documentation should be reviewed in *supervision* to mediate risk for the supervisor and clinician while increasing quality of care. Supervisors can be held liable for the errors of their supervisees.
5) *Service evaluation* occurs on multiple levels. Agencies, insurance panels, and certifying organizations all evaluate either individual cases or do some program evaluation, which at times require individual charts.
6) *Accountability* may be initiated through client requests, insurance contracts, interagency collaboration, litigation, licensing boards, ethics committee oversight, and utilization review bodies.

Policy of Health Insurance Companies Sets Content Standards

Insurance companies will set policy for documentation standards that providers must maintain. An incomplete session note translates into not being paid for services rendered. It is not uncommon for an agency or practice to be required to pay back money to the funder for inadequate or inappropriate documentation. Outlined in these policies are the minimum standards for the session note. Consider the following minimum standards set by the insurance company Value Options, listed in Table 13.2 (Value Options, 2014).

Considering also Value Options' requirements of documentation of specific services and/or interventions, the following in Table 13.3 are expectations of the content:

"Medical necessity" is a term used by insurance companies to guarantee that there is evidence of clinically appropriate services and interventions useful for the condition being treated. For any intervention to be a medical necessity,

Table 13.2 Minimum Standards for Session Notes

Date of Service
Service intervention of service coed
Location if other than office
Time providing billable service
Documentation of specific services and interventions
Signature and credentials

Table 13.3 Required Documentation of Services Provided

Reason for the contact
Assessment of the client's current clinical presentation
Relevant history
Specific mental health/clinical interventions by provider
Client's response to interventions
Unresolved issues from previous contacts
Plans, next steps, and/or clinical decisions
Indications of progress or lack of progress and indicate reason
Date of next planned contact and/or next clinician action
Indication of any referrals made
Documentation of any issues of risk and how they were managed

there must be evidence that the intervention is effective in improving health outcomes. It needs to be the least restrictive and cost effective for this condition compared to alternative interventions, including no intervention. To have medical necessity, the clinician would only provide services for client problems that cannot be treated by physical health interventions.

Each session, then, needs to demonstrate medical necessity. Each session note should stand on its own to meet the medical necessity requirement. Linking the session note to the treatment plan helps meet this requirement (Value Options, 2014).

Models for Documenting the Therapy Session

Clinicians can mistakenly believe that taking time to document the details of a session takes away from their client care, but documentation is, in fact, one primary aspect of client care. A carefully written session note will improve and enhance the treatment process by helping the clinician track the couple's progress in treatment and help them stay focused on the treatment plan. Documentation that is completed correctly demonstrates how the interactions and interventions in session were directed by the treatment plan. It is one of the best possible measures of the clinician's abilities as a professional.

Models of Clinical Documentation

In my own experience working in a children's psychiatric hospital many years ago, the model for documenting the group or individual session at the hospital

Table 13.4 Models for Clinical Documentation of the Therapy Session

DART	Description, Assessment, Intervention, Plan
PIRP	Problem for that session, Intervention provided by the clinician, Response of client in session and to the intervention, Plan for the next appointment
DAP	Description, Assessment, and Plan
BIRP	Behavior, Intervention, Response, Plan
TALP	Topic, Assessment, Level of Participation, Plan
APIE	Assessing the client, Problem, Intervention, Evaluation and Response
FAIRS	Focus (goals and objectives), Assessment, Intervention, Response, Subsequent plan

was the SOAP model. This model is still used today. SOAP is an acronym for Subjective Complaint, Objective Findings, Assessment of Progress, and Plan for Next Session. This allows the clinician to be concise and focused in writing their session note. The challenge with this model is that it is problem based and developed from a medical model. It is not conducive, though, to a strength-based model of couples therapy.

In Table 13.4, I have identified several common note-writing models that have been adopted by agencies across the US. Take a moment to notice the similarities in the various structures. Though many of these have their roots in hand-written clinical records, these same content areas show up in electronic records-management programs. Many electronic records-management programs available to private practitioners allow the clinician to develop their own templates. Clinicians should consider the benefits of content-driven session notes versus notes that are minimalistic and have pre-selected check boxes.

Content Areas of the Session Note

In the era of managed care, maybe we have forgotten that the primary purpose for the session note is for the use of the clinician to document and plan services. Since clinicians have the opportunity to develop their own templates in a private-practice setting, I suggest that the session note be content-driven and include three primary sections: description, intervention, and response and treatment planning. Within each of these content areas are components outlined in Table 13.5.

Description

The description section serves as a concise outline of what occurred in session. It should convey the purpose of this particular session and include a discussion of what was planned for this session. It should certainly exactly indicate the billable service implemented by the clinician. A simple method of describing and identifying billable service is to consider the use of verbs and nouns.

Table 13.5 Primary Content Areas of the Session Note

Content Area	*Component*	*Purpose*	*Elements*
Description	Description	To outline what took place in the session To identify the billable service, including assessments and interventions	Simple outline of the session content Purposeful use of verbs
Intervention and response	Reflection Intervention and response Counseling relationship	To describe each clinical intervention and the client's response specifically to the intervention To document the clinician's conceptualization that was shared with the couple To document the strength of the counseling relationship	The session reflection statement Paragraph-by-paragraph identification and discussion of the clinical intervention and the client's response to each Client and counselor assessment of the counseling relationship Purposeful use of nouns
Treatment planning	Current conceptualization Between-session task Plan/intervention for next session	To articulate clinical case conceptualization Articulate progress/ lack of progress To plan the next session To identify any between-session task To develop reflection statement for the following session	Current clinical conceptualization Client conceptualization of their situation Between-session task that has been selected Plan for the next session

From Mitchell's perspective (2007), verbs indicate the billable service, and nouns indicate what was the focus of the clinician's attention in session, such as depression, anger, cognitions, or affection. The billable service should be clearly discussed in the description section of the session note. Verbs used in the description section could include *taught*, *demonstrated*, *facilitated*, *challenged*, *assessed*, or *explored*, just to name a few. As an example of how this can be used, consider this statement: "The clinician taught the Imago dialogue strategy as a means of effective communication." It is important to understand that activities of the client and clinician in session should be directly related to the treatment plan. Allegheny County Department of Human Services (2014) offers an expansive list of action verbs that can be used in writing progress notes. Not all pertain to working with couples, but reviewing the list could help expand your verb vocabulary.

Adapted	Empathized with	Planned
Advised	Empowered	Practiced
Analyzed	Encouraged	Prepared
Applied	Engaged in	Prescribed
Assessed	Evaluated	Provided
Assessed for	Examined	Provided education on
Assisted	Facilitated	Provided positive feedback
Assisted in exploring	Formulated	Provided supportive listening
Assisted in identifying	Gathered history	Recommended
Clarified	Gathered information	Redirected
Collaborated	Generalized	Referred
Compared	Gently confronted	Reflected
Confronted	Implemented	Reframed
Consulted	Integrated	Reinforced
Contrasted	Interpreted	Reorganized
Created	Made recommendations about	Reviewed
Defined	Made referral to	Role played
Described	Mirrored	Specified
Designed	Modeled	Summarized
Developed	Monitored	Utilized
Discussed	Observed	Validated
Distinguished	Organized	
Empathized	Performed	

Also, included in the description section are the clinician's observations of the client at the beginning of session and how it compares to the last session, including current mood, actions, gestures, and body language (HPSO, 2014).

Intervention and Response

Reflection

Typically, sessions begin with an opening session summary, which I call a reflection. I see the reflection as an intervention in itself, not just a way to start the session. It is a short statement to the couple on how I am conceptualizing their situation. I keep it very tentative, as I do not state any opinion strongly and recognize that my opinion is only one perspective in the room. Following the few minutes used for the reflection statement, I ask the couple to respond. Following their responses, I validate the perspective and move on with the session.

This reflection is helpful to be documented in the session note. In doing so, the clinician is able to read through the reflections from time to time and become aware of patterns that emerge in their own writing. It is important that the clinician share with the couple the patterns in their own thinking, when appropriate, to help the couple expand their perception of their situation and relationship.

Intervention and Response

Interventions are why we get paid. It is important that we document the billable service and how the couple responded to it. Interventions are the discussions that you *facilitated*, skills that you *taught*, thinking that you *challenged*, assessments that you *conducted*, and crisis situations that you *managed*.

The couple's response to intervention should be documented in the session note following the discussion of the intervention. This could include topics spoken or avoided, cognitive distortions, tone of voice, and any changes to the initial mood, attitude, actions, gestures, and body language (HPSO, 2014).

As an example, here is a simple excerpt from the Intervention/Response section of a session note written at my practice:

> Counselor facilitated a discussion about the challenge of keeping secrets in marriage. At the beginning of session Marty shared his opinion that secrets are acceptable. Counselor challenged this perspective and gave the couple a handout with definitions for a variety of terms, including privacy, confidentiality, secrets, and transparency. By the end of session, Marty had stated that privacy was more important to him than he understood. He also was more open to the perspective that his close relationship with a woman outside his marriage, shrouded in secret, was harmful to the marriage relationship.

Counseling Relationship

Towards the end of session, it is a nice idea to ask how the clinician and couple did with helping the couple meet their expectations for the session and treatment goals. Any ruptures in the relationship are more likely to be identified when there is a direct discussion about the relationship. This offers an opportunity to continually assess the strength of the relationship and to strengthen it by repairing any ruptures. This also models good skills in repairing ruptures. Opportunities to strengthen the client/clinician relationship increase the potential for positive outcomes for clients and reduce drop-out rates. Document in this section of the session note any comment the couple make about their assessment of the therapeutic relationship and any success or struggles in their meeting goals.

Treatment Planning

Current Conceptualization

In this section, I offer my conceptualization in first-person language. In other words, I use the much-shunned word in clinical documentation: the word *I*. The reason I do this is because I am my primary audience for this section. I recognize that there are other audiences that may in fact read my notes, but on the week-to-week basis, it is me.

Now, I am not the only clinician who uses this naughty word. Barbara Lichner Ingram (2011, p. 93), in her comprehensive book *Clinical Case Formulations*, states that "You are allowed to use the word 'I' " and that sometimes good writing requires breaking habits from prior educational experiences. Her argument is that the American Psychological Association (APA) manuscript style is for journal articles, not for all psychological writing.

Documentation in this section is much more than just what the client said or did. It should be grounded in the theoretical lens of the clinician so that the reader can recognize the clinician's model of treatment.

In our team meetings at my practice, I will challenge the clinicians to conceptualize before stating interventions to other team members. During case presentations, it can be easy just to offer possible interventions to other clinicians, so I ask them to first conceptualize their understanding of the client from their theoretical lens. This is more beneficial than just offering an intervention for a clinician to use for a particular couple. I will ask the clinicians to use a general method of conceptualization, typically focused on three broad areas: diagnostic, clinical, and treatment. Using these broad categories in session notes can also be helpful. The clinician can discuss their diagnostic impressions; clinical concerns such as perpetuating factors, themes, and patterns; and treatment considerations for interventions or strategies for future sessions.

Breaking down conceptualization a bit further, there are a number of topics that capture my attention for conceptualization. In Table 13.6, I list a number of these. I would suggest taking the list and practicing writing about some of the topics in your next note. It will make your session note better and over time will increase your effectiveness as a clinician.

Using the "power statement" adds professionalism to the conceptual section of the session note. The "power statement" is a strong diagnostic statement that has a specific structure to clearly state the clinician's diagnostic impressions. The structure includes 1) the problem, 2) the evidence for the problem, and 3) the resulting consequence. For example, "Dave has increased depression as evidenced by a score of 35 on the Beck Depression Inventory, resulting in a decrease in activity level as reported by his wife, Jen." You can add to the strength by also noting frequency or duration. For example, "Reduced physical activity level was noted for the past week by the couple."

Table 13.6 Recommended Content for Conceptualization

Presenting, ongoing, or unresolved issues and context
The couple's understanding of the problem or issues and the clinician's understanding
Themes, problematic or coping relational patterns, factors perpetuating the problem, vicious circles
Interventions that that might be beneficial and considered for an upcoming session
Symptomology present or assessed and plan of action for reduction
Progress, lack of progress towards goals
Strengths and barriers towards achieving treatment goals
Emotional experience or cognitive distortions
Clinical hypothesis
Clinical decisions considered or made
Recommendations of the clinician or referrals made
Any risk for the couple or individual risk, assessment procedures, and plan for safety

Between-Session Task

I favor using the term *between-session task* versus *homework*. I worry that for some couples, the term *homework* may have a negative connotation. The between-session tasks can be assigned by me or developed in collaboration with the couple. I prefer to make the between-session tasks as specific as possible and write it in this section much the way I write a treatment goal. For example, stating the task, the context (who will do what, when, and how), and frequency/ duration (once a week on Wednesdays, daily at 6 p.m.).

I also ask the couple to participate in "experiments." These are assigned as a method to get the couple to do something differently with the intent of coming back to report on the outcomes of the experiment. This helps the couple notice change and increases their observation of the relationship. Both the between-session tasks and experiments should be clearly and explicitly documented in this section.

Plan/Interventions for Next Session

This section should first identify any immediate needs that need to be addressed before the next session. This should also include who will be responsible for addressing the need and a time frame for implementation.

Next, include any agenda items that the couple has stated that they want to focus on for the next session. Also, include any interventions planned for the next session that were identified in the conceptualization section of the session note.

A Few Good Rules

Effort should be made to complete the note as soon as possible after the session and preferably the same day. Writing notes within twenty-four hours is considered best practice. A session note that is written on the same day of service will be more accurate and have more detail. A detailed note assures that someone unfamiliar with this case can understand exactly what has occurred in treatment.

When writing the note, make sure to avoid tentative language such as *may* or *seems* or *appears*. When I started working in mental health, these words were recommended. Clinicians are trained at a high level and know when someone is depressed, so never say "seems depressed." Use a power statement such as "Mr. Jones is depressed as evidenced by [list of symptoms] resulting in [identify the outcomes of the depression]." Similarly, avoid absolutes such as *always* and *never*. Always and never rarely, if ever, occur.

Session Notes for Crisis

Additional information needs to be documented in session notes for crisis intervention. Of primary importance is a detailed description of the emergency and immediacy of the situation, including the client's immediate danger to self or others. Interventions should be documented to show what has been done to decrease, eliminate, or alleviate the danger, reduce trauma, or ameliorate the crisis. It is important to note that any time there is an assessment of risk, the clinician must document what they did to reduce the risk. Lastly, a safety or aftercare plan can be developed and documented, noting collateral and community contacts who will participate in follow-up or support.

Collaborative Documentation

A newer concept that has certainly taken it roots in Ohio is the process of collaborative documentation. Collaborative documentation, sometimes referred to as "concurrent documentation," is a process in which clinicians and clients collaborate in the documentation, assessment, service plan, and session note (Hirsch, 2014). Hirsch believes this process is an opportunity for clients to provide their input and perspective on services and progress, and it allows clients and clinicians to clarify their understanding of important issues and focus on outcomes. Hirsch (2014) identifies a number of benefits of collaborative documentation, including the following:

Improves quality or care by increasing engagement with the client in treatment.
Improves client outcomes.
Increases the quality and objectivity of the documentation.
Improves the quality of life for the clinician because they are involved in less paperwork!
Creates structure in the session.
Allows the client to feel heard and understood.

Certainly, collaborative documentation will require a shift in thinking. As has been mentioned throughout this chapter, writing session notes is an essential part of the treatment process. Viewing it as a valuable interactive process will help your couples see it that way. The clinician will need to adjust their writing style so that the client can understand the concepts and language (Hirsch, 2014).

There are several common concerns that clinicians state about participating in collaborative documentation, including that the client will be resentful, it wastes valuable session time, or it takes more time to do documentation with the client. However, client experiences with the process are more favorable. A survey conducted with over 6,000 clients indicated that 82% of the clients said that reviewing session notes were either "very helpful" or "helpful" while 77% said that they would want their provider to continue to review the notes at the end of session (Schmelter, 2014).

Collaborative Documentation

"Aren't we going to do that thing?" That thing? I froze, seized by bewilderment and panic. To what on earth was my client referring? To set the scene, I was rushing to wrap up a school-based mental health session with a sixteen-year-old client and return the client back to class on time. "That thing?" Those of us who work with children, adolescents, and even couples know there are very few constants in mental health practice. A client's remembering the promise of a counselor is one of those steadfast truths. I wish I could chronicle this story with my tactful navigation of this minefield. However, my recollection of the exchange includes stammering something along the lines of, "That thing?" To my surprise and amazement my client responded, "That thing we do on the computer where you write and I tell you what we did today." There it was, served up to me so nicely, my first realization that collaborative documentation works!

A few weeks prior, the agency I work for had instituted a collaborative documentation declaration. I must admit I did not immediately jump on the collaborative documentation train. I think, like many clinicians, I was practiced in a documentation style that didn't include the client and occurred behind closed doors. I couldn't see collaborative documentation for the valuable clinical tool that it is.

In a profession like counseling that is focused on best practice and client-centered treatments, collaborative documentation, sometimes referred to as "concurrent documentation," meets both standards for clinicians. Collaborative documentation "is a clinical tool that provides clients with the opportunity to provide their input and perspective on services and progress, and allows clients and clinicians to clarify their understanding of important issues" (Schmelter 2012). The beauty of collaborative documentation is that it can be molded for use in progress notes, treatment-plan development, yearly reviews, medication updates, and even termination summaries. All a clinician needs to put collaborative documentation to use is flexibility, a little creativity, and a client.

Perhaps the most advantageous aspect of collaborative documentation is the amount of time saved when the clinical documentation is completed, or at least begun, in session. Aside from the hours of time saved, collaborative documentation will open a window into the minds of our clients. It provides greater insight into what the client latched onto in the session, what they found helpful, and which skills the client is planning to use outside of the session. Additionally, utilizing the client's influence in documentation can reduce unnecessary fillers clinicians fall victim to using and keeps documentation from being skewed by the clinician's perspective. Lastly, it is important to remember that to collaboratively document, a clinician does not have to rely on an overabundance of client quotes. I have found that simply engaging the clients in a structured session review will support more positive client outcomes, and clients leave the session feeling more hopeful.

In honest disclosure, instituting collaborative documentation with my clients did not come without its struggles. A barrier encountered when incorporating collaborative documentation into my progress note was the concern of how to include information the client did not voice for the note. After much pondering, I realized this was collaborative documentation, after all, and I was just as much a part of this collaboration as the client.

Short prompts like:

What about . . .
I thought . . . was important
I would love your thoughts on . . .

Or a simple, more direct:

Can we include . . .
How do we say . . .

Serve to help me include all the important information.

I discovered in my practice that collaborative documentation supports a more strengths-based, goal-driven treatment. Collaborative documentation assists the development of the initial treatment plan. I utilize the VIA Institute on Character's list of character strengths to support struggling clients in identifying personal strengths. Goals are written in the client's words, and the treatment plan is printed to be utilized at the end of the session for progress monitoring. I prompt the client to identify the goal and objectives we addressed in session that day and how we addressed them.

I follow up with the standard questions:

How can we summarize what we did today?
What did you find useful/helpful from the session?
What will you use out of session?
What will you take with you from today?

Just as clinicians instill in clients the use of therapeutic skills, so too can clinicians instill a climate of collaborative documentation. It may take some weathering of the storm to perfect the practice, but the end results will be well worth the effort.

Jennifer Johnson, B.A., is a lead community-based mental health provider for Child Focus Inc. She began working in the field of mental health in 2001. She received her Bachelor of Arts from Xavier University in 2007. She has been working as a school-based mental health provider for a non-profit community mental health agency since 2007. Prior to working with children, she worked with adults diagnosed with co-occurring mental illness and substance abuse as a community case manager and as a halfway house residential manager. She has been a member of the Clermont County Crisis Response Team since 2009, co-leads a court-ordered family group, and is a member of her agency's Corporate Compliance committee.

Jennifer can be reached at
513–460–1433
jennifere.johnson@yahoo.com

Progress Evaluation Report

As you can see, the session note is a very useful clinical tool to conceptualize and prepare for sessions. The session notes can also be integrated into the client session in more direct ways. Collaborative documentation is just one way to integrate the session note in the counseling session.

David Kats from Therapist Consultants (Kats, 2014) suggests offering a progress evaluation report that should be prepared prior to session and discussed in session. This report is given every ten sessions and is based on the clinician's review of the last ten session notes. The clinician discusses the report, seeks feedback from the client, and gives the report to the client.

I believe the progress evaluation report is especially useful for clients who feel stuck because it helps the client see the subtle changes that have been occurring from the clinician's perspective. Getting feedback from the clinician about the work the couple has done can be the freeing agent that moves the client closer to achieving their goals.

Kats (2014) notes that something interesting happens when you perform a progress evaluation and report. The client becomes re-enthused about their care. And, obviously, an enthusiastic client will never drop out of treatment and is more likely to continue and achieve greater benefits from counseling.

References

Allegheny County Department of Human Services, Office of Behavioral Health. (2009). *Documentation guidelines for service coordinators*. Retrieved May 18, 2014 from www.alleghenycounty.us/dhs/spa.aspx

Hirsch, K. (2014). *Collaborative documentation with children & youth*. Extracted May 8, 2014 from www.thenationalcouncil.org/wp-content/uploads/2012/11/NC-C-and-A-CD-Training-3-21-12.pdf

HPSO. (2014). *Good documentation brings peace of mind*. Retrieved May 4, 2014 from www.hpso.com/resources/article/233.jsp

Ingram, B. L. (2011). *Clinical case formulations: Matching the integrative treatment plan to the client* (2nd edition). Wiley: Hoboken, NJ.

Kats, D. (2014). Personal communication.

Mitchell, R. W. (2007). *Documentation in counseling records: An overview of ethical, legal, and clinical issues* (3rd ed.). Alexandria, VA: American Counseling Association.

Reamer, F. G. (2005). *Documentation in social work: Evolving ethical and risk-management standards*. Faculty Publications, Paper 163. Retrieved May 15, 2014 from http://digitalcommons.ric.edu/facultypublications/163

Schmelter, B. (2014). *Implementing collaborative documentation: Making it happen!* Retrieved May 8, 2014 from www.integration.samhsa.gov/pbhci-learning-community/jun_2012_-_collaborative_documentation.pdf

Value Options. (2014). *Clinical record documentation standards*. Retrieved May 3, 2014 from www.valueoptions.com/providers/Network/California_Counties/Documentation_Requirements_and_QA_Standards.pdf

14 Using Reflecting Team in Couples Therapy

Tom Andersen is generally credited with developing the term *reflecting team* (Paré, 1999) in the 1980s and for creating the model that is now used in modern practice. At the time, clinicians were using teams of professionals to observe the interaction in session from what they called "behind the glass," using short breaks in the session. Andersen became frustrated with several aspects of the process, including the hierarchical nature of a team that announced their impressions unilaterally to the client via the counselor, ultimately supporting the idea that the team members were the experts. Remaining hidden, the team was inaccessible to the client, and important conversations that could offer a more integrated, multi-perspective view of the client's experiences were unavailable to them. Andersen rejected several tenets of the practice and worked to create a non-hierarchical approach to therapy using a reflecting team that was collaborative, non-directive, multi-perspective, and not drawn into the pessimism of the family (Paré,1999).

A newer model of reflecting team that I propose is for the client to have direct access to the team, no longer only communicating "behind the glass." The team is in the room with the couple, so the couple can observe the team and have opportunities to interact directly with the team. This approach gives the couple an opportunity to observe the reflecting team in action and at times have direct dialogue with them. Once solely used in family therapy training programs, reflecting teams are now used in private practice for couples.

Benefits for Couples

The basic premise of the reflecting team is that multiple realities exist in any situation, and the reflecting team's responsibility is to share with the couple a number of alternative perspectives to how the couple views themselves (Harrawood, Parmanand, & Wilde, 2011). The team attempts to stay non-directive, reflects out loud, and hypothesizes about the client's situation. They reject the couple's negative impression of the client, preferring to positively connote negative transactions, and in doing so can more objectively view the couple and their situation.

At specific times in the counseling session, the team has a dialogue in the presence of the couple, and these thoughtful conversations can create dissonance and dilemmas for the couple that need to be reconciled. The couple is put in the position of choosing from several different perspectives, those of each individual team members and their own. People generally are more open to new perspectives when they receive not just one, single, final version, but several variations from which they can choose the versions that best fits and reject the ones that don't (de Barbaro et al., 2008). The sharing of information by team members can offer new insights for the couple that may not have previously been in their awareness (Harrawood, Parmanand, & Wilde, 2011). This can be freeing for the couple and create opportunities for change.

Reflecting team clinicians work to focus on the positive aspects of the couple relationship in the first and subsequent sessions, demonstrating that they are multi-perspective and in no way the expert in the room. This perspective can reduce mistrust and create an environment of caring that can lead to a strong therapeutic alliance. As Janis Sanchez-Hucles (2001) contends, the clinician should work to show they care before they show what they know.

With many private practices unwilling to accept insurance, and insurance panels refusing reimbursement for couples therapy because they consider it not a medical necessity, the use of reflecting teams can be a cost-effective alternative for couples. Private practices that train interns can use interns to be both the lead clinician and/or members of the reflecting team. In my practice, the supervisor of the session is a licensed professional who has been trained in the facilitation of reflecting teams. Since interns generate a small revenue stream, some of the intern revenue is redirected to pay the cost of the supervisor for their time in session. For this reason, I will describe the reflecting team process as we utilize it at my practice, with an intern taking the lead-clinician role and a supervisor participating as the lead reflector, with two other interns also serving as reflectors.

Benefits for Interns

There are several benefits for adopting the reflecting team model in teaching interns in a clinical practice. First, the reflecting team is a method for helping interns develop a wide range of clinical skills. In particular, interns learn core skills that help develop the therapeutic alliance, such as active listening, empathy responding, and circular and reflexive questioning. Interns also learn how to structure the session, develop treatment goals, and manage termination. Through interaction with the team they learn the process of conceptualization and learn how to use this skill to develop interventions for the client.

Interns regularly speak of the supportive nature of the team and the confidence it gives them with their core skills. Interns who participate in the reflecting team develop the confidence to use language and conversation therapeutically (Cox et al., 2003) because as they practice, they are highly supported by the supervisor. This translates into the intern's receiving immediate feedback in a supportive way since by their very nature, reflecting teams are positive and supportive. This support also helps interns be more receptive to feedback when compared to an intern who is not in an encouraging environment.

The reflecting team encourages interns to practice reflection processes and therapeutic responses while challenging them to be less focused on delivering successful interventions. Since interns tend to be over-focused on implementing interventions, there is a risk that they will focus on interventions at the detriment of their own development of process skills. Reflecting teams are non-directive (but influential) and therefore guard against this.

The multiple perspectives of the supervisor and fellow interns of the reflecting team also challenge interns on the black-and-white thinking often characteristic of novice clinicians (Harrawood, Parmanand, & Wilde, 2011). Interns move through right-or-wrong thinking to a deeper understanding of client problems and solutions. Reflecting teams promote the concept that there are no absolute truths, resulting in less-rigid conceptualizations among interns (Shurts et al., 2006).

Additionally, Cox et al. (2003) state that in the reflecting team context there is no one right way of responding to a couple, so interns feel less constrained by having to "get it right." This can reduce dualistic thinking and open the intern to more possible perspectives. Interns become more accepting of feedback from other team members and the supervisor since interns are less concerned with defending what they have done and more open to learning from the input of others.

Clinical Orientation for Reflectors

There are a few primary guidelines critical to effective reflecting. Following Anderson's early prescription, any comment from the team should be non-directive and avoid any suggestions or interventions. Reflectors should be told to avoid statements like "has the daughter tried talking to her mother?" or "I think it would be helpful if the couple spent more time in the evening together," and so forth. These are typical strategic statements from reflectors that are violating the principle of non-directive reflection.

Reflectors are also cautioned that reflections from the team are not just restating and paraphrasing. The focus should be on the observations, questions, curiosities, and hypotheses of each team member. As reflections occur, team members should attempt to create a cohesive dialogue about what they observed in the counseling session that builds on the comments of other team members' curiosities. Table 14.1 lists orienting underpinnings that guide the reflecting team.

Reflectors are asked to be polite, affirming, and personal in their demeanor. Since they are non-directive, their language should not include specific interventions or any clinical jargon. Their reflections need to be relevant and focus

Table 14.1 Orientation for Reflecting

Be polite and affirming
Reflect only on what has been discussed, observed, not observed
Focus on the positive aspects of the client
Be speculative, tentative, and not the expert
Multi-perspective; use both/and orientation
Use positive connotation
Use common language
Approach problems non-strategically

on what has been discussed, observed, or not observed. Statements made by the reflecting team should be tentative and not give the impression that the reflecting team is the expert. The key orientating word reflectors are asked to remember is *curiosity*. Creating curiosity opens up many possibilities; being the expert, however, creates resistance. They are also asked to maintain a multi-perspective view and not advocate for any one perspective. Reflecting teams that maintain a multi-perspective orientation help expand the client's perceptual field.

Since the reflecting team does not adopt the negative view of the couple situation, reflectors are encouraged to focus on the positive aspects of the client. When a challenge is offered to the couple's negative view, the reflector is asked to use positive connotation, in other words to positively connote the underlying motive of the problematic behavior or thought. Positive connotation can help the client hear a positive perspective for something they view negatively; negative attributions and blaming should be avoided. For example, "I understand that you are frustrated that Natalie is not listening, and when you yell at her, she listens less."

Reflectors are required to plan their open-session reflections and share them with the team prior to saying it in front of the client. Since they are new to the process, interns are expected to use only one of the pre-selected, directed reflecting team responses outlined in Table 14.2.

An interesting feature of the reflecting team model is the use of self-disclosure and the sharing of personal stories. As noted previously in Table 14.2, reflectors have an opportunity to use self-disclosure under the guidance of the supervisor. Clinician self-disclosure is considered a major process within clinical practice, with the recommendation that when used sparingly, it has the potential to be very influential (Hill, Helms, Tichenor, Speigel, O'Grady & Perry, 1988; Watkin, 1990; Knox & Hill, 2003). Most clinical theories support clinician self-disclosure to some degree (Edward & Murdock, 1994), which is defined by revealing positive or negative personal information about oneself, which includes positive or negative statements about the client's behavior in the here and now (Watkin, 1990).

The use of self-disclosure is not that uncommon in clinical practice. Edward and Murdock (1994) found that all clinicians in their study used a moderate amount of self-disclosure, with the most frequent type of disclosure being about professional issues. Psychoanalytic practitioners reported significantly less

Table 14.2 Directed Reflecting Team Strategies

Pose a question.
Hypothesize in an "appropriately unusual" way.
Offer an affirmation.
Offer a different perspective.
State something you are curious about.
Normalize something.
Talk to each other; comment on another team member's idea.
Disagree with another team member, politely and respectfully (positively connote first).
Define the problem from a circular perspective or differently from the client's definition.
Emphasize something positive.
Positively connote a difficulty of the client (after rapport is clearly established).
Notice a metaphor or image you have while listening; share it and connect it to the client story.
Share a personal story about the reflector and relate it to the client narrative—be brief.
Share a story about another client (respecting confidentially of course).
Reflect on the themes of your reflections.

disclosure, while humanistic and behaviorally oriented counselors used self-disclosure to increase similarity and demonstrate modeling behavior. Offering self-disclosure can have a variety of benefits for the couple. Jourard and Jaffe (1979) highlight the potential benefits of effective use of clinician disclosure, including increased client disclosure, improved client growth, greater client trust, and better therapist-client rapport (Hill, Mahalik, & Thompson, 1989).

The primary purpose for disclosure is to strengthen joining with the couple by placing the couple, clinician, and team in a more authentic context (Cole et al., 2001). Self-disclosure through the team process also flattens the hierarchal nature of counseling because the couple will hear the reflections in an egalitarian manner (Freedman and Combs, 1996).

Knox et al. (2003) present at least seven subtypes of disclosures, which include disclosure of facts, feelings, insights, strategies, reassurance/support, challenges, and immediacy. For the purpose of interns, they are only permitted to use self-disclosure to offer reassurance or support or to normalize an experience.

If reflectors choose to use self-disclosure, these personal statements need to be brief with the attention on the client and not the team member. Sharing a personal story by the team member does not mean baring one's soul to the client. The personal story should be concise and relate to the client narrative.

Informed Consent for Reflecting Team

The reflecting team process as a clinical intervention is a strange set-up to the couple and should be recognized as such. Special care should be taken to provide detailed information about the process through informed consent. It is important to be careful to emphasize the differences of the reflecting team from traditional therapy, and care should be given to acclimate the client to the setting prior to session. It is interesting to note that when couples are asked to identify when reflecting teams are not effective, they report that they are ineffective when rapport between the clinician and couple was not established or they did not understand the process (Pender & Stinchfield, 2012). Client participation is always voluntary, and following this preparation the client should be asked if they want to participate in counseling.

Following is an outline of topics for informed consent with couples participating in the reflecting team. This could be read verbatim to the couple if so desired by the clinician. At the end of each category, the clinician asks, "What questions do you have about [confidentiality, your role, etc.]?" Following the conclusion of informed consent, the clinician asks the client what they are still curious about and whether they want to continue their involvement with the team.

Unusual Nature of the Reflecting Team

The reflecting team is an unusual set-up in couple counseling. Much of the experience is what you would expect from traditional counseling. One obvious difference is that there is a group of people observing you and that initially you will feel uncomfortable. However, in our experience, couples tell us that this goes away quickly and they focus on their conversation with their lead clinician. They also feel supported by the team. Another difference is how the team interacts with you. Our team is challenged to see your problem in a different and positive way and then share those perceptions with you. What do you think will be most unusual for you?

Why a Team?

We believe that the reflecting team process is an effective way to help find solutions to your problem. We also know the reflecting team has many benefits. Our clients tell us that the approach is comforting, trusting, and even nurturing. It can offer new insights and allow you to consider a range of options to address your problem. These insights are positive and constructive. We hope that by providing a variety of thoughts from the team, we create multiple perspectives for you to consider.

The team approach does have risk. If we are too wordy in our reflections to you, we can create confusion and stall the counseling process. Since several of us are interns, they may stray from the structure that I, the supervisor, have set. As the supervisor, I may need to stop the intern and have them do something different. What questions do you have?

Reflecting Team Orientation

Our team has a specific way that we require ourselves to interact with you. We have to be speculative and multi-perspective. Our goal is to create many perspectives that you may or may not want to consider. Another goal is to be non-directive. We know that you are the best person to solve your problems. We hope to expand your perspective so that it creates new opportunities for solutions. So, you will not hear us telling you what to do.

Structure of Session

We will offer a team reflection midway through our session. During this time the team will discuss what they heard so far in your session. We ask that you and the lead clinician quietly listen and take notes as needed. The reflection lasts just about five minutes. After the reflection is completed, you and the lead clinician will discuss your reaction to the reflection.

Structure of Reflecting Team Sessions in Private Practice

The reflecting team counseling session follows a specific structure. We have found it helpful for everyone involved to have a clear schedule, as follows in Table 14.3:

Table 14.3 Reflecting Team Session Structure

Pre-Session	Thirty minutes
Session A	Thirty minutes
Reflection	Five minutes
Session B	Fifteen minutes
Closing Reflection and Open Discussion	Ten minutes
Post-Session	Thirty minutes

Pre-Session

The pre-session meeting begins thirty minutes before session and does not include the couple. Pre-session is primarily for the lead clinician and reflectors to plan the session. The team is expected to review the client record and conceptualize the case, utilizing theme and context analysis. Theme analyses include identifying themes both within and between sessions and includes the perpetual stress/presenting problem, underlying feelings of the client, productive and maladaptive coping, patterns that the team has identified, individual and social resources, and strengths of the client. Context analysis includes prior learning and the social and environmental factors that may contribute to the problem.

The next task of pre-session is to prepare a reflection and plan the structure of the session. The team is asked to offer their reflections using the Directed

Reflecting Team Strategies in Table 14.2. As the team shares and discusses their reflections, the clinician listens and takes notes. The clinician uses these notes to create an open-session summary to offer the couple at the beginning of the couple session.

The couple joins the pre-session planning at the end of the pre-session meeting. This tends to be useful because it increases the couples' comfort with the process. Cohen et al. (1998) found in their practice that when couples were in their pre-session and post-session discussions, it made therapy more comfortable for the client because it allowed them to understand what was happening in session and feel equal to the team.

Session Part A

In the interest of making the team accessible to the client, sessions are conducted with the team and the couple together in the same room. As the session begins, the clinician and the reflectors start with an open-session summary. The focus of the summary is on the content of the last session, any themes between sessions or within the previous session, the key affect, and setting an agenda for the session. The session continues for thirty minutes. At any point in the session, the supervisor may interrupt to direct the clinician to focus on specific content or affect components, or to direct away from interventions or strategies.

Reflection

At the end of this thirty-minute period, the clinician is signaled by the reflectors to begin the reflection and discuss their thoughts about the session. The reflectors use the Directed Reflecting Team Strategies outlined in Table 14.2 as a guide to provide the reflection for the couple. One reflector functions as a facilitator of the reflection and helps make connections with the other reflectors ideas. They also should help to make sure that the discussion is perceived by the couple as a coherent and fluid discussion among the reflectors.

At the completion of the reflection, the counselor facilitates a short discussion with the couple to get their reaction to the reflection. As the counselor listens, it is important to paraphrase and validate the couple's response. The expectation is that the clinician does not challenge the couple's ideas or add additional comments from the clinician's perspective during this short discussion about this mid-session reflection.

Session Part B

The session then continues as before. After approximately fifteen minutes, the clinician will stop the session for the final closing reflection and open discussion.

Closing Reflection and Open Discussion

During this stage, everyone in the room is offered the opportunity to reflect on the session. This is an open discussion with interaction between all participants. The session ends with the clinician's asking the couple to consider how they might translate their ideas into action.

Post-Session

After the couple leaves, the team meets for thirty minutes to reflect on the session. The team is asked to 1) hypothesize about the couple diagnostically, 2) identify the clinical issues noted in terms of themes, patterns, and the conditions that might be perpetuating the problem, and 3) consider treatment strategies for upcoming sessions.

References

Andersen, T. (1987). The reflecting team: Dialogue and meta-dialogue in clinical work. *Family Process*, *26*(4), 415–428.

Brownlee, K., Vis, J., & McKenna, A. (2009). Review of the reflecting team process: Strengths, challenges and clinical implications. *The Family Journal: Counseling and Therapy for Couples and Families*, *17*(2), 139–145.

Cohen, S. M., Combs, G., DeLaurenti, B., Freedman, J., et al. (1998). Minimizing hierarchy in the therapeutic relationships: A reflecting team approach. In M. F. Hoyt (Ed.), *The handbook of constructive therapises: Innovative approaches from leading practitioners* (pp. 276–292). San Francisco, CA: Jose-Bass.

Cole, P. M., Demerrit, L. A., Shatz, K., & Sapoznik, M. (2001). Getting personal on reflecting teams. *Journal of Systemic Therapies*, *10*(2), 74–87.

Cox, J. A., Banez, L., Hawley, L. D., & Mostade, J. (2003). Use of the reflecting team process in the training of group workers. *Journal for Specialists in Group Work*, *28*(2), 89–105.

de Barbaro, B., Drozdzowicz, L., Janusz, B., Gdowska, K., Dembinska, E., Kolbik, I., & Furgal, M. (2008). Multi-couple reflecting team: Preliminary report. *Journal of Marital Therapy*, *34*(3), 287–297.

Edward, C. E., & Murdock, N. L. (1994). Characteristics of therapist self-disclosure in the counseling process. *Journal of Counseling and Development*, *72*(4), 384–389. doi:10.1002/j.1556-6676.1994.tb00954.

Freedman, J., & Combs, G. (1996). *Narrative therapy: The social construction of preferred realities*. New York: W. W. Norton & Company.

Harrawood, L. K., Parmanand, S., & Wilde, B. J. (2011). Experiencing emotion across a semester-long family role play and reflecting team: Implications for counselor development. *The Family Journal: Counseling and Therapy for Couples and Families*, *19*(2), 198–203.

Hill, C. E., Helms, J. E., Tichenor, V., Speigel, S., O'Grady, K. E., & Perry, E. S. (1988). Effects of therapist response modes in brief psychotherapy. *Journal of Counseling Psychology*, *35*(3), 222–233. doi:10.1037//0022-0167.35.3.222.

Hill, C. E., Mahalik, J. R, & Thompson, B. J. (1989). Therapist self-disclosure. *Psychotherapy: Theory, Research, Practice, Training*, *26*(3), 290–295. doi:10.1037/h0085438.

Jourard, S. M., & Jaffe, P. E. (1979). Influence of an interviewer's disclosure on the self-disclosing behavior of interviewees. *Journal of Counseling Psychology, V77*, 252–257.
Knox, S., & Hill, C. E. (2003). Therapist self-disclosure. *Journal of Clinical Psychology*, 59(5), 529–539. doi:10.1002/jclp.10157.
McCarthy, P. R. (1982). Differential effects of counselor self-referent responses and counselor status. *Journal of Counseling Psychology*, 29(2), 125–131. doi:10.1037/0022-0167.29.2.125.
Paré, D. A. (1999). The use of reflecting teams in clinical training. *Canadian Journal of Counselling*, 33(4), 293–306.
Pender, R. L., & Stinchfield, T. (2012). A reflective look at reflecting teams. *The Family Journal: Counseling and Therapy for Couples and Families*, 20(2), 117–122.
Sanchez-Hucles, J. (2001). Staying the course: Psychotherapy in the African-American community. *Quest*, 4(2), 13–15.
Shurts, M. W., Cashwell, C. S., Spurgeon, S. L., Deggs-White, S., Barrio, C. A., & Kardatzke, K. N. (2006). Preparing counselors-in-training to work with couples: Using role-plays and reflecting teams. *The Family Journal of Counseling and Therapy for Couples and Families*, 14(2), 151–157.
Watkin Jr., C. E. (1990). The effects of counselor self-disclosure: A research review. *The Counseling Psychologist*, 18(3), 477–500. doi:10.1177/0011000090183009.

15 Post-Treatment Planning

Termination is more than an act signifying the end of therapy; it is an integral part of the process of therapy.

—Irvin Yalom

Termination is the last phase of treatment and an important one. It should not be seen as an abrupt end to treatment but more of a transitional phase. It is possibly the most transformative phase of therapy.

Irvin Yalom (1975) expressed the importance of termination when he stated, "Termination is more than an act signifying the end of therapy; it is an integral part of the process of therapy and, if properly understood and managed, may be an important factor in the instigation of change."

Termination involves a number of important issues and activities. There are three primary functions for successful termination. First is the function of assessing the client's readiness for the end of counseling. Some behaviors of the couple that might indicate that they are moving toward termination include less-intense discussions, cancellations that extend session intervals to two or three weeks, increased laughter and joking in session, or statements that they increasingly have less to talk about.

A second function of termination includes both resolving remaining affective issues and bringing about appropriate closure of the significant and often intense relationship between the client and the counselor. This is the act of appreciating one another and saying goodbye.

The third function is to maximize the transfer of learning and to increase the client's self-reliance and confidence in their ability to maintain change after counseling has ended (Ward, 1984).

Termination should not be seen as just one session but potentially a series of sessions to close out therapy. Following are some of the primary tasks for the sessions related to termination.

Assessment of Goal Completion and Outcomes of Treatment

Goal assessment can be accomplished in a variety of ways. I begin by administering any formal assessments or outcome measures that I had originally administered at the beginning and middle of treatment. These are completed, scored, and reviewed in session. These assessments are then compared to the original assessment scores. Couples are usually quite amazed to see the changes they have created in their relationship.

Next, the couple can be asked to identify the broad outcomes of treatment. Sometimes, clients will forget the achievements that they have made in counseling, or they neglect to give themselves credit for their accomplishments. Most often, though, clients in my practice are able to identify a number of achievements. For this reason, I offer no direction on this because couples tend to identify a broad range of outcomes that may not be directly linked to the treatment goals or symptom reduction. I do not want to restrict their exploration of the outcomes.

Lastly, I will read each treatment goal with the couple. I will ask the couple to rank each goal based on the level of change that has occurred: mild, moderate, or strong.

Closure of the Affective and Relationship Issues

The couple is encouraged to discuss feelings associated with ending therapy, particularly around grief and loss. It is natural to have these feelings, and it is important to discuss these for the successful completion of therapy. I also encourage couples to share how I was helpful as a clinician and how I might improve for future couples.

Post-Treatment Planning

I ask couples to create one or two post-treatment goals. These are developed in the same way as the treatment goals. Renewed goal setting can rejuvenate the couple and create a new energy and interest to continue creating change in their relationship. Learning not to discount or forget that new development should continue in the relationship will be important.

References

Ward, D. E. (1984). Termination of individual counseling: Concepts and strategies. *Journal of Counseling and Development*, 63, 21–25.

Yalom, I. D. (1975). *The theory and practice of group psychotherapy*. New York: Basic Books.

Index

For Product Safety Concerns and Information please contact our EU
representative GPSR@taylorandfrancis.com
Taylor & Francis Verlag GmbH, Kaufingerstraße 24, 80331 München, Germany

www.ingramcontent.com/pod-product-compliance
Ingram Content Group UK Ltd.
Pitfield, Milton Keynes, MK11 3LW, UK
UKHW022204190926
475702UK00003B/189
9781138780309